A Collection of Canadian Plays Volume 1

GENERAL EDITOR: ROLF KALMAN

Bastet Books, Toronto, 1972

Live theatre has existed in Canada for more than three hundred years, yet the history of Canadian live theatre, in terms of professional production and mass entertainment, is very short. For many years the only regular paid outlet for original Canadian plays was the Canadian Broadcasting Corporation, which to its everlasting credit, nurtured and showcased many outstanding theatrical talents, and brought much good theatre to millions of people to whom live theatre was unavailable. A curious paradox was thus created, however: when professional live theatre finally became an active and integral part of Canada's cultural life, it found itself in competition with the very medium which had helped to create it — radio, and later on television, drama. In spite of the fact that this "competition" existed, however, hundreds of thousands of paying audiences became involved with live theatre, and continue to be involved, every year.

Canada, politically and economically, has always functioned on a regional basis within Confederation; this is also true of the arts. Even though a great many Canadians are still isolated from theatres, it is not uncommon for people to travel for hours to see live productions, which are now readily available because of the tremendous growth of regional theatres. Canadian playwrights are now receiving unexpected prominence; and while we are the first to admit that not enough is being done for the Canadian drama writer at this time, we must point out that there are now at least three theatres in Toronto alone devoted exclusively to the production of Canadian plays. What major city in Europe, where theatrical tradition is hundreds of years old, can make such a claim on behalf of its native playwrights?

The selection of plays in this first Volume was not, of course, a random one. We have tried to include one play representative of its particular genre, from the open stage production, the traditional proscenium stage, the school and/or university production and plays suitable for amateurs through to the frankly experimental.

We have also taken care to select plays from a variety of regions in Canada, and this will remain an established policy for all future volumes, though naturally it will not be possible to include all regions in every publication.

The purpose of "A Collection of Canadian Plays — Volume I" and of the similar volumes to follow, is to present to the Canadian public good plays which have received regional acclaim but not national publicity. Concurrent with the publication of each book, we will make available copies of the individual plays to organizations such as schools and theatre groups. In this way we hope to achieve the widest possible dissemination of original Canadian plays, not only for those who may be interested in mounting their own productions, but also for those playgoers who may wish to recapture the pleasures of an evening well spent in the theatre.

R.K.

Bastet Books are published and distributed by Simon & Pierre Publishers, P.O.Box 280 Adelaide Street Postal Station, Toronto M5C 1J0, Ontario, Canada.

Publishing Editor	Rolf Kalman
Associate Editor	Mark Dwor
Staff Writer	Jean Stewart Hannant
Designed by	Design Workshop

Printed and bound in Canada by T. H. Best Printing Company Limited.

ISBN 0-9690454-0-9

98378

Glasgow-born **Stewart Boston** was educated in Manchester, where he graduated in 1954 with a B.A. (Hon.) in English and he has followed a distinguished teaching career in England, Kenya and Alberta, where he now holds the position of Assistant Principal at Sir Winston Churchill High School in Calgary. Mr. Boston's interest in dramatic writing, with special emphasis on historical and biblical themes, began in 1964, and has developed steadily since then. His work includes seven plays and one short story broadcast by the CBC, among them The Form of the Thing, Cressida, Dialogue, The Kingdom of the Blind and the popular Easter production Problem in Judaea. In 1970, another radio play The Coming of the Wild Flowers was nominated for the Prix Italia, and the late Nathan Cohen suggested in a review that Mr. Boston was a writer "well worth watching".

In March, 1971, the Citadel Theatre of Edmonton opened its sixth season with a production of Stewart Boston's Counsellor Extraordinary, possibly the author's best work to date. Intensive research and Mr. Boston's special knowledge of English and English History resulted in a play of considerable strength, and was performed to impressive critical acclaim.

The visual material accompanying the text of this play was provided through the generous co-operation of the play's designer, Mr. Phillip Silver of Edmonton.

The founders of the Citadel were also especially fortunate in their choice of Artistic Director for the project — none other than the well-known and multi-talented Irish actor, director and lecturer, **Sean Mulcahy**. Colourful, charming and flamboyant offstage, Mr. Mulcahy brought to his work all the serious application and dedication bred of a long and distinguished career in Ireland, England and Canada. His training and experience endowed him with one essential ingredient for artistic and commercial success: discipline. It shows, not only in every play he produces, but also in the sound business sense he brings to the running of the theatre itself.

Illustrations on pages A26 and A36 courtesy Fine Arts Department, Metropolitan Toronto Central Library.

A4

EXTRAORDINARY
BASIC SET   SILVER 71

"Counsellor Extraordinary" was first produced
March 24 — April 17, 1971 at the Citadel
Theatre under the direction of **Sean Mulcahy**
and the set designed by **Phillip Silver.**

FRANCIS 1
SILVER 71

Francis Bacon's house at Twickenham. Francis and Anthony are sorting through legal documents, scattered on a large oak table. A cape lies over a chair. The year is 1600 A.D.

Francis: There, all in good order. Though how our mother got her leases and estates in such a muddle I'll never understand.

Anthony: She grows old, Francis, it's natural — we must watch her more carefully, help her more.

Francis: Of course, Anthony, that's understood. Now that . . .

Anthony: Now that my Lord of Essex has no further need of our services.

Francis: *(sharply)* Don't say that.

Anthony: Why not, Francis, it's true; a dead man needs neither adviser nor secretary. God rest his noble soul.

Francis: *(irritably)* Amen. Amen.

Anthony: Why, Francis, you sound peevish. Can it be that, now the chief support to your ambition's gone, you regret what you did?

Francis: Don't bait me, brother.

Anthony: Not for the world, Francis. I know how dangerous it is. All men saw how you served your dearest friend, the lord to whom you swore support. It would be foolish for a mere brother to rely on ties of blood for protection.

Francis: You feel I should have helped him more, don't you? You think I sought to bolster up my credit with the Queen. Oh, Anthony, this is unjust! I swear to you that my dearest wish were that I could turn back the clock five years, to when we served him jointly, faithfully, to when he strove to get a place for me at court, before the horror of diseased ambition destroyed the blessed harmony of the times. Then was there laughter in the air and dalliance acted out to music . . .

(Music and laughter are heard. The lights dim

Cast of characters

Francis Bacon
Anthony Bacon
Musician
Robert Devereux (Earl of Essex)
Queen Elizabeth I
Lady-in-waiting
Sir Robert Cecil
Sir Thomas Egerton
The Earl of Nottingham
A Messenger
Sir Christopher Blount
Sir John Davies
The Earl of Southampton
Sir Charles Davers
The Lord Chief Justice
Sir William Knollys
Sir Edward Coke
A Counsellor
A Guard
A Clerk of the Court
Assorted Lords, Rebels, Counsellors, Guards

and rise again on a room in the palace. A musician sings to Queen Elizabeth and Robert Devereux, the Earl of Essex. It is 1595 A.D.)

Musician:
Blow, blow, thou winter wind
Thou art not so unkind
    As man's ingratitude.
Thy tooth is not so keen
Because thou art not seen,
    Although thy breath be rude
Heigh ho, sing heigh ho, unto the green holly!
Most friendship is feigning, most loving mere folly;
Then heigh ho, the holly,
This life is most folly.

Freeze, freeze, thou bitter sky
That dost not bite so nigh
    As benefits forgot.
Though thou the waters warp.
Thy sting is not so sharp
    As friends remembered not.
Heigh ho, sing heigh ho, unto the green holly!
Most friendship is feigning, most loving mere folly:
Then heigh ho, the holly,
This life is most folly.

Essex: *(laughing as the musician continues quietly)* 'Twould have gladdened any heart alive to see the judge's face.

Queen: Robert, you're a rogue — such pranks will lead to scandal.

Essex: Nay, no scandal, madam; he was well recompensed — we must respect the pillars of the law, *(laughter subsides)* Which makes me think how much more we should concern ourselves with such pillars of justice where they touch closely to Your Majesty's sway and honour.

Queen: Robert, I prefer you joking. I know now that you speak obscurely that you're being serious. Today is not a day for serious affairs.

Essex: I only meant, madam, that if we must respect the dignity of a village magistrate, how much the more must we be careful in our choice of senior legal counsel near your throne.

Queen: So, you have a candidate for the place of Solicitor-General.

Essex: If I might . . .

Queen: Don't tell me. I know it already. None will do but Francis Bacon.

Essex: He does possess some qualities . . .

Queen: I know his qualities well enough: wide learning and independent notions of what is fitting. All excellent qualities in a prince, but not suited to my needs. I need a mature, serviceable lawyer, who, if he thinks at all, has the good grace to keep his notions to himself.

Essex: Gloriana, Divinity, be serious a moment —

Queen: Why, so I am, Robert. Your young friend lacks a due sense of his position. I don't want a thinker of novelties, a bold schemer, nor yet an ambitious politician. I want a dull, steady, effective practioner of law — my law.

Essex: Let me speak on his behalf —

Queen: Robert, I'm weary of this topic. Pray don't bore me with such talk.

Essex: Just one word.

Queen: Later, Robert, later.

(Cecil enters with papers. Looks confused and is about to retire. The Queen sees him.)

Essex: Very well, *(he kneels and kisses her hand)* but still . . .

Queen: Sir Robert, pray come forward.

Cecil: Not if inconvenient to Your Majesty.

Queen: Quite the reverse. *(she signals for music to stop)* My Lord of Essex was e'en now on his way to prepare our masque. We will not detain him.

Essex: *(stiffly)* Your Majesty has but to command.

Queen: Quite so, Robert.

Essex: *(bowing stiffly)* Your servant, Sir Robert.

Cecil: *(returning the bow more deeply but equally stiffly)* My Lord of Essex.

(Essex exits in a huff)

Queen: Sir Robert, I am glad to see you. I need your advice.

Cecil: Of such worth as it is, Your Majesty, it is yours, as ever, to command.

Queen: Its worth and **quality** I know, Sir Robert. I am gladdened though by your willingness to have it commanded.

Cecil: You Majesty need not be concerned about the reception of the Spanish Ambassador —

Queen: Nothing Spanish ever worries me, Sir Robert. Spanish matters I deal with, not worry over.

Cecil: Of course —

Queen: I want your views on the Solicitor Generalship. To whom should we give it?

Cecil: Your Majesty doubtless has a candidate in mind?

Queen: Several.

Cecil: It is an important appointment. Next to the Attorney General's duties, so ably discharged by Sir Edward Coke, it is the most important legal position in the realm.

Queen: This I know, Cecil, knew it indeed before you were born.

Cecil: Your Majesty must not think I would instruct you . . .

Queen: Must I not, knave? Why you would all instruct me, if you dared, and you probably will instruct my successor, especially if it's that simpering fool from Scotland.

Cecil: *(casting eyes up and clasping hands)* May

God in his infinite mercy long delay the day when England has to consider a successor to your Majesty.

Queen: *(grimly and with feeling)* Amen! But come, whom do you favour for the Solicitor General? Speak out, no shilly shallying, Sir.

Cecil: Perhaps Your Majesty has thought on my cousin, Francis Bacon?

Queen: My Lord of Essex makes me think of little else.

Cecil: Ah, quite so, and, now I remember, his lordship advised Your Majesty to appoint Francis Bacon Attorney General instead of Sir Edward Coke.

Queen: What of that?

Cecil: Why nothing, but that your final choice in that regard confirmed your loyal council in their belief in your queenly wisdom. Francis is doubtless an able man . . .

Queen: I'm waiting, Sir Robert.

Cecil: Your Majesty must know how reluctant I am to criticize a cousin and indeed the great favour shown him by my Lord of Essex has gone far to make me revise my judgment on Francis Bacon yet . . .

Queen: Leave posturing, Sir: strike, if you will.

Cecil: Strike? Oh, I would not strike my cousin, a man whose learning is so generally admired and whose legal knowledge, if not formidable or the fruit of overmuch experience, is at least adequate, no question of it, it is adequate.

Queen: Adequate say you. Is that good enough for a Solicitor General?

Cecil: Perhaps not now, but with time and experience I'm sure that in a year or two Your Majesty would have few causes for complaint, just the odd lapse which maturer years would avoid, nothing more.

Queen: Lapse me no lapses, Sir; there's no room for lapses in my council, nor in those who sustain it with legal advice.

ELIZABETH I
SILVER 41

Cecil: Your Majesty must forgive me. You'll think I wish to oppose Mr. Bacon's interests in the case because he's young.

Queen: I did entertain some such notion.

Cecil: Nothing could be further from my mind. I try to forget kinship ties when advising your Majesty.

Queen: I've noticed this, Sir Robert.

Cecil: Yes, well, as I say I try not to let ties of blood bias my judgment and, I must confess, in general terms I favour young Francis; in general terms, you understand me.

Queen: Aye, well so much for the general; now how goes it in the particular?

Cecil: Ah, the particular, yes, indeed, the particular; now that saddens me.

Queen: Does it so? Pray be good enough to tell me why.

Cecil: In a word, Mr. Francis Bacon has too independent a spirit. He means well, means very well, if I judge him rightly, but like so many of his age and ambition, he tends to judge events in the light of what he feels and thinks is right. Now this is a noble trait in a youth. Who would have it otherwise? If youth were as circumspect and careful of offending as maturer spirits, we'd think them cunning, a base quality in a servant of the Crown.

Queen: Say you so, Sir Robert?

Cecil: Most assuredly, madam. I'd rather my cousin suffered for showing too lively and independent a spirit than for being shifty and cunning, a vile thing in a young man.

Queen: You want him to **suffer** then in the matter of his candidacy for Solicitor General?

Cecil: I would not have Francis suffer in any endeavour and, sometimes, as I say, I doubt my own judgment when I see and hear my Lord of Essex plead his cause for this position so earnestly . . .

Queen: Indeed.

Cecil: Why, yes, knowing as I do the great esteem in which you hold my Lord of Essex and knowing that such esteem would not be bestowed without deserving.

Queen: The loyal and devoted manner in which you seek to undermine your cousin's hopes does you credit, Sir Robert.

Cecil: Madam, I would not be so construed for the world.

Queen: If not for the world, then for whom?

Cecil: Madam?

Queen: Come, Sir, in whose interest would you tear down your cousin's claims; have you a pawn you would play to strengthen your party in my council?

Cecil: Madam, I must disclaim all thoughts of attempting to influence you for reasons of base faction.

Queen: If you must disclaim it, you must, but I still want your candidate's name.

Cecil: Busied as I have been with the affairs Your Majesty knows of, I have not been as dutiful in sifting through the various candidates for office in the way I should. However . . .

Queen: However?

Cecil: There is a man whom Your Majesty might be gracious enough to consider. In short, I would advance Sergeant Fleming to the post. He's able, experienced, tried in affairs of state and lacks the strong self-willed presumption which led my cousin to vote against your tax bill in Parliament.

Queen: Aye, Mr. Bacon did so vote against me; I had nearly forgot.

Cecil: A youthful error only, Your Majesty, I'm sure that in time Mr. Bacon will learn that Your Majesty's interests and the well-being of the realm are one and the same. I hope, too, that with such an advisor and patron as my Lord of

Essex the time may well come when I shall be able to recommend my cousin to your Majesty's bounty and favour. My Lord of Essex is younger still, but the esteem in which you hold him and the high offices and honours you have lavished on him must steady him beyond his years and curb his youthful enthusiasms.

Queen: Must they so of necessity, Sir Robert?

Cecil: Not of necessity, madam, but it would be the most vile ingratitude else, and so I think it must at least be likely, for my Lord of Essex has noble qualities and is very sensitive of his honour and reputation in the eyes of the common people.

Queen: So you'd advise Sergeant Fleming for the position of Solicitor General?

Cecil: I believe it would be a prudent appointment, Your Majesty.

The lights dim and rise again on a room in Essex House. Anthony Bacon is busying himself with papers at a desk S.L. Occasionally while Francis Bacon is speaking to him, he writes, as though not listening properly. Francis Bacon paces C.S. and S.R. from time to time he picks up a document from another desk S.R. to conceal his nervousness.

Francis: He's about it now, brother; right now he's in the presence.

Anthony: Our Lord of Essex is in high favour . . .

Francis: Go on, go on.

Anthony: You wish me to prejudge the outcome?

Francis: Can we fail now? Well, out with it, Anthony.

Anthony: *(looking up for the first time)* Is it solace or encouragement you're wanting? I've given both since Essex regained access to Her Majesty's favour —

Francis: She dotes on him lately; it's unthinkable he'll fail —

Anthony: *(dryly)* Then let me be the first to congratulate you on your appointment.

Francis: This is not kind, Anthony; I need help.

Anthony: *(putting down his pen and sitting upright in his chair)* I offered help before, Francis; you called me craven and timid. Both you and our lord preferred a frontal attack on our Lady Elizabeth. You would overpower her with love, gallantry and so forth. She's not to be won that way.

Francis: She's a woman, Anthony, a woman; gallantry and flattery have worked on her before. Whatever the outcome, mealy-mouthed submissions would have failed. Has Essex risen so high by prudence and fear? She revels in his spirit and bravado; he'll carry it. I'll be Solicitor-General; she can't refuse him; her passion blinds her.

Anthony: Her Majesty is a woman, doubtless, Francis. She is also a Queen, a prince, jealous of her honour and renowned for her statesmanship.

Francis: So I'm unworthy for Solicitor General — I, who was considered for Attorney General and would have had it only . . .

Anthony: Yes, tell me why Lord Essex failed to get you such a place. I have my views on it of course, but as I was out of England at the time they must perforce take second place to yours and my lord's, who both were basking in the Queen's favour.

Francis: You know full well. The Cecils had her ear and Essex urged his suit too boldly. She sought to pique him in their lovers' tiff and I was the means to do it. I had it all from Essex and wrote you of it. Can you deny it?

Anthony: In your present state, Francis, it would be cruel to deny you anything. I serve our Lord of Essex as well as you, I think, but my loyalty is settled and sober; it will last. I expect little. I know his faults and also a favourite's limitations.

Francis: What am I then, a callow youth, an impetuous fool?

Anthony: (throws up his hands in a deprecatory gesture) No, no, Francis, but you stand like a man at the mouth of a cave about to move out to the sun's glare. In the cave one sees well enough and so would you clear out of it in the sun, but just at the entrance you're dazzled and mistake things.

Francis: What an absurd conceit! We've both been in the sun through our father. We've always had access to Her Majesty. I'm not at the mouth of any cave; I'm not obscure.

Anthony: In that you're right, brother, and so it was doubly foolish to vote in parliament against the Queen's proposals.

Francis: Against the tax bill, not against the Queen. In any case, she knows my reasons; I wrote them out in full. She must realise that in forwarding the business of the state my conscience has to be my guide. She knows I never meant offence. I went further; I expressed regret, even obsequious sorrow for seeming to affront her needs.

Anthony: There you might succeed with her Majesty as prince, as statesman, but as you tell me, she's a woman. It's not enough to stand as loyal servant in parliament, voting as your honour would deem best for the state. You're no great lord to urge your wisdom in defiance of the Crown's desires and then apologise for giving offence but still maintain the rectitude of your judgment.

Francis: (sitting down) Aye, but the offence made, what could I more than grieve for it?

Anthony: (spiritedly) What could you more? Why, grovel on your belly, Francis, grovel. Disclaim not only your offence, but also the judgment which led you to it. Pray for better wisdom to serve your queen as she deems best. Avoid and quit the notion that the son of a knight knows better his queen's business than the queen herself. You irritate by keeping the offence while begging pardon for it. Quit the offence, reject your clownish independence, act a courtier if you'd be one.

Francis: But my honour.

Anthony: Honour costs dear, brother. It's lost you one post and may lose you another.

Francis: The Queen must know —

Anthony: Know! Know! Certainly she knows; she's learned and well read as any prince in Christendom, but when it comes to court appointments, when it comes to Attorney and Solicitor Generalships, the woman's out; she feels. Then your dutiful independent honour's an irritant, a cause for her displeasure.

Francis: You forget the Cecils, urging Coke for Attorney — they proved too strong for Essex.

Anthony: Who can forget our cousins and their smiling disservice to our hopes? Coke is no fool though. His claims were strong.

Francis: Were they stronger than mine, the son of her Majesty's Lord Keeper of the Seal? Am I less able than that bumbling old sheep?

Anthony: Perhaps not, but less experienced certainly. He knows the law —

Francis: Better than I?

Anthony: Longer, he's more service in it, and then the chief legal servant of the Crown must be —

Francis: A learned fool, must he be that?

Anthony: Fool or no he must be . . . reliable, compliant to the Queen's demands.

Francis: And I wouldn't be such?

Anthony: "Wouldn't be" is not the issue; "haven't been" is.

Francis: Your sojourn abroad's embittered you, Anthony. I'd hoped for greater comfort.

Anthony: Comfort of what quality, little brother? Of you, my Lord of Essex and myself, only I see clearly and speak the truth, unpalatable or no.

Francis: Aye, but how you do enjoy it.

Anthony: Don't be childish, for my sake and your own. You aspire where I do not for both our honours, I know that, but you must not let the strain unman you.

Francis: Certainly you give good advice, but would you stomach it yourself?

Anthony: One aspiring star's enough. (he gets up and limps painfully over the stage) The firmament might else be crowded out. (he stops, stooped and frail) I have not the humour or the constitution to (begins painful limping again) dance at Her Majesty's pleasure. My infirmity prevents me. However, I'll not fail you or my Lord of Essex. My loyalty and strength, such as they are, are yours and my lord's to use. To you I'm tied by blood and to my lord and patron I have chosen to be bound. You'll never find me lacking in your cause or his, whatever may befall.

Francis: We both respect your policy, brother —

Anthony: But my loyalty you wonder at because I'm sometimes waspish, and cannot trip a galliard to your measure. Well, Francis, we shall see. (Moving off) We shall see. I'll leave you to receive our Lord of Essex.

(Anthony begins to hobble off, Essex enters before Anthony leaves.)

Francis: (expectantly) My lord!

Essex: I'm sorry, Francis.

Francis: Then it goes to Sergeant Fleming?

Essex: As you say; he is commissioned as Solicitor General.

Francis: I must thank you, nonetheless, my lord, for pressing my case with the Queen. Were you less in Her Majesty's confidence, I would fear you had disabled your credit in so zealously promoting my interests.

Essex: Our interests, Francis, our interests. Fleming's a tool of Burleigh and the Cecils.

Francis: Anthony feels, if we had settled for the Solicitor, and not sought for Attorney first, we might . . .

Essex: Anthony, you're an old woman. I love you dearly, but your maddening caution's not for me. These things have to be done with eclat, or not at all.

Anthony: Perhaps, my lord. Our agents at the Court of France await instructions. With your permission I'll withdraw to draft some letters.

Essex: Do so, Anthony. That business cannot wait another day.

Anthony: Francis, I am sorry for your disappointed hopes.

Francis: I thank you, Anthony.

(Anthony exits. There is a pause)

Francis: I'll stay awhile in London. Anthony's received some fresh dispatches from his foreign agents. These sifted, I'll request your lordship's favour to withdraw.

Essex: Withdraw! Unthinkable! In any case, where to?

Francis: Cambridge.

Essex: Come, Francis, I'll not have you play the hermit.

Francis: Forced to, my lord, with my debts. There's no other part to play. I'll purchase an annuity and devote myself to study and repose. My schemes . . .

Essex: Wonderful schemes, Francis; you shall pursue them here.

Francis: Impossible, my lord. They all require power, influence and money. Reforming abuses in the state, revoking bad, old laws and encouraging science by scholastic endowments, these are not the projects of a pauper lawyer grubbing for paltry fees. Besides, I cannot contemplate with ease the rise of base men into favour. Jealousy and a sense of wronged worth gnaw at me constantly. At Cambridge, I'll be spared the pains of long thwarted ambition and services ignored. Of course, should Her Majesty, or you, my lord, require my services from time to time . . .

Essex: Come now, Francis, this won't do. We have a duty, Anthony, you and I, to save the Queen from fawning Cecils and that doddering Coke. Besides, I have long meant to repay you for your many services on my behalf. Now the time has come.

Francis: I know not what your lordship means. True, I have invested more time in your interests than either in my own or the Queen's, but I have ever felt your lordship's zeal on my behalf whether successful or no . . .

Essex: Ah, but that's just the point. I failed you. First the Attorney Generalship to Coke and now the Solicitor's post to Fleming.

Francis: My lord, the failure is more . . .

Essex: Peace, man, you shall hear me. I wish to confer on you my manor of Twickenham.

Francis: But, my lord —

Essex: Don't interrupt. I can spare it and it will serve to buttress up your faltering credit. It will make you a new man, Francis, serviceable and independent. Come, speak now, will you have it of me?

Francis: What can I say, my lord, but thank you? I am overwhelmed. Let me, though, say this. I would not have you snared by openhandedness as was the Duke of Guise in France. He, having turned his lands all into obligations to bind his followers to him, found at the pinch that he had bought bad debtors. For my fortune it is nothing, but you my lord should take this warning —

Essex: Come, Francis, no fencing; it's yours. I'll brook no other answer.

Francis: What option have I when my Lord of Essex presses?

Essex: Then it's settled. I'll draw the deed; you'll be ensconced at once. It will serve your designs and make you more serviceable to some of mine. Which yet lie brooding, disclosed to no man.

Francis: Again my humble thanks. I see then I must be your liege man and hold land of your gift, but do you know the manner of doing homage in law?

Essex: What (laughing) nonsense now, Francis?

Francis: (gravely) Always it is with a saving of one's faith to the Queen. Therefore, my lord, I can be no more yours than I was, and it must be between us as with that ancient saving clause.

Essex: (slightly disconcerted but recovering well and in a bantering tone) Why, of course, Francis, I agree not to lead you into treasonable practice. 'Fore God, you're a dull, legal dog at times!

Francis: My lord is pleased to say so.

Essex: (archly) Come then, my refurbished counsellor, tell me, if it be not against Her Majesty's interests, how I might strengthen my standing in her favour. For, believe me, we parted unfriendly just now over our friend Fleming's o'ertopping you.

Francis: Three things, my lord, are necessary both to strengthen your position and your standing with the Queen. For the first, avoid military glory. You've had enough; to seek for more is dangerous.

Essex: How dangerous?

Francis: The successful exercise of military power renders you suspect and creates imbalance in the state.

Essex: How imbalance? Am I not serving the Queen?

Francis: I speak, of course, of how your enemies may construe it. Perhaps Lord Burleigh says: "How well my lord becomes command of armies and how his soldiers love the Earl of Essex!" You've proved yourself successful in the field of war; nobody doubts your courage. Leave it betimes, for if too much success can cause the Queen unease, 'tis certain just one failure can lead to your disgrace.

Essex: This is cautious lawyer talk and suits me ill.

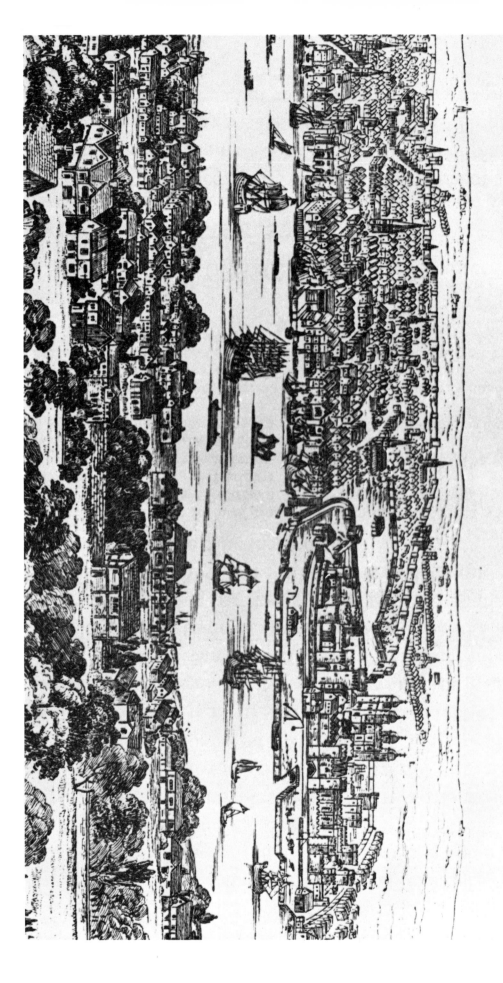

A16

Francis: Ignoring it will suit you even less, believe me.

Essex: Very well; for the second?

Francis: Aye, for the second. Avoid or at least seek to avoid an obvious popularity with people at large. It may gratify you to ride as through a sea of sweaty caps thrown upwards in your lordship's honour. The truth is no mob ever saved its darling from displeasure and royal displeasure you are tempting by such a course. Again the fact may be innocent, but what construction can be put on it. "How fortunate your Majesty's so well enshrined in all the realm's affection, else would the following of my Lord of Essex prove displeasing at the least" and so forth.

Essex: Faith, Francis, your new gained wealth has made you a sad counsellor. I must sheath my sword and frown on my citizens. Cannot I do something positive? These don'ts will make me a cipher, a non-courtier. Perhaps I should dress out of fashion and say my prayers more frequently.

Francis: My lord is pleased to mock me.

Essex: Nay, Francis, I'll hear you out.

Francis: Finally, my lord, move not from court and if you'd seek an honour or position from the Queen make it a civil one. Eschew foreign and military affairs, but be on hand to advise Her Majesty. Remember, the Queen's favour is the beginning and ending of all affairs.

Essex: Is that all?

Francis: Not quite, my lord. You should take steps to show yourself submissive to the Queen's desires, her whims even. Perhaps you might seek leave to tour your Welsh estates and when she demurs at your departure from her as being inconvenient, why gladly abandon the project as worth naught besides Her Majesty's pleasure.

Essex: I thought that, having revived your prospects with a fair estate, I'd deserve brighter counsel from you, but it seems you're the same worthy wise friend I had before. Will nothing shake your wisdom?

Francis: I hope not, small as it is, for I use it only in your lordship's service.

Essex: It seems well enough Francis, but tell me — say there were trouble in Ireland again. They say that villain Tyrone's astirring. What then? Do I stay holding a white wand by my sovereign lady while lesser men cover themselves with glory putting rebellion down?

Francis: My lord, could I presume to make you swear to anything, it would be this: go not to Ireland. Rather send your worst enemy there that he may founder in their bogs and treachery. There is no regular warfare, there no firm engagements, but only an eternal skirmish through rough country, whittling away your spirit and resources, until you find a mocking will o' the wisp has bled you haggard. Then back in shame and ignominy to court to suffer royal displeasure.

Essex: Think you so, Francis? Could not an ample force of soldiery ably led truss up that base Tyrone?

Francis: Not so, my lord. Indeed, if you follow Roman example you'll avoid it. Their generals ever suffered from the hardy savages who held rough country. Believe me, nothing but shame will come out of Ireland for the lord foolhardy enough to go and fetch it.

Essex: This advice I'll take then Francis. Who should we send in such a case?

Francis: If that Tyrone's behaviour impugn Her Majesty's honour, so that by general vote his treasons must be answered, why then I think one of the blood or faction of the Cecils would prove the likeliest general. There'd be no honourable solution. Do nothing, we lose Ireland, but whoever acts for the Queen as general will destroy himself and damage those of his alliance.

Essex: You Bacons chime together; I think that Anthony would advise the same.

Francis: He would, my lord, believe me.

Essex: (turning to leave) Be ruled by me in some things, Francis, it will redound to your credit and honour.

Francis: *(As Essex exits)* I am, as always, at my lord's disposal, *(With Essex off stage, quietly)* saving that ancient clause.

(The lights dim and rise again on a meeting of the Queen's Privy Council in 1597. Queen Elizabeth is seated. Sir Robert Cecil stands obsequiously on Queen's right. Nottingham and Egerton are also present)

Queen: . . . which brings us to affairs of Ireland and the heinous treason of the base Tyrone. For long our natural patience bore with this insolence hoping by our well-known generosity of purpose to bring this rebel to his sense and duty. It now appears the times do call for sterner measures. This then is the chief cause for this privy council wherein your loves and wisdoms are entreated to offer comfort to the state and further to propose a fitting course of action. My Lord of Egerton, pray begin.

(As Egerton steps forward to speak, Essex runs in. He wears a magnificent court costume and he smiles like an infatuated boy as he throws himself down at the Queen's feet. She smiles indulgently at her favourite as she extends her hand. Essex kisses it fervently several times.)

Queen: Robert!

Essex: Divinity!

(A pause. Cecil and Nottingham exchange glances of distaste at this exhibition. Essex takes up a position on the Queen's left. He scowls at Nottingham, who scowls back. Some of the council members pore over documents together. The Queen and Essex smile at each other. Egerton clears his throat to get attention.)

Queen: Sir Thomas, continue.

Egerton: Your Majesty has indicated that this council leave the vexed issues of France and Spain as being more amenable of solution when the problems in her realm of Ireland have received our care.

Essex: And yet, Lord Keeper, some would say this realm is not so beggarly that a war on both fronts could not be fought.

Egerton: Quite so, my lord —

Essex: Some would say that those who offer caution to Her Majesty express a craven fear or worse, reluctance that others should achieve what they cannot.

Nottingham: This is intemperate language, Essex. We'd hoped that those who caution you in these affairs had tempered your impetuous desire to settle all by the sword.

Essex: My advisors caution, as you put it, not dictate.

Nottingham: This is apparent. Nonetheless, we'd hoped your own debacle in Europe would teach you that to win a war is not the same as wishing it won. Her Majesty's resources are not at the disposal of tiltyard heroes, nor can they be squandered in unskilled soldiering.

Essex: Take care, sir, what you say; I'll not be taunted, no not in the presence.

Queen: My lords, this is not council room behaviour; desist from this brawling or I'll seek maturer counsel.

Nottingham: *(Half bowing)* Your Majesty.

(Essex takes a step backward, folds his arms and looks down petulantly.)

Queen: Sir Thomas Egerton, proceed.

Egerton: Why yes. It seems then fitting to consider measures for suppression of Tyrone in Ireland, as neither censure nor expostulation can bring that traitor to a due and just demeanour in his dealings with Her Majesty. A merciful indulgence being spurned, there seems no other course than to suppress him as a first measure to pouring balm on the traitorous wounds so late inflicted on this Her Majesty's realm of Ireland.

Cecil: On this we have been long agreed. It yet remains to estimate the need in terms of men, supplies and moneys to effect the cure of Ireland and the destruction of Tyrone.

Essex: First we should name the commander and being agreed on him we could the better with his judgment advise Her Majesty on the wants of such an undertaking.

Nottingham: Agreed, and with Her Majesty's permission, I advance the name of Sir William Knollys, uncle to my Lord of Essex. He is a tried commander and no doubt *(looking hard at Essex)* could profit from his nephew's failures in Europe. I'm sure my Lord of Essex would discourse with him at length on futile sorties, lost supplies, unaccounted losses in money, and the neglect and abandonment of diseased and sickly subjects of Her Majesty, all to the benefit of this new enterprise.

Essex: Nay, I'm with you and your game; you do not catch me so. You'd send my uncle sparsely provisioned, poorly equipped and set his failure at my door. Your Majesty, this is a trick to discredit me and mine and at the expense of your honour and dignity and the peace and prosperity of Ireland. Those vipers would sell your honour and the lives of honest men so that they could achieve my downfall. This is treachery in another guise. We'll not have it so . . .

Queen: Peace, Essex. We'll have it as it seems us best. Lord Keeper, your views on this.

Egerton: Sir William is a tried commander and, should it please Your Majesty to appoint him, I'm sure we all could more than satisfy my Lord of Essex that nothing reasonable will be spared to effect our purpose, which is to bring a lasting, prosperous peace to subjects long beplagued with treachery and violence and to help Your Majesty's realm of Ireland enjoy once more the blessing of your kind, solicitous governance.

Queen: Sir Robert Cecil, what think you of Sir William Knollys? Is he fit for such a venture?

Cecil: Eminently so, Your Majesty.

Essex: Aye, for your plans, not for suppressing rebellion; for suppressing me, "eminently" fitted as you say. I'll not have it. Your Majesty give me leave —

Queen: Essex, you grow unruly. Silence.

Essex: But, Your Majesty —

Queen: Silence, Essex, silence! Must I raise my voice to council members? Remember who I am and where you are. Remember also what you were before I made you what you are.

Essex: Forgive me, Majesty; I only speak to save your honour.

Queen: None is more jealous of my honour than I, Essex. Hitherto I've saved it, without breach of decorum. I think you may safely leave my honour in my hands, or the hands of those to whom I may entrust it.

Essex: As Your Majesty wishes.

Queen: Cecil, proceed.

Cecil: As I said, Your Majesty, Sir William Knollys would be a sound appointment. Indeed, for such an enterprise, I would advise either him or one of his age and service. I do not think the pacification of your realm is fit employ for hotheads and young firebrands *(looking at Essex)* however jealous they may be to save Your Majesty's honour. In brief, the Irish project would involve so much discretion, both in dealings with the rebels and the Irish Council, to say nothing of the safe and prudent use of Your Majesty's warrant, that sobriety would be a prime virtue in your new governor there. The power, moreover, which must of necessity be delegated to such a man, is such that would suit ill with any but those of riper years, maturer wisdoms and known excellence in the delicate exercise of both military and civil powers. I know my Lord Burleigh, were he here, would endorse my views.

Queen: It likes us well. Sir William Knollys we will send. It but remains to study with him the necessary wants of this endeavour. Sir Thomas.

Egerton: Your Majesty.

Queen: Summon Sir William to my presence and at such times following as may be most convenient to us and our council, we will convene with him to certify supplies and forces.

Egerton: As you wish —

Essex: He shall not go. By God, he shall not go. I'll not stand by and see my noble uncle's name besmirched and stained by such a pack of jackals, tricked out inadequately to founder in Ireland to his shame and my dishonour.

Queen: Essex, enough. It is resolved —

Essex: Not yet. Hold off. Send Sir George Carew. He has the years you value and the experience too. He is, moreover, leagued with the Cecils and a friend to Nottingham. Send him and leave my uncle to enjoy the dignity and honour he has fairly won.

(The Queen stands and confronts Essex)

Queen: Essex, this is dangerous.

Essex: I care not. Send Carew. My uncle shall not go. I defy you all —

(The Queen takes a step towards Essex and slaps him hard on the face. Essex recoils and places his hand on his sword. Cecil moves solicitously towards the Queen. Nottingham places his hand on his sword.)

Queen: Leave, sirrah!

Essex: By God, Madam. You go too far with me! I neither can nor will swallow this affront, nor would have endured such from your father!

(The Queen displays shock and horror at Essex's words. Essex turns abruptly on his heel and exits. There is a pause.)

Queen: Leave me, all of you!

(As the others bow and leave, the lights dim on the Queen, alone. The lights rise again on Essex House. It is two years later, in 1599. Anthony working, as in Scene I. Francis enters wearing travelling clothes.)

Anthony: *(As he rises to meet Francis.)* A good journey, Francis?

Francis: The worse for being speedy; your letter alarmed me. I've been out of touch awhile.

Anthony: I thought you should know of our lord's doings in Ireland.

Francis: Of that I'd know and more. Who would have thought the Queen would commission him governor of Ireland? His disgrace, their unbreached quarrel, our advice, his own common sense even all cry out against his going forth, and yet he goes, leader of the largest army the times have known, better supplied and victualled than I could have imagined and with such a sweeping mandate of power.

Anthony: I won't be trite, but you know the extravagant results of love and war.

Francis: Love! The Queen is sixty-seven.

Anthony: Exactly so, and my Lord Burleigh's dead, the only man who could or would have restrained her.

Francis: And yet the breach between our lord and the Queen is not entirely healed?

Anthony: They tell me, and I must perforce believe it, having no personal experience of these matters, that love and hate grow frantic in decline.

Francis: Very like, but come, of Ireland.

Anthony: *(Standing and hobbling over to fetch some papers from S.L. desk.)* They tell me that our lord does poorly, fritters his forces away in futile processions through Munster which is all but pacified and refrains from confronting Tyrone in Ulster. They say he's lost thousands in men and supplies, that he overplays the viceroy's part and dubs scores of knights for their mere presence at a skirmish.

Francis: Why, why does he so?

Anthony: That much I'm sure of, indeed it's public property. *(Anthony burns a pile of letters in the fireplace. Occasionally he ferrets through his files and adds another to the blaze.)* There's worse, however. Letters for my eye alone hint at things of which I dare not speak except to you.

Francis: Go on, go on!

Anthony: There's talk of correspondence with the Scottish king to arrange his succession.

Francis: *(Quietly)* Treason?

Anthony: If my reports are true, certainly. But my reports are just reports.

Francis: What else?

Anthony: Understandings with Tyrone.

Francis: To what end?

Anthony: To match his might with Scotland's and compel the Queen to grant James the succession.

Francis: And Tyrone, what would he?

Anthony: Undisputed sway in Ireland acknowledging only the vaguest suzerainty of the English Crown.

Francis: *(Spiritedly)* I'll not believe it. Why, this is madness.

Anthony: Whom God would destroy, He first sends mad.

Francis: You believe it then?

Anthony: How much is substance, how much ill construed conjecture it is impossible to say. Again it might be the reports of Cecil's agents designed to destroy him. Or . . .

Francis: Or what?

Anthony: It still could be something else; wild thoughts and fancies that our lord has ill advisedly let loose. All words and no substance.

Francis: This is true; it ever was a fault with him to utter wildness when smarting under slights or some denial of his will, illusory or actual.

Anthony: Heaven make it so, but there is more.

Francis: Can there be worse?

Anthony: I think so. At his first going into Ireland, so fearful was he of the Cecil faction,

that he demanded, and received under the royal seal, permission to return when e'er he would.

Francis: I remember. He called it guarding his back.

Anthony: Her Majesty of late revoked that privilege. Irked by his losses and incapacity to beard Tyrone in Ulster, she bade him stay until she personally gave him permission to report to her of his success.

Francis: A blow to his pride, but what of that?

Anthony: It's said, by those who whisper of his treating with the Scots and Irish, that having knit the plot to affront Her Majesty with a show of force, he plans to land his army, augment it from his Welsh estates, and march on London.

Francis: If this be true, he's quite undone and so are you for harbouring information against Her Majesty's peace.

Anthony: *(Dropping a final bundle of letters on the fire)* I have no information now.

Francis: Don't be foolish, Anthony. If it is known that you've received such letters, there are ways to make you remember their contents.

Anthony: It won't be known. I've other papers kept intact to destroy my Irish correspondent should he talk.

Francis: And they, have they not papers of yours?

Anthony: None. I send verbal instructions only.

Francis: But the messenger.

Anthony: There I'm fortunate. He threatened me the last time we met, said he'd have us both and our lord arraigned for treason.

Francis: You paid him off?

Anthony: Yes, I paid him off.

Francis: How much? Our resources . . .

Anthony: Your journey's tired you, Francis.

You're normally not obtuse or more dainty than the case has need of.

Francis: Anthony, what peril do you lead us into?

Anthony: No peril, Francis, no peril.

Francis: But of the treason, what of that?

Anthony: I know of no treason as yet. There's grounds for much suspicion, but as yet, no treason.

Francis: Is it just wild talk then?

Anthony: I'm disposed to think so. Firstly, the plot is too extravagant to hope of success. Secondly, our lord of late has grown both wild and peevish.

Francis: 'Tis so. Ambitious men if they rise not with their service, they will take order that their service fall with them.

Anthony: Quite. Thirdly, we are bound to him to believe nothing absolutely to his disgrace until it is more evident than it is.

Francis: I find it in myself to believe he thought or said such things out of spleen, but that he would act on it, I'd rather not accept.

Anthony: Our duty is to bring him back to his allegiance, in will and spirit, as well as deed. We should not forsake him just because he's wild. He rose to fame too fast for one of his humour; we must see he doesn't pay for a doting Queen's indulgence to a favourite.

Francis: But if he's guilty?

Anthony: You know the law. Our patron or no, treason's treason. However, it still would be our duty to extenuate his guilt, out of our love and service, and in gratitude for benefits conferred.

Francis: So that in doing so we fail not to keep our allegiance clear unto our lady, the Queen.

Anthony: (Irritated) Of course, of course.

(A furious banging on the door. The messenger's voice is heard. "I must see Master Bacon at once." He enters.)

Messenger: Good Sirs, I bring strange news, and letters from Nonsuch to confirm it.

Anthony: Do you so, sirrah, then let us have them both and quickly.

Messenger: My payment first.

Anthony: Are you mad, were you ever not paid?

(Anthony throws him a purse. The messenger counts out the money and then throws it down.)

Messenger: The price is up. There's talk of treason. I could talk, nay, will, 'twould be my duty. They'd take you both as traitors.

Anthony: How much?

Messenger: You know the value of my silence, if not of the news I bring.

Anthony: How much, villain?

Messenger: Offer me gold; I'll tell you if it will suffice.

Anthony: We're trapped, Francis. We must pay.

Francis: Is there no . . .

Anthony: Patience, Francis! This does not contain much. Pray God it satisfy you.

(The messenger warily accompanies Anthony who limps painfully over to the chest. Francis stands dumbfounded and inactive. Anthony opens the chest. He takes out a leather bag and hands it to the messenger.)

Anthony: Count it.

(Anthony moves round to the messenger's side, draws a dagger and plunges it into the messenger. Anthony then moves back at a nimble limp to survey his handiwork. The messenger clutches the dagger, looks about him wildly and falls. Francis is stunned.)

Francis: My God, Anthony, what now?

(Anthony moves forward and removes two letters from the messenger. He opens the first, glances at it and throws it aside. He opens the second, reads it and then turns to Francis.)

Anthony: Our Lord of Essex has disobeyed his orders and returned to England. He's thrown himself on the Queen's mercy at Nonsuch.

(The lights fade slowly to black.)

End of Act One

A24

Act Two *Essex House, later in 1599. Essex is seated alone. On Francis' entrance, he rises in great agitation and rushes over to greet him, and grasp his hands. Francis is embarrassed at the warmth of his reception.)*

Essex: Francis, thank God!

Francis: *(Disengaging himself gently)* My lord, you are indeed distraught — Had I known . . .

Essex: Francis, I don't feel safe, not in my own house even, whence as you know I am forbidden to stir by the Queen's order. Ah, Francis . . .

(He allows Francis to help him to a chair, but a settled posture is impossible for him.)

Francis: You received my letter at Nonsuch?

Essex: Yes indeed, but then nothing.

Francis: My lord, this agitated way of acting will not do. You invite danger by seeming to endure it.

Essex: Ay, but the Cecils, are they not even now plotting my destruction?

Francis: Certainly, they are constant in their enmity, but what of that? It is with Her Majesty that you must treat and you have been closer to her than any Cecil. If you act as though lost you will be. Think of your present plight but as a mist, if it go upwards it may perhaps cause a shower, if downwards, it will clear.

Essex: This may well be, but what of your advice? Does it stem from my loyal friend, Francis, or from a servant of the Queen, the newly appointed Counsellor Extraordinary?

Francis: Good my lord, you know how I stand; I am more yours than any man's and more yours than any man.

Essex: What think you then of the Queen's dealing with me?

Francis: Not so bad but that your lordship's wisdom can yet turn it to good account.

Essex: Perhaps so, but what course can I take?

Sᴿ F. BACON.

A26

Francis: Complete abasement.

Essex: Even so, I am denied her presence — but you, Francis, you are not banned; you can . . .

Francis: Only so much. It will little help us, if, while I portray a meek and chastened Essex, begging favour of attendance, you, my lord, maintain an ill beseeming coldness, a sort of proud ill-used disdain. Nor will my picture of palefaced penitence prevail, if those whom you consort with are frantic soldiers of fortune, younger sons of beggared lords; no, these frantic conclaves with former comrades are not to the point. *(Pause)* I take it you've written no letters?

Essex: *(Abject)* No, none, except to my sister.

Francis: Or received any.

Essex: *(Offering letter)* Only her reply.

Francis: *(Reading extract)* "I have written to Her Majesty on your behalf to quarrel with her base usage of you, for never was a noble viceroy so despicably repaid for constant service to the Crown of England. Indeed, it causes wonderment where'er one turns." *(Francis thrusts it back at Essex abruptly)* Burn it!

Essex: You think she's wrong?

Francis: The Queen will.

Essex: But can she use me so? Have I deserved . . .

Francis: My lord, your confinement was a shock, no doubt, and, doubtless, I was wrong to delay my visit to you. I thought my letter would suffice. So much I am to blame, but cannot you see the danger of your present course? 'Tis not the time to think of honour or ill usage. The Queen's the fount of honour, dignity, virtue, nay, the source of life itself. There is no appeal from her sway.

Essex: But is it right?

Francis: I don't know what you mean by "right", but, if its meaning lies outside the governance of Her Majesty, I'll not enquire.

Essex: Francis, forgive me, but you're not of noble blood; you lack the terror of a tainted name.

Francis: My father was knighted, my lord, yours was made the **first** Earl of Essex.

Essex: Francis, I meant . . .

Francis: Let's leave this talk of blood; it is a foolish fantasy we cannot afford. Let's talk of reinstatement, favour and power, and also of shame, imprisonment and death.

Essex: *(Pause)* Very well.

Francis: Good. First, importune the Queen by all and every means to grant you access to her; beg, flatter, promise, wheedle, grovel — at least three letters a week; I'll write some for you.

Essex: You think it's easy . . .

Francis: Next, banish all wild companions and cease all correspondence. I'll see your sister's letters both to you and to the Queen are intercepted. Her crazed notion of family honour will lead you to the Tower.

Essex: Nay, sir, you do presume too much . . .

Francis: I should be loath to accept the consequence of your thinking that. I should be loath to see your lordship sink under the Queen's displeasure.

Essex: You'd hinder my aims?

Francis: I would not presume to usurp a role your lordship would fulfill.

Essex: Me? Do you think I'd ruin myself, left to my own devices?

Francis: Fortune is so variable. I'll not prophesy, but I would fear it.

Essex: *(Standing up and pacing)* Go on, go on, what else must I do?

Francis: But this; if by good fortune you gain an audience do not present yourself as the sole saviour of Ireland whom Her Majesty must perforce send back with such additions of forces and honour as will soothe you for your forced detention.

Essex: What then?

Francis: Offer your services to be used as Her Majesty may deem best, how Her Majesty may deem best, and when Her Majesty may deem best.

Essex: (Ironically) If Her Majesty may deem best?

Francis: Ay, that too.

Essex: (Sitting down, but still not at ease) But if my letters fail, what then?

Francis: (Thoughtfully) They shouldn't . . . I have it! We'll have some letters — I'll write them — purporting to be between you and Anthony. In them, we'll paint your woes in terms of humble and loyal despair.

Essex: My fears, my enemies?

Francis: That as well, if need be. After a while, I'll show them to the Queen, as offered to me by my brother, in duty bound. It cannot fail but move her.

Essex: What does the Queen purpose next with me?

Francis: A judicial enquiry of your conduct in Ireland and other disloyal acts.

Essex: Disloyal acts . . .

Francis: It pleases her to see them so.

Essex: Then I am ruined surely?

Francis: Not so. First the enquiry will be private with no written records.

Essex: Why the secrecy?

Francis: A public hearing would destroy your honour.

Essex: The Queen cares for my honour?

Francis: Some would say, more than your lordship does.

Essex: There is honour and honour.

Francis: That there is; the Queen's version leads to preferment and riches, the other kind to ruin.

Essex: Why else in private?

Francis: (Hesitating) A public outcry would be unseemly.

Essex: (Brightening) She fears that, does she?

Francis: She fears that any public outcry in your favour would compel her to deal more harshly with you than she wishes.

Essex: (Mocking) I am touched at this concern.

Francis: (Serious) You should be; it is a fear for your welfare that she is not compelled to entertain.

Essex: This crawling will kill me.

Francis: Not so, you will rise up a new man and the Queen and yourself be better acquainted for it. Bend, my lord, bend, or of a surety you'll break.

Essex: What do I do at the hearing?

Francis: Why, admit all and humbly crave Her Majesty's pardon, while making yourself amenable to whatever's advised in her interest by the noble judges present.

Essex: So, I must endure disgrace without complaint from lesser men who in my palmy days begged a fortnight but to make a gift to me?

Francis: At last, your lordship understands. Which reminds me, I have requested Her Majesty that I might be spared the task of prosecuting you on her behalf.

Essex: (Mocking) Your honour prompted this?

Francis: My loyalty to your lordship without which I would not now be troubling you with my advice.

A28

Essex: I am sorry, Francis.

Francis: It may be that as counsellor extraordinary to the Queen, I can't avoid this duty, odious to me though it is; for which I must needs beg your pardon, for I shall press my charges hard, so be advised and flinch not.

Essex: You will not suffer by it in my regard.

Francis: (Getting up) I thank you. My lord, I'll not detain you longer. (Pause) Remember Icarus though, who sought to fly to the sun on waxen wings and plunged to his death.

Essex: Ambition I have, but what are my wings of wax?

Francis: Why, nothing but pride and a lack of due proportion.

Essex: I'd accept that from no man else.

Francis: My loyalty makes me bold. Good-day my lord.

Essex: (Rising) Good-day, Francis.

(Francis leaves as the lights dim on Essex and rise on Francis Bacon's house at Twickenham. The year is now 1600 A.D. Anthony is limping around the room affecting pleasure at hangings, carved chests, pictures and other items of furnishing. The room is more lavishly furnished than the room at Essex House. Francis enters, with a portfolio of papers)

Anthony: Well, Francis, the Queen herself when she came over the river for supper, must have found you very comfortable here at Twickenham.

Francis: Her Majesty was pleased to thank me for my poor provision for her ease and comfort.

Anthony: Tell me, Francis, was any part of that ease and comfort an assurance to violently attack the Earl of Essex at the York House hearing?

Francis: (Putting down papers and giving Anthony his undivided attention) You know very well, Anthony, that the mildness of the Queen t'wards Essex is in large measure due to my good offices with Her Majesty. By taking part in the enquiry, and by taking the Earl to task for some slight matter, I was able to maintain decorum. It was an odious task for me to attack my patron, but I'd warned him of it and he accepted it as I advised. Had I not been there, Sir Edward Coke, our brave Attorney General, would so have enraged the Earl by stout abuse, that all would have been lost. As it was, decorum was maintained. The earl accepted mildly all the court's rebukes and humbly begged that pardon Her Majesty was happy to bestow.

Anthony: Our lord accepted your advice?

Francis: That he did. His words were: "You will not suffer by it in my regard", or some such phrase.

Anthony: It may be as you say, Francis.

Francis: It is as I say. I visited him. He begged me for advice; I gave it and he agreed to all.

Anthony: From what you say, it was the same advice I remember giving to a brother of mine some years ago, to be humble and complain to the Queen's will.

Francis: You know it was the same — I'll not deny it.

Anthony: Was that wise, think you?

Francis: Would I have given it else? Do you think I meant to ruin him?

Anthony: The advice I gave to you and which you hourly profit by, for certainly there never was a busier servant of the Crown, was good advice to give an ambitious clerk. But advice is only good or bad in terms of its being taken. Do you think our Lord of Essex, a high spirited noble, forced to stand at bay while Cokes and Cecils, aye and Francis Bacon too, yelp and snap at his heels, can stomach such advice as I gave you and you gave him?

Francis: Stomach it or no, it is the only way. Be he as noble and high spirited as he will, the Queen is sterner mettled yet and he will wreck himself by any other course.

Anthony: I believe you think so, yet I could not be party to my lord's abasement as you have been.

Francis: Is he not free now to come and go with all restraints of movement lifted?

Anthony: This is true, but still I'd be a better guardian of my lord's good name and reputation, a reputation not enhanced by cringing like a scolded schoolboy in York House. He who took Cadiz must now beg pardon of such as you and Edward Coke and bite his tongue when ink stained hands are pointed at him.

Francis: Pardon was begged of Her Majesty — the court was but an instrument, a tool, to convey it to her.

Anthony: A tool of your fashioning, brother. Were you not ashamed to see our lord's humiliation?

Francis: Essex took my advice willingly. It was given in his best interests and taken with good grace.

Anthony: (Looking about him at the furnishings and perhaps touching a silver bowl or some such object of value) Certainly he has paid enough for it. How would you value this manor and land he gave you?

Francis: 'Tis not a subject to be thought on, much less discussed in vulgar terms.

Anthony: I remember how "vulgar" it was when he bestowed it on you, "vulgar" enough to prevent your burying yourself in Cambridge, "vulgar" enough now to enable you to maintain yourself in style as Queen's Counsel Extraordinary and attack your former patron with slander and abuse before his peers at York House.

Francis: Essex was and is my patron. I serve the Earl still.

Anthony: "Essex" is it now? Or "the Earl"? Where has "our lord" gone? Where is "my sweet lord", "my dear lord", "my singular good lord"? (Pause) Alas he's gone for you, Francis; he exists no more.

Francis: So, it's out at last, is it? Anthony Bacon, private secretary to the Earl of Essex, alone can understand him, alone supports him. Why then are you not received at all his present councils? Why are you not welcomed by the wild young sprigs of nobility who now frequent his table? When, when were you last in his confidence? Is it you he leans on now, or is it that adoring youth, the Earl of Southampton?

Anthony: I never have intruded upon my lord, as you have, brother, never fawned and stabbed alternately. It is enough for me to have served and keep myself in readiness to serve again, whenever my lord commands. I am not a servitor in the modern fashion.

Francis: That you're not! Your sentiments are mouldy and rotten. They smack of the old wars before Henry VII. They smell to me of the folly that kept Lancaster and York at each other's throats while England bled for their antics. You're the model of the dedicated squire who'd hand his lord a lance to commit whatever folly his lordship might wish; aye, or any treason too.

Anthony: I'm not treacherous, speak not to me of treachery — I serve.

Francis: Cannot you think too? Must you serve blindly any cause my lord embraces whether it's dangerous or no to his ultimate peace, or the Queen's, or the state's? Can't you see those days are past, that now best service lies in keeping that accord the nation's blessed with and not go wrangling after one lord's reputation while good government is shaken and comfort's given to those unwholesome elements who'd mar Her Majesty's peace? How can my lord have any honour, any dignity, that's not encompassed by the Queen's, and how can you serve any man by failing to preserve a sane relation between him and his sovereign?

Anthony: The Queen knows my lord's worth; she has recognized it in the past and she is not so overserved with valiant followers that she can afford to neglect him.

Francis: Aye, but he's changed; our loyalty now must be tempered with caution. You've changed too. There was a time when you'd call folly, folly; failure, failure. What's unmanned you, Anthony, that you must dance to one man's tune and he the wildest piper of them all?

Anthony: I've said before, I dance not, Francis. I leave that to courtiers. Were you as kind and attentive to my concerns as I have ever been to yours you'd notice that I limp more, stoop more, grow more frail. I would not have a forced compassion; pity that's forced from one's own kin is poor comfort. However, as I say, I'm failing . . .

Francis: Nay, Anthony —

Anthony: I know it and my physician confirms it. In such a state, I'd rather devote what energy is left me to old loves, old causes. I've no use for your modern sterile concepts: "the state", "the nation", they are true possibly, but they hold no charm for me; my blood cannot race the faster for them. They are of the mind, of theory and suitable for those who can shift with politic fashions. In my case, I'll serve my old allegiance in the old way whatever you say of me. If it's folly, it's a folly I've grown used to and, to my fading vision, it has an aura of nobility; it recalls the ancient decencies. Remember me to our lord, Francis, should you see him on affairs of state *(Pause)* or out of an old loyalty. Tell him his secretary has strength yet still to serve should he require it.

(Anthony exits. Francis returns to his work but cannot. He crumples a paper and flings it down. Blackout. Out of the darkness voices are heard: "My brother will not join us".; "Is all bestowed as needed?"; "The city has been pledged."; "Three hundred of us at least!"; "They suspect nothing."; etc. The lights come up on Essex House. Essex and the Earl of Southampton are standing by a table on which are scattered papers and rolled documents. They are dressed for fighting, though lightly, with no armour. Essex is flushed and frantic and moves with the jerky decisiveness of a hypertense individual in the grip of paranoia. Southampton exhibits a boyish enthusiasm. Groups of armed men are seen. They are conferring excitedly among themselves. Their number is augmented during this scene up to the entrance of the Lord Keeper Egerton when the stage should be as full of them as is practical.)

Essex: *(Speaking to Southampton)* With the Queen's person seized we'll dismiss Raleigh, Cobham and proud Cecil. The realm will then be ours. Tyrone from Ireland and James from Scotland will not fail us if there's risings in the West and North to support the government. Sir Christopher.

Blount: My lord?

Essex: Have you determined on the seizing of the palace gate? Is all prepared and do all know their places?

Blount: In point exact, my lord.

Essex: Good. Sir John, know they who would assist you hold the hall how they should act?

Davies: In all particulars, my lord; also, Sir Charles has organised the gaining of the presence chamber; indeed our plans therein are interlocked.

Essex: 'Tis well. My Lord Southampton and myself will succour you and take the custody of the Queen.

Southampton: I like not this summons to the Council —

Essex: 'Tis nothing — they're told I'm sick and cannot go; it will suffice.

Southampton: Let us pray so. So much depends on timing, on horses even.

Essex: If lack of horses worry you, bring them up now.

Southampton: That would precipitate events the more. Who would imagine three hundred horses gathered together for innocent employ? No, we must do without them till the very last, else we'll provoke alarm at court and give them time to muster arms in force.

Essex: Well, leave it so then; if fortune can but smile on us a few hours more we're safe.

Southampton: She's in our debt, we cannot fail at this stage.

DAVIES
SILVER 71

Essex: (*Addressing the company at large*) Lords, gentlemen. My thanks for your adventuring yourselves gainst tyranny and to save my life from those who plot against it, can yet, at this stage, but express itself in words. But if our push succeed, which in such company I doubt not, my thanks will manifest themselves in solid recompense that those who held off from us, to whom our life's peril was a cause indifferent, will have reason to grieve in jealousy alone. However, those, far worse in my opinion, for I do not count my life as much, when weighed against the safety of the realm, those who would play the sluggard while Cecil and Raleigh trample our liberties and sell the succession to the Infanta, those whose coffers daily swell with Spanish bribes, they will have greater cause to grieve than jealousy at your rewards. For, believe me, we mean to bring all to account who'd sell the crown for private profit and subject our nation to a Spanish usurpation.

(*Cheers of encouragement from all on stage.*)

Davers: (*Entering*) My lord.

Essex: Sir Charles?

Davers: Sir Thomas Egerton is without with three accompanying lords from the Council. They seek an audience with you.

(*Consternation*)

Essex: Why then, show them in.

Southampton: What! Let them see the scope of our assembly. Make excuses, my lord. You said you were sick; be sick still, unable to receive them.

(*hub-bub*)

Essex: We cannot hide our numbers at this stage — of that they will have guessed, probably knew of it before, and therefore come to question it.

Southampton: Yet to confirm all, my lord, it cannot . . .

Essex: Courage, Southampton.

Southampton: That I lack not, but common prudence . . .

Essex: Sir Charles, pray show in my Lord Keeper Egerton and the lords accompanying him.

Davers: Very well, my lord. (*Exits*)

Minor hub-bub. Sir Thomas Egerton enters accompanied by Sir William Knollys and the Lord Chief Justice. The crowd parts for them grudgingly. Sir Thomas Egerton, leading, glances coldly around him until the chattering subsides, then fixes Essex with a cold stare.

Essex: (*Nodding to each*) My Lord Keeper; My Lord Chief Justice; Uncle (*to Knollys*)

Egerton: My Lord of Essex, it grieves me that your swift recovery of health should manifest itself by your capacity to lead a riotous assembly for though it's yet contained within your grounds, it is one.

Essex: My lord is pleased to mock.

Chief Justice: The Queen in Council sent us hither to question this assembly and to receive from you a fitting explanation.

Essex: Well or ill, I'll not go to Council.

Knollys: There's no need of that, nephew, the Queen is satisfied that you report to us the cause for this assembly. If you wish, in private at your discretion.

Essex: And if I say no, I'll not be questioned?

Egerton: My lord, I do not think you understand. We are not instructed by the Queen to parley or debate with you as you see fit. Rather are we sent to make demands why you are leading such a gathering here which might be interpreted as meaning disrespect unto Her Majesty's peace.

Essex: I have no explanation for the Queen in Council, none.

Knollys: Nephew, take care. This rude defiance of the Queen's demands coming so shortly after her sustained displeasure —

Essex: I defy the Queen's displeasure.

Egerton: I cannot accept you'd be reported even so in council. Think again, my lord; be guided by your uncle's wisdom and we will suffer for you a lapse of memory on what has just now passed.

Southampton: Do not listen, good my lord, who can claim a lapse of memory of what has passed such an assembly? Defy them and the Council.

Lord Chief Justice: Would you defy the Queen too, Southampton, is that your drift?

Southampton: Aye, her too, together with all the pack of traitors that advise her.

Knollys: Nephew, this is treason that you purpose . . .

Essex: Call it what you will, uncle, I've done with satisfying demands from both the Council and Her Majesty while she's beset with rogues like Cecil.

Knollys: Then, nephew, you are lost, for this is treason clear and must be so reported.

(Jeering)

Egerton: *(After glancing about him to still the clamour)* One final time. Robert Devereux, Earl of Essex, I charge you on the warrant of Her Majesty in Council to give a fitting explanation of this assembly.

Essex: You shall have none, Lord Keeper.

Egerton: Then must we report you even so, that, and the treasonous complexion of your following.

Southampton: Let them not return, my lord.

Voices: Keep them fast. Kill them. Let's be done with them now. An end to tyranny. Let them not leave my Lord.

Essex: Silence! *(To Egerton and lords)* My lords, I'm left no other course than to detain you here. The honour that I hold you in forbids my loosing you into the streets where followers of mine out of excessive zeal for my cause and too mindful of my wrongs might do your lordships violence.

Lord Chief Justice: Would you seize the Queen's officers, traitor?

Voices: Why keep them? Kill them! The devil have their lives. They shall not leave this place. End it now.

Knollys: *(Shouting above confusion)* Nephew, for God's sake and your own, if not for ours, do not lay violent hands on the Queen's officers.

Essex: *(As hub-bub subsides)* Uncle, have no fear, you'll suffer no ill usage at my hands, but only honourable confinement to save you from the enmity which, brewed by fault of Cecil and the Council, might else destroy you. I would not suffer any of you to risk the chance of mischief. Sir Christopher.

Blount: My lord?

Essex: Pray you and some others secure these lords within our inner library and mount guard on them. *(To Egerton and lords)* My lords, if you would follow out Sir Christopher, he'll see you safe bestowed where danger shall not reach you.

Egerton: This is treason, Essex, treason.

(They accompany Blount off stage to the accompaniment of some jostling and jeering.)

Southampton: What now, my lord?

Essex: My lords, there's only one course now.

Voice: Aye, arm and out!

Essex: Right, arm and out it is. Raise the City. Their trained bands will rally to us I've no doubt; indeed, they have assured me so. Then on to the palace. They cannot withstand us with the City at our back.

Southampton: But what of horses, good my lord?

Essex: Talk to us not of horses now Southampton. Our Fortune's beckoning. We've done with plans and parleys. Now is the time for action. My lords, are you with me?

All: Aye!

Essex: Shall we wait for the government to gather arms?

All: No!

Essex: Then it's arm and out and raise the City. *(He draws his sword)* The call's "Essex and the Queen"!

All: Essex and the Queen! Essex and the Queen!

(Essex leads the whole gathering out on the run. The shouts of "Essex and the Queen" mount in volume as the lights dim. Suddenly there is silence. A bell sounds and the lights slowly fade up on the trial of Essex and Southampton. They sit in a dock S.R. flanked by guards. Above them sits the Lord Chief Justice: at his sides are Egerton and Nottingham. To the left of this group sits the clerk of the court at a table with bibles, papers etc. On S.L. sits Sir Edward Coke and behind him at a table covered with documents, Francis Bacon and two other counsellors.)

A36

Essex: *(Spiritedly)* So you would wave aside the treason of Sir Walter Raleigh — Do so then, there's others. I can name them, if the Court is not bent on shielding traitors!

Chief Justice: My Lord of Essex, you lack decorum. Remember that it is you and my lord of Southampton who stand trial for treason here. Remember too the awesome penalties which must follow conviction and give some thought to your behaviour.

Essex: May I speak; am I to be silenced? Are traitors to sell the succession to Spain and the Pope? Do you want the Papists' claims recognised above those of Protestant Scotland? Are we to be priest ridden again in England? "Decorum" you say, "behaviour" — Aye, there are some that it would suit well to have "decorum" and "behaviour" stifle the truth; some who even now are selling us to Spain.

Chief Justice: My Lord of Essex, your charges against Sir Walter Raleigh have been proved groundless. The chief base of your defence has been the need you felt to take up arms to put down Spanish plots. So far we have heard little to induce us to an acceptance of your views and, even if we had, armed insurrection can never have excuse.

Essex: But plotting and bribing can, is that it? Never take up arms for the Queen and our protestant faith — no that's treason, but plot and scheme for Catholic Spain to swallow us up, that's the mark of a patriot. Can it be my lords, that you would so blind yourselves, not to the danger of my life which is nothing, but to the slow treachery of shuffling clerks and supposedly loyal advisers?

Chief Justice: My Lord of Essex, you must either produce evidence or desist from idle slanders.

Essex: Evidence you want? You shall have it. I see Sir Robert Cecil is not in Court. Strange that so valuable a member of council cannot be present. Where is he, think you! ! I'll tell you where he is. He's in his cellar counting out his Spanish gold, that's where he is. Send for him there and, if you can drag him from his vile hoard of Judas gold and silver, ask him how he came by it. Ask him how he and Sir Walter

Raleigh just now excused by you, plotted my life and Southampton's here because we would oppose his treason. Ask him how the estates and property of the Cecils wax so fat in the land.

Chief Justice: This court cannot . . .

(Sir Robert Cecil, wild eyed and frantic, rushes into the room. He stands momentarily C.S. then throws himself down before the Lord Chief Justice.)

Cecil: Lies! Lies! My lord, hear me, hear me. Let me clear my name from the evil slanders of this traitor. Let me speak!

Essex: Speak on, traitor! Tell us of your Spanish wealth.

Chief Justice: *(Raising Sir Robert Cecil up)* Sir Robert, there is no need nor warrant to disturb the Queen's justice in this distracted fashion.

Essex: No need, say you. Look at him, he's shaking with fear. Sweat away, Cecil, sweat away your Spanish fat if you can!

Cecil: My lords, I heard all —

Essex: Aye, like an eavesdropping lackey spying out his betters' business. The knave should be whipped. Thinks he this court's a play, or masque to spy on it as unlawful audience?

Cecil: Let me but speak, but hear me, lords.

Chief Justice: Fear not, Sir Robert, you will be heard. Though I fear we waste the court's time in these delays, yet I would not have it said the prisoner was not allowed a just chance of defence, nor would I have your dignity outraged by the intemperance of the prisoner's attacks.

Cecil: I thank your lordship. It is not my intent . . .

Essex: Swear him in, if we must hear his lies, let him perjure his soul for them and go to hell for it.

Chief Justice: Swear in Sir Robert Cecil.

Clerk: *(Advancing on Cecil with Quarto Bible)* Do you Robert Cecil . . .

Essex: Nay, look to what he swears on; is it a bible?

Clerk: My lord, it is a quarto bible such as . . .

Essex: *(No longer rational or displaying any semblance of control)* Quarto will not do. Bring in the great Folio Bible we all have sworn on. Though quarto will suffice to damn that greasy villain, I'd have him damned in folio like Raleigh. Bring out the folio.

(Francis goes and fetches the heavy folio from the back of the court and places it on the table.)

Cecil: *(Placing his hand on the folio and shaking with fear and anger.)* I swear by Almighty God to bear true witness this day in the cause of the Queen's justice.

Chief Justice: The prisoner Essex may put questions to Sir Robert Cecil.

Essex: I will be brief, lest his perjured soul prove too strong a temptation for the Devil himself and Satan come into this court to drag him off like Faustus in the play.

Chief Justice: Proceed, my Lord of Essex.

Essex: Oh, vile man, relate why and from whom you took your Spanish bribes.

Cecil: Bribes I never took, Spanish or other.

Essex: Bribes, I say, bribes! Answer me, answer me.

Cecil: *(To Lord Chief Justice)* My Lord Chief Justice, much as I spurn the prisoner's frantic ravings yet will I make answer. Spanish gold I have. Who has not who works in the courts of any realm? If one performs a service in the course of duty to the Queen and an ambassador chooses to feel himself favoured and is pleased to pay for what is his free and for gratis, none but a madman would refuse. My refusal of such gold, imperial or Spanish, would be taken as discourtesy. The sums I have received are common knowledge — I have never sought to make a secret of it. Far from it, I have made jest with Her Majesty herself about it. This, then, my lords, is the sum of all my treason. Would it

were true my Lord of Essex, it were the sum of all of yours.

Essex: He lies.

Chief Justice: Sir Robert Cecil, be free to leave us or remain as you judge best. Your honour never was in question here. However, I welcome your testimony as confirming what all have judged before, namely the wild and fanciful nature of such defence as my Lords of Essex and Southampton have seen fit to bring to the atten-

(Cecil leaves)

Chief Justice: Pray proceed now with the business in hand, Sir Edward, we waste time with these digressions and delays.

Coke: *(Bumbling)* May it please your grace, *(To Lord Chief Justice)* my lords, it was not, has not been the intention of Crown Counsel, that is we never wished to open enquiry general into the question of succession —

Essex: *(With spirit)* Aye, it would not suit some of you to do so. Yet have we seen Sir Walter Raleigh and Sir Robert Cecil begging the court on bended knees to acquit or forget their plotting in the cause of Spain. *(Exchanges confident smiles with Southampton)*

Chief Justice: I must request the prisoner Essex to desist from further interruption. Proceed, Attorney General.

Coke: Why yes, it never was the purpose of this court to open issues so extraneous. Indeed, were it not for your grace's indulgence, Lord Chief Justice, in allowing free and, some would say, wilful irreverent interference, had it not been for that, we may well have advanced our case more clearly.

(Francis Bacon all this while evinces an infuriated impatience with Coke's handling of the case.)

Coke: My Lord of Essex, it has been shown by deposition and witnesses here appearing, that you, with divers other disaffected, sought to seize the person of Her Majesty and, by such a treasonable course, grasp into your hands the ordering of the state. All of which is in any terms in law a treason which —

Essex: I never sought nor never would to harm Her Majesty's person, but driven by plots, both on my life and on the true succession of the Crown which some would sell to Spain, I took what course I could, both to preserve my life and protect the Queen and nation.

Coke: In law, my lord, such seizure or attempted seizure, for praise be to God, it was but attempted, constitutes a treason. Again, detention of Her Majesty's officers, sent to demand account of you for treasonous gatherings, the defiance of the herald and the clash of arms provoked by you with government forces under my lord High Admiral all, all point to treason in law.

Essex: My intent was never treason. I defy your law. My conscience was ever clear.

Coke: It could be, my lord, as you say, but we are met . . . *(Begins fumbling through books and papers)* We are met, that is this court is now assembled to determine treason as a point of law which *(To Lord Justice)* with your grace's kind indulgence, I will now make plain *(Further fumbling)* The statute that I seek of Mary — nay of Stephen, Stephen clearly states . . .

(During the last moment Francis Bacon, quietly and determinedly, rises and walks in front of the long table and Coke, who is still muttering in his parchments. As Bacon begins speaking Coke looks up absently and then sits down with a glance of mild and timid expostulation to the Lord Chief Justice. The latter does not meet his glance for his eyes, and the eyes of everybody else in the court are fixed on Francis Bacon.)

SOUTHAMPTON

Silver '71

Francis: *(Speaking calmly and distinctly)* My lords, in speaking of this late horrible rebellion, which has been in the eyes and ears of all, I will not presume to bore your lordships with matters that are obvious to so learned an assembly. Yet must I in the discharge of my duties speak out plain in several matters. Firstly, it is well known that traitors never never dare attack the person of a prince without a pretext. Some claim to protect the sovereign, others to remove evil advisers who would corrupt religion or destroy the people's ancient rights and liberties. For God has imprinted such a majesty in the face of a prince that no man durst approach his sovereign with a traitorous intent. So the Earl of Essex seduced from their allegiance such as are charged with him by a pretense to save the state. The same was his excuse to fly to the City, seeking armed aid against Her Majesty, claiming the while his person was in danger from such imaginary foes as he has told you of. Alas for the Earl, his life was in no danger, nor was the state till he himself assaulted its good order with rebellion. *(Turning to Essex)* For you, my lord, should know that though princes give their subjects cause of discontent, though they take away the honours they have heaped upon them, though they bring them to a lower estate than they raised them from, yet ought they not to be so forgetful of allegiance that they should enter into any undutiful act; much less upon rebellion, as you, my lord, have done. *(Pause)* All whatsoever you have or can say in answer to this are but shadows. Therefore, I think it best for you to confess and not to justify.

Essex: My lords, to offer a defence against this Queen's Counsel Extraordinary, who seeks to be so busy in this case, I call forth Mr. Bacon against Mr. Bacon. It is as yet unknown to you, my lords, how, when I was late suffering Her Majesty's ill favour, this Counsel Extraordinary, just now speaking, was so moved by threats to my life and fortune that he composed forged letters between me and his brother, Anthony. These were brought to the attention of the Queen to show her the state of my loyalty and the patience with which I bore, not alone indignity and neglect, but also threats against my very life. Indeed, while they were written by Mr. Bacon here, I swear I could not better myself have stated my own case. It now appears that Mr. Bacon has undergone a change, so that what

he believed before he now discounts, and what he wrote down he would deny. Mr. Bacon may suffer a change of mind about my merits and deserving — such changes are not unknown when a man's ambition drives him to ally himself with strength and not with justice, but the letters, my lords, the letters stand to rebuke him and justify my cause.

Francis: My lords, these letters I do not deny. They belong to a period when I wasted time and fortune in a vain attempt to bring the traitor Essex to a better understanding with the Queen. The letters themselves are harmless and irrelevant. How sadly I failed to curb the Earl's rebellious nature and make him a loyal and useful servant of the Queen is quite apparent. Would I had spent my energies in a cause more serviceable to Her Majesty's peace and profit than to have laboured so to cure the pride and treacherous folly of the Earl of Essex. May I conclude with this: I have never yet seen in any case such favour shown to a prisoner; so many digressions, such delivery of evidence piecemeal and so foolish a defence of such great and notorious treasons. The Earl of Essex claims he would have gone a suppliant to Her Majesty. How can a "suppliant" be armed: To take secret counsel, to run together in numbers armed, to ignore the warning of my Lord Keeper and a herald and still persist? We need no niceties of law to come to judgment. Will any simple man, when told of what they did, take it to be less than treason?

Essex: *(Jumps up screaming, madly)* Treason, is it, Mr. Bacon? It is lies, all lies! Tis your "good advice" that . . .

Lord Chief Justice: Silence, my Lord of Essex! Silence in Her Majesty's Court!

Essex: I defy Her Majesty's court! I appeal to . . .

Lord Chief Justice: Remove the prisoners!

(Confusion breaks out as the guards drag Essex and Southampton screaming from the court. The others exit as cries of "Lies, Lies!" "Treason! etc. continue. Francis is left alone as the lights dim.)

A42

(A room in the Palace. The Queen is seated behind a desk S.R. Sir Robert Cecil stands before her S.L. The Queen is haggard and drawn and a little unkempt. Sir Robert Cecil is grave but otherwise unchanged.)

Queen: What said he then in the Tower?

Cecil: He begged forgiveness of Your Majesty for his manifest and black treason. Then, he gave us a list of such as were implicated with him. He begged you not to ignore their treason and, in particular, he stressed the wildness of his sister, the Lady Rich, whom he called vicious and treacherous.

Queen: What else?

Cecil: Continually he asked us to pray for his soul. *(Pause)* He also wept with gratitude when told that Your Majesty had granted his last request, to be executed privately in the Tower grounds.

Queen: Nothing else?

Cecil: Merely a repetition of the names of traitors that we had not discovered, together with pleas to Your Majesty to move against them and spare not their lives. This and begging forgiveness for his treason and beseeching us to pray for his soul was the sum of all his discourse. He was, moreover, distracted in his speech and bearing and spoke his words wildly like a man bereft of his wits.

Queen: That puritan preacher of his brought him to that and shamefully unmanned him.

Cecil: Very likely, my Lord of Essex received no other visitors but his spiritual adviser, and remained closeted with him, confessing and praying, for hours at a stretch.

Queen: But he made a good end, they report — no weeping there?

Cecil: None. At the scaffold he spoke well and steadily; all was as seemly as Your Majesty could wish. Sir Walter Raleigh had the ordering of the guard and . . .

Queen: "Seemly", say you, Sir Robert?

Cecil: Aye, madam, "Seemly". *(Pause)* Your Majesty wishes the late Lord Essex's confession published with amendments?

Queen: No. Mr. Bacon is commissioned to write a true account for publication.

Cecil: And the traitors' names supplied by him in the Tower? Do we proceed against them?

Queen: Not so, investigate and record only. We have spilt enough blood, Sir Robert. I do not wish the closing years of my reign to be a byword in times future for the shedding of blood. God give me a better memorial than that!

Cecil: I'm sure Your Majesty has many years . . .

Queen: Don't be foolish, Cecil. The time for flattery's past and the time for gallantry too. They can lead to sad conclusions. The times call now for duller and more prudent qualities. It's the age of the **sensible** man, Sir Robert. Sensitive, high spirited youth belongs to the past, the glorious past, almost a different age now. Which calls to mind the work of Francis Bacon at the trial. He took over it seems from that donkey, Coke, you and the council saddled me with.

Cecil: As Counsellor Extraordinary to the Crown, my cousin did his duty certainly.

Queen: Has Mr. Bacon been rewarded for this **duty** to my court of justice?

Cecil: Not yet, Your Majesty.

Queen: See his work is paid for. There's twelve hundred pounds seized off the traitor Catesby; bestow it on your cousin. I would not have his efforts in our service grow sluggish for want of that encouragement the coming generation most appreciates.

Cecil: Twelve hundred pounds, Your Majesty! Would not five do just as well? It is not wise to . . .

Queen: Twelve hundred pounds, Cecil, is barely enough to pay a man that loved a lord who went mad. Essex was his patron and his friend. There are conflicts of the heart in such cases, for those who have hearts to entertain them. The foolish, lying and splendid young men of the past always had hearts, Cecil, for all their faults. They felt things.

Cecil: *(Embarrassed by her nostalgia)* Will that be all, Your Majesty?

Queen: That will be all, Cecil, Nay, that *is* all. The rest is routine the council can devise as they see fit.

Cecil: Then with Your Majesty's permission I'll withdraw.

Queen: Aye do, Sir Robert, withdraw and pay your cousin for his services in helping the court destroy a traitor. Twelve hundred pounds now, no juggling.

Cecil: As your Majesty pleases.

(The lights come up again on Bacon's House at Twickenham. The papers of the opening scene are still in place.)

Anthony: I must leave you now, Francis. Remember the leases and seal all with the notary as agreed. I'll attend on our mother shortly.

Francis: Can't you stay a little longer?

Anthony: No Francis. I only came to settle the business of our mother's leases and estates. *(He puts on his cape slowly.)* I've nothing more to talk of with you now.

Francis: So you'll go, thinking I betrayed him? Can't you see it was impossible to help him at that stage? Had I failed in my duty to the Crown, I'd have been branded a traitor too. I did all a man could do to help him. But when his crazed pride led him, sword in hand, to raise rebellion in the streets of London, he was lost.

Anthony: I'm sure you acted in good faith, Francis, your motives don't worry me, your actions only cause me pain.

Francis: Oh, Anthony, can't you see.

Anthony: I see only that the Earl of Southampton, who lacked the benefit of your advice before the trial, and your attentions during it, lives on, even has hope of ultimate release, while my lord, not *our* lord now, but *my* lord, suffered execution in the Tower. It seems to me that all the court was charged with was to establish guilt and pave the way for the Queen's mercy, mercy ever ready to be shown her favourite. There was no need for your officious interfering. So Coke irritated you, did he, Francis? And because you cannot stand a little fumbling at a treason trial, you have to make all orderly? So orderly you made it that my Lord Chief Justice and attendant counsel ordered my lord's head severed from his neck. Your impatience of the Attorney General led the Queen's favourite to the block. Southampton, never a favourite with her Majesty, goes to imprisonment. He lives Francis, the object of the Queen's displeasure lives and breathes. How fortunate for him that he never gave you ought in property or favoured your ambitions with the Queen! How fortunate for him that you never served him, never smiled on him, never claimed to love him or be bound to him! I won't call you fool, Francis, nor yet knave, though I hear they paid you well for your betrayal. I'll just say your ways are not my

FRANCIS 3
Silver '71

ways. *(Pause)* My growing sickness keeps me in now, and prevents encounter with my friends or kin. This way I meet with few whom I do not invite to visit me. I'd rather you were not a visitor, Francis, except upon our mother's business.

Francis: *(Pleading)* Anthony, I beg you stay till I have read you this. It is an account of my part in the trial, which I have felt needs best be written to explain my cause aright. It's short, the part I'd have you hear. Just stay for that.

(Anthony says nothing. Francis rummages through papers and finds what he seeks. He glances over his shoulder to ensure Anthony's presence. He smiles at his brother pleadingly. Anthony is grief stricken and impassive. As Francis begins to read, Anthony unknown to him, limps slowly, painfully and silently off stage, so that half way through Francis' speech he has left.)

Francis: Here it is. *(Turning his back on Anthony he reads from a manuscript)* Whatsoever I did, concerning that action and proceeding, was done in my duty and service to the Queen and to the state; in which I would not show myself false-hearted or faint-hearted for the sake of any man. For while an honest man should forsake his own profit and even risk his life to save his friend, yet should he also forsake that friend rather than oppose his King and forsake his King rather than forsake his God. *(Pause)* I hope the world has not forgotten these degrees.

(On the last phrase Francis turns to where his brother was for confirmation of his views. His face changes from smiling ingratiation to lonely horror when he realizes he is alone. The lights fade.)

The End

Wu-feng

Munroe Scott

Photo by John Juliani

In 1948, Canadian writer **Munroe Scott**, while still attending Queen's University in Kingston, distinguished himself by winning first prize in the one-act category of Queen's Drama Guild's nation-wide playwriting contest with a blank verse farce entitled Sunstroke. Since then Mr. Scott has gone on to become one of Canada's most prolific and widely-travelled writers. On the staff of Crawley Films from 1950 to 1957 Mr. Scott wrote, among other things, six half-hour episodes for the TV series RCMP produced by Crawley Films, and in 1957 Mr. Scott went freelance. In 1959, he was in Holland writing for Carillon Films Limited, and in 1960 researched and wrote a documentary film On the Rim of Tomorrow — work undertaken during extensive travel in Japan, Korea, Okinawa, Taiwan and Hong Kong. Mr. Scott has since travelled to Africa and Asia, has been round the world twice, and in the course of his film writing has visited almost every region in Canada. A long list of credits for the CBC includes The Devil's Petition for General Motors Presents; work as writer/director on such public affairs series as Inquiry, The Sixties, Citizen's Forum and Intertel; four one-hour segments for Hatch's Mill; a 90-minute play plus its 90-minute sequel, Reddick, starring Donald Harron; and writer/director for five one-hour segments for the eight-part series The Tenth Decade, a distinguished CBC-TV public affairs series.

A significant factor in Mr. Scott's writing career was his meeting, during his travels in Taiwan, with Canadian missionaries Bruce and Marnie Copeland. Marnie Copeland introduced the author to the Formosan folk hero Wu-feng, who died in 1769. In Mr. Scott's own words "Wu-feng then haunted me for the next decade". In 1970 he wrote his play Wu-feng in a style especially suited to the open stage.

Because the setting of "Wu-feng" is so foreign to the Canadian experience, care had to be taken in selecting the illustrations used to illuminate the text. The artwork had to properly mirror the mood of the play with some of the flavour of the setting. Yet it couldn't be so physically exact as to inhibit the future work of designers and directors.

Wu-feng was written after Mr. Scott journeyed to the Orient and by a fortunate coincidence the paintings accompanying the text of the play were done by someone who journeyed from the Orient to Canada: Madame Ma Shiu Yu.

Ma Shiu Yu, who is a Canadian citizen, was born in Canton China. She now lives in Toronto, has taught at the Ontario College of Art, and is on the faculty of the Artists' Workshop of the Three Schools. Ma Shiu Yu, who paints in both traditional and contemporary styles, has had shows in Hong Kong, Osaka, Tokyo, Toronto, Atikokan, as well as at York, Queen's, and McMaster Universities.

Time: 1769
Place: A mountain in Taiwan

Cast of characters

Wu-feng, a tribesman, appointed by the Emperor of China to govern the Mount Ali Tribe
Serenity, Wu-feng's daughter
Stranger, a Chinese wanderer
Piong-shih, head chief of the Mount Ali Tribe
Margama, son of Piong-shih
Tsai-yu, Commissioner of Protectors, Heir to the chieftanship, nephew of Piong-shih
Tranquility, sister of Tsai-yu
Li-yu and Poolee, friends of Margama
Han-sun, a Chinese merchant
First Elder and Second Elder, counsellors to the head chief, Piong-shih
Margama's followers, beautiful young people
Elders, tribal fathers
Ai-lee, the oldest of the elders
Protectors, tribal police
Assorted children, servants, and coolees

馬笑如

B4

Act One, Scene One

A young man, plainly dressed in the manner of a Chinese wanderer, comes on stage and walks to a convenient resting point. He takes a look at his surroundings and finding them satisfactory he sits down. He produces a small leather pouch from which he extracts a few miserable and unsatisfying crumbs of food which are consumed in a twinkling. He then curls up for a snooze.

Enter Margama and his followers. They are moving quietly, stealthily, and in single file. Each youth carries a large, wicked-looking machete-type knife. Their clothing consists of sparse leather costumes that emphasize rippling muscles and gleaming bronzed skin. They are not really hunting. Their movements have more of a ritualistic rhythm to them. The stealthy, winding procession moves around the stage until Margama sees an imaginary victim and signals. The line forms quietly and swiftly into a circle. Machetes are slowly raised high overhead with both hands. Suddenly, with a large explosion of breath, the youths take one great step inward, each going to one knee as he does so, and each swinging his machete forward and down with a tremendous sweep. The machetes all but clash in the centre of the circle. For a moment they remain kneeling, then Margama rises abruptly.

Margama: That can't be right!

Poolee: It was beautiful, Margama!

Margama: Ten knives, ten chops, ten pieces! What are we going to do with ten pieces!

Li-yu: *(Also rising)* Margama is right. We don't need ten pieces. Two are sufficient.

All rise and look somewhat disconsolate.

Li-yu: It is obvious. Two knives are enough.

Margama: Much of it is correct. I am sure. I can remember the old ones telling how it was. The hunt. The surround. The offering. It feels right. It feels good.

Poolee: It is magnificent Margama. I feel fulfilled just going through the motions.

Li-yu: Ten knives make the offering aesthetically unacceptable!

Margama: *(Nods agreement with Li-yu)* Come brothers. Let us try again.

Margama exits, with the others all following him in single file.

Piong-shih enters. He is an elderly gentleman, dressed conservatively in Chinese fashion.

Piong-shih: *(Calls)* Margama! Margama!

As Piong-shih crosses the stage he almost trips over the sleeping Stranger. He stops, goes back a couple of paces, and gives the Stranger a rousing kick, then turns to leave.

Stranger: *(Sits up)* Thank you, Father.

Piong-shih: I am not your father.

Stranger: No, Father.

Piong-shih: You are a wandering beggar?

Stranger: Yes, Father.

Piong-shih: I am not your father!

Stranger: I use the term out of respect for your great wisdom.

Piong-shih: You know me!

Stranger: Who has not heard of you, Father? But being an illiterate unlearned beggar this poor brain of your humble servant has difficulty remembering the full glory of your name.

Piong-shih: Piong-shih.

Stranger: Of course. Piong-shih. Simple and unadorned for strength and dignity, as befits one of your exalted rank.

Piong-shih: I am High Chief.

Stranger: The mightiest High Chief of all the mountain tribes of Ali!

Piong-shih: *(Gives him a coin)* Here is something to keep you from starving in the streets. It's been a bad year. We can't afford to bury any strangers.

Stranger: Thank you, Father. Blessings of Buddha and Confucius be upon you and upon the bones of your ancestors.

Piong-shih turns away and the stranger lies down again.

Piong-shih: *(Calls)* Margama!

He hears no reply and recrosses the stage. This time he does not trip over the recumbent stranger but does pause long enough to give him another rousing kick.

Stranger: *(Sits up)* Thank you, father Piong-shih. *(Lies down again)*

Piong-shih: Remember, no starving to death around here.

Piong-shih exits.

Enter Margama and his followers. They are still stealthily proceeding on their ceremonial hunt. This time they spot the sleeping Stranger. They surround him. The machetes are all raised rhythmically on high. This time, however, only

Margama and Li-yu take the one step forward, going to one knee as they do so. They pause for a moment, machetes raised for the strike.

Margama: Ah, that feels much better. Now — two strokes, two pieces.

The Stranger sits bolt upright.

Stranger: Forgive me, tall and handsome brother. Two strokes will make three pieces.

Li-yu: He is right, Margama!

Margama rises, breaking away from the circle. The formality disintegrates.

Margama: *(Frustrated)* This is ridiculous. We need a manual. One manual. There must be one manual somewhere in all these Ali mountains.

Li-yu: If we ask the old ones again — discreetly — by the fire at night while old memories drift in the smoke — your own father the Chief — surely he remembers?

Margama: Piong-shih is a fool!

Poolee: *(Shocked)* He is your father!

Margama: Then I was fathered by a fool. *(Calls to the others)* Brothers. *(To Li-yu)* I use the term "brothers" not to imply family ties but merely to emphasize that we were all fathered by fools.

Poolee: I thought you promised a rebellion without disrespect!

Margama: Why Poolee, I have great respect for fools. Particularly fools in authority. The damage they can do demands respect, I assure you.

Poolee: *(Alarmed)* Governor Wu will hear you!

Margama: Governor Wu knows all about fools. He deals with our fathers. *(The others have by now all gathered around Margama. He talks to them all.)* Brothers, we need a manual. Somewhere in these mountains, lost in some cave, hidden beneath some family altar, cunningly concealed in the thatch of a roof, fondly preserved in an old man's medicine pouch, reverently entombed with an ancestor's bones — somewhere there is still a Manual of the Ancient Rites. Go. Search the four winds and the five tribes. We must have a Manual.

The youths all hurry off in various directions, with the exception of Li-yu and Poolee who remain with Margama.

Poolee: Why don't we write a new one?

Li-yu: On old paper.

Margama: It may come to that.

Margama has wandered over to the Stranger who is engaged in trying to extract a few more food crumbs from his leather pouch.

Margama: You are a stranger.

Stranger: *(Agreeing)* I am a stranger.

Margama turns away and looks at Poolee and Li-yu as though this is a very interesting information.

Li-yu: *(Low)* He may have powerful friends.

Margama: *(To the Stranger)* You have no powerful friends?

Stranger: *(Obligingly)* I have no powerful friends.

Poolee: Travelling alone?

Stranger: Accompanied only by my dead ancestors and unborn children.

Again the three friends turn away from him and walk a few paces in earnest, low, conversation. They return to the Stranger.

Margama: You will be in the mountains a few days?

Stranger: *(Bows in agreement)*

Margama: Do not hurry. Enjoy the languid mornings, the sultry afternoons, the music of twilight. Do not hurry.

Poolee: We are planning a festival. A stranger will be useful.

Margama: Forgive our clumsy use of the High Tongue. Poolee means that a stranger, travelling alone and with no powerful friends, will be "welcome".

Li-yu: It is a folk festival.

Poolee: There will be music, dancing, and a beautiful, beautiful ceremony. It will touch you deeply.

Li-yu: You can participate.

The three back away from the Stranger, bowing politely to him, their hands folded palms together in front.

Margama: Do not hurry.

Li-yu: Enjoy our mountains.

Poolee: Enjoy our sisters.

Margama : Do not hurry.

They are almost offstage. They turn away from the Stranger.

Margama: Well and good. Now if we can only find a manual.

Margama exits.

Li-yu: Sisters indeed!

Poolee: A mere figure of speech. Governor Wu has taught us politeness, has he not?

Poolee and Li-yu exit.

Stranger: *(Musing)* I wonder why they wanted to cut me in two? Why two? *(He gathers up his few belongings.)* Three wouldn't do. *(Begins to move off but stops again to puzzle over it.)* Thank goodness I haven't fallen amongst those barbarous Christians one reads about. They'd have made a trinity of me in no time.

He is about to exit but collides with a very pleasant looking, active, middle aged man. This

happens to be Governor Wu, but there is nothing about him at the moment to denote rank. Both men bow deeply to each other in apology.

Wu-feng is followed at a discreet distance by his daughter, Serenity.

Stranger: I am sorry sir. I do not know with whom I have had the honour to collide.

Wu-feng: The Master said, "It does not grieve me that others do not know of me . . ."

Stranger: "But only that I do not know of them."

Wu-feng: *(Looks delighted)* Aha. *(He walks around the young man, eyeing him.)* Clothes, well cut, but in bad taste. Hair, long, but untidy. A look of hunger. You will notice the eyes, daughter, how they sparkle.

Serenity: He's cute.

Wu-feng: The man is most certainly a scholar.

The Stranger bows low to Wu as though acknowledging that he has been unveiled.

Serenity: *(Clapping her hands)* May we keep him?

Wu-feng: He may be an impostor, of course. That sparkle in the eyes can come from madness.

Serenity: I never meet any interesting people.

Wu-feng: But still, a scholar is a very difficult thing of which to make even a reasonable facsimile.

Serenity: He does look hungry.

Wu-feng: You are welcome at our humble table, sir. *(Breaking off)* Ah, come along child. It would be too good to be true to think that a scholar might actually have strayed into the Provinces.

Serenity: *(To the Stranger)* Please come.

Stranger: Gladly.

Serenity: Father?

Wu-feng: *(Almost off stage)* Very well.

But Wu-feng keeps on going and Serenity has to follow.

Stranger: *(Bewildered)* Is it far? Wait. Whose house do I ask for?

Serenity: *(Torn between following her father or staying)* Father! You offer hospitality without introductions!

Wu-feng: *(Returning part way)* Introductions? Names? What use are names? A man's character is not in his name. I am a virtuous man, I trust he is the same.

Wu-feng is about to leave but stops cold in his tracks as the Stranger speaks.

Stranger: "The ruler will first take pains about his own virtue."

Wu-feng turns slowly and looks at him, then walks back and confronts him.

Wu-feng: "Possessing virtue will give him the people."

Stranger: "With the people goes the territory."

Wu-feng: *(To Serenity, delighted)* He knows the game!

For just a moment it looks as though Wu-feng could almost dance with his daughter through sheer delight. He restrains himself and turns to the Stranger.

Wu-feng: "Possessing the territory will give him wealth."

Stranger: "Possessing wealth he will have resources."

Wu-feng: "Resources are to be used for the welfare of the people."

Stranger: "Thus virtue is at the root."

Wu-feng: "And public good is the result."

The two men bow to each other.

Both: Thus said the Master.

Wu-feng cannot resist taking Serenity's hands and doing a little circle of pure delight. Serenity laughs to see her father so pleased.

Wu-feng breaks off abruptly.

Wu-feng: Serenity, my child, we shall have soup and noodles and a marvelous hot pot. I shall send everyone away and this young man and I shall talk all night.

Serenity: Everyone?

But Wu-feng is already heading off stage.

Serenity: Don't mind father. He gets so excited when he finds anyone who **knows** something. Oh, I must hurry.

Serenity moves to leave in the wake of her father.

Stranger: Wait. You don't even know who I am.

Serenity: *(Calling as she goes)* A nobleman. A prince even. From the Emperor's household. Don't worry. *(Stops and looks back)* It's quite all right.

Wu-feng returns to the edge of the stage.

Wu-feng: *(Impatient)* Serenity! Hurry up, child. I think we may be out of noodles.

Wu-feng exits.

A ferocious looking being comes onstage. He is dressed in leather armour. Two lesser, but also ferocious characters are with him. They, too, are leather clad in a fashion similar to the first man, but less flamboyant. These three men are Protectors. Those onstage do not, as yet, see them.

Serenity: I must go.

Serenity exits.

Stranger: Wait! Who are you? *(Calls)* How do I find you? What house? Where?

The lead newcomer gestures to one of his companions.

Sergeant: You, seize that man.

Protector: Yes, Sergeant.

The Protector comes forward and puts an armlock on the Stranger. The others remain immobile.

Stranger: Who was that man? Who was the girl? In the name of heaven, who was the girl?

Sergeant: You want to know who they are, eh?

Stranger: Yes. Yes, most noble sir.

Sergeant: I know your kind. You want to wheedle your way next to the Governor so you can rob him. Ah yes, I know you. You, sir, are a thief!

Stranger: *(Submissively)* Yes.

Sergeant: Seize this thief.

Protector: I have, Sergeant.

Sergeant: That was on suspicion. We now have a confession. Away with the villain. Take him to the Magistrate.

The Protector takes the Stranger away. The Sergeant glares around at no one in particular.

Sergeant: Criminals, criminals, criminals. *(Bellows at second Protector)* You! Protect somebody.

He exits. Second Protector exits smartly in his wake.

Scene Two

Piong-shih and Elders enter. They seem very agitated.

1st Elder: The granaries are almost empty. I personally conducted the survey.

Piong-shih: I know, I know. You think I don't know? My sister says there's not enough food for one more meal. She's been saying that for five weeks. How could I not know?

1st Elder: Surely the Governor can get help — another caravan from Peking?

2nd Elder: It's more Protectors we need. And a garrison. *(Wagging his finger at Piong-shih)* I tell you that son of yours is dangerous.

Piong-shih: I know, I know. You think I don't know? Revolution and change. Change and revolution. That's all I hear. How could I not know?

2nd Elder: Surely the Governor **can** get help from Peking?

Piong-shih: Don't worry about Margama. You don't understand him like I do. After all, I'm his father. So he wants to revive the Old Culture. Well, was that all bad? We can't ask our children to turn their backs forever on the ways of the ancestors.

2nd Elder: The Emperor will turn his back forever on us.

1st Elder: *(Lamenting)* At a time when trade is already dropping off! And two bad harvests in a row!

Piong-shih: Margama is a good boy at heart.

2nd Elder: They've been drilling in the woods. *(To other Elders)* Did you know they've been drilling in the woods?

Piong-shih: Boys will be boys.

2nd Elder: They're sharpening knives and there's no harvest.

Piong-shih: Ah, the insecurity of youth. *(Sits down crosslegged and the others follow suit)* The poor boy is frustrated. Can you blame him? My son. The son of the High Chief, Piong-shih. And he must take second place to that — that — *(Words fail him)*

1st Elder: Sh-h-h. "That" comes.

The Elders all immediately scramble to their feet, but Piong-shih does not move an inch.

Tsai-yu enters, followed by his sister Tranquility. Tsai-yu is about the same age as Margama, but a foppish character, dressed in Chinese manner but much too ornately, and bearing little resemblance to the rugged dress and style of Margama and the youths we have seen with him. The Elders all bow low to him.

Elders: Welcome to Tsai-yu, much beloved and highly respected Soon-to-be-Chief of our unworthy tribe.

They also bow to Tranquility.

Elders: Welcome to Tranquility, niece of High Chief Piong-shih and sister of Soon-to-be-Chief Tsai-yu.

Tsai-yu sits down crosslegged. His sister stays discreetly behind him.

Tsai-yu: Let us begin, Uncle.

Piong-shih: Margama is not here.

Tsai-yu: For which I give thanks. Han-sun the trader has not·come and I have run out of perfume.

Piong-shih: Nevertheless, I have called Margama.

Tsai-yu: *(Sarcastically)* But Margama does not come?

There is a long pause while the two men sit and the Elders continue to stand. Tsai-yu fusses with his clothing and ornaments. He snaps his fingers and his sister brings him tobacco and a long pipe.

Piong-shih: Must you smoke in front of the elders?

Tsai-yu: I need the incense. I fear Margama may come, and he smells so strong these days of heather and moss and dripping woods that I frequently faint at the mere thought of crossing his path downwind.

The Sergeant and the two Protectors pass through with the Stranger. The Protectors are driving the Stranger with blows.

B11

No one really watches them, but when they have gone an elder speaks.

1st Elder: Who was that?

Piong-shih: Some beggar who was intending to starve to death in the village. *(To Tsai-yu)* I see your people had the good sense to move him while he was still mobile.

Tsai-yu: *(Acknowledging the compliment with a bow)* Protective custody, I imagine.

Children run in, laughing and looking over their shoulders as though something is after them.

Piong-shih: The Governor must be coming.

All present except the children bow forward where they sit, and cover their faces with their hands. They hold this position.
There is more laughter and more children enter. They are dancing around Wu-feng who is wearing a blindfold and is being led by two children. They turn him around three times then suddenly scatter, laughing as they go. Wu-feng suddenly gives a little shout and slaps his hands. The children all freeze where they are standing. They are mingled with the grown-ups, none of whom has deserted the bowed, face-covered position of respect.

Wu-feng, hands outstretched, gropes around.

He comes to Piong-shih and carefully runs his hands over the Chief's face.

Wu-feng: Piong-shih! *(Removes the blindfold)* I didn't know you were playing!

Piong-shih: Tribal brother, beloved Governor, reflection of the Emperor — you called a conference.

Wu-feng: *(Remembering)* Ah! Yes.

He makes a fast circle shooing children away, swatting a few smartly on the rear to accelerate their departure, then one by one raises Piong-shih, Tsai-yu, and the elders to an upright position. He slaps his hands vigorously. Two black and red throne-like chairs are brought for Piong-shih and Tsai-yu, who now occupy these seats. A third is brought for the Governor.

Suddenly Wu-feng is all business.

Wu-feng: Where is Margama?

Piong-shih: No doubt my worthless son feels he is not worthy to enter the presence of Governor Wu-Feng.

Wu-feng: *(A little snort. Then continues)* I am expecting a guest for supper. Noodles and a hot pot, I thought. *(Looks slowly around the assembly)* No noodles. One might consider the hot pot an unnecessary frill, but noodles!

1st Elder: Alas Governor Wu. It is as we have been saying. The rain does not fall. The crops do not grow. The animals flee to the far mountains.

Piong-shih: It's a bad year, there's no doubt about it.

2nd Elder: The young men are blaming it on the ancestors. We have deserted the Old Culture, they say. The ancestors intercede with the gods to punish us, they say.

Piong-shih: That's a fact. At least there's no denying they say it.

Wu-feng: If it is so simple the problem only has two faces. Famine and rebellion.

Piong-shih: Why I suppose you are right!

Wu-feng: *(Making himself comfortable)* Very well. I am open to suggestions.

1st Elder: Food from the Federal storehouse.

2nd Elder: Troops from the Federal army.

Wu-feng: Please, one at a time. I heard a venerable voice ask for troops?

2nd Elder: *(Bows)* If there is danger of rebellion it is quite obvious we must have troops. The Protectors are quite inadequate.

Tsai-yu: Begging the learned Counsellor's pardon, *(To Wu-feng)* it is their equipment that is inadequate. As you know I have been asking that they be issued cross-bows.

2nd Elder: If there is a rebellion the Emperor in his infinite mercy will send Federal troops to pacify us all. I would much prefer that we invite the troops now, that their presence might thus prevent the need for pacification. *(To Wu-feng)*

A few good troops and nothing need change.

Wu-feng: If there is famine what are the troops to eat?

1st Elder: Indeed, it is only a month since the government sent a caravan of relief food into our mountains. Already it is gone.

Wu-feng: Am I to request the Emperor to start pouring Federal troops and Federal food into these mountains in ever increasing streams? I would be a poor servant to the Son of Heaven were I to ask that. I can just see the entire empire gradually disappearing, like the fabled bird, up its own orifice! *(To 2nd Elder)* Let us turn our minds to this problem of famine. *(To Piong-shih)* When one has political problems first look in the cooking pot, eh brother? *(To 2nd Elder again)* I looked in your cooking pot on the way here. You are having tan-mi for supper. My congratulations. You feed, at last count, eleven persons at the family fire. Now tan-mi requires noodles, but of course the secret, correct me if I'm wrong, is in the sauce. Ah, the sauce. For your family I would recommend, let me see, three handfuls of chopped pork loin, lean, ten green scallions, cut fine, enough sugar to give delight, a slight inspiration of salt, a small gourd of soya sauce, one handful of mushrooms from a mountain crevice, all boiled lovingly in crystal water. On the side, of course, one must have a generous quantity of ocean shrimp, shelled, with the tails on, bean sprouts, bamboo shoots, and pork spareribs. All of which, I can assure you, your beloved wife has been preparing for you. I greatly fear, because of the terrible famine that afflicts us all, that you may have to forget a dash of pepper, sesame seed oil, crushed garlic, malt vinegar, and parsley. I am not certain about the parsley. *(Apologetically)* I only had time for a quick glance.

Piong-shih: *(To 2nd Elder)* A few troops and nothing need change, eh?

Wu-feng: The status quo can be eminently satisfying to one's stomach. *(To Piong-shih)* Didn't we work out a law having to do with drilling holes in the Federal rice bowl?

Tsai-yu claps his hands and the three Protectors enter.

Wu-feng: We wrote it the day after the festival of the Double Fifth in the fifth year of my Governorship. It is scroll one hundred and sixty-seven, the pertinent clause being found in columns eleven, twelve and thirteen. I'll have a boy run it round to the magistrate.

Piong-shih: *(Patting Wu-feng gently on the knee)* Beloved Governor — **you** are the magistrate.

Wu-feng: So I am.

Tsai-yu indicates the 2nd Elder and the Protectors take him away as a prisoner.

Tsai-yu: You will notice that they are armed solely with two-edged daggers. The officer has a spear. An anachronism, of course. Merely a badge of office surviving from more primitive times. I see no reason the Protectors should not have crossbows. A powerful weapon, it is true, but clumsy at the best of times. In the event of minor disturbances their display would have a highly salutory effect — psychological, of course. No one could abhor physical violence more than I.

Sounds, offstage, of violence and conflict.

Margama enters.
Tsai-yu holds a handkerchief to his nose and turns half away.

Tsai-yu: How the wind does shift.

Piong-shih: Margama, where have you been?

Margama: Dear cousin Tsai-yu, one of your men is meeting with an accident. *(To Wu-feng)* Your humble servants were hurrying to attend upon the Representative of the Son of Heaven when we met three protectors dragging an Elder.

Piong-shih: They were doing their duty.

Margama: Be that as it may, beloved father, the victim cried out to us in the Elder Tongue in a manner that compelled us to intercede on his behalf. *(To Tsai-yu)* So violently did your man react to our friendly inquiries that he, ah-h — *(Slight pause — Sounds of conflict end abruptly)* I greatly fear he has just been killed by his own brutality.

Tsai-yu: *(To Wu-feng)* There! A couple of crossbows and all would have been well.

Margama: *(To Wu-feng)* The prisoner, taking advantage of our solicitous intercession, has escaped.

Tsai-yu: We'll have an inquiry into this!

Margama: So we should. When the mere sound of the Elder Tongue causes the Protectors to so over react that —

Tsai-yu: *(Outraged)* Causes **them** to over react!

Wu-feng: Tsai-yu, I suggest you go and protect the tan-mi supper. When it is completed have it distributed impartially to all.

Tsai-yu exits angrily, followed by his sister.

Wu-feng: *(To Margama, annoyed)* I want to talk to you. Privately. Come around later. *(To Piong-shih)* I just remembered where I can get some noodles.

Wu-feng exits.

Margama's young men come in bearing the body of the Protector. It is on a bier, draped with bark cloth. The youths are chanting a weird processional. Piong-shih and the remaining elders join the procession as it winds across stage and off. Poolee and Li-yu drop out momentarily beside Margama.

Margama: Well?

Li-yu: Two pieces, but messy.

Poolee: The climax is right. After all, when you get down to it, how many ways are there to cut off a head?

Li-yu: But there is a polish lacking somewhere. Ritually it's still all wrong.

Margama: By all the little clay gods, when will we find a Manual!

They exit in the wake of the procession.

B14

Scene Three
Wu-feng enters with a Servant who is carrying a large pot. He is followed by some Children and is met by Serenity.

Wu-feng: Ah, my dear, we have fortune. There has been a sudden redistribution of food.

He gestures and the servant takes the pot to Serenity for inspection. Wu-feng speaks to a child.

Wu-feng: Find Margama. I want to speak to him.

The Child exits.

Serenity: Noodles! *(She looks delighted)* How wonderful. Now, indeed we can feed the stranger!

Wu-feng: I was afraid I would have to stand in line a very long time, but I arrived there early. I must have been one of the first to hear the news!

Serenity: But so many noodles! Are you sure — is this really — **our** portion?

Wu-feng: She made a good trade. There is more status in two mushrooms than in a pound of noodles, and that woman relishes status.

Serenity: You made a good trade.

Serenity: We've not much time. Our guest should be here soon.

Serenity and the Servant exit.

Wu-feng, by himself now, paces slowly. He looks deeply pre-occupied.

Wu-feng: Famine and rebellion, eh? There are two fine bedfellows for you, Governor. They always lie together, those two. Famine! Bah! A mere tightening of the belts. My people haven't seen famine since the Federal authorities moved into these mountains and well they know it.

Margama enters. He is carrying his machete. While Wu-feng paces, Margama begins to stalk him, stealthily, quietly, like a lithe, leather clad panther.

Wu-feng: Very well then. Rebellion has seduced innocent Hunger; and now Hunger, betrayed, swells into the pregnant spectre of Famine.

Margama has reached a high spot, just behind Wu-feng.
Margama is crouched as though about to spring.

Wu-feng: What is required then, and speedily, is an abortion. *(Puzzled)* But does one treat the mother or the father? Certainly, Governor, your inclination is to treat the father, a conclusion that throws some doubt on the validity of your diagnosis.

Margama, with a very deliberate motion, drops his machete and uttering a yell launches himself upon Governor Wu. But the sound of the machete falling is just sufficient warning for the Governor to meet the attack with an evasion that sends Margama flying over Wu-feng's back. They fight, wordlessly, quietly, and with great efficiency in holds, rolls, trips, and evasions. After a few moments they pause for breath as though by mutual consent, and both men are laughing! They lean a moment on each other, then throw themselves on the ground like a couple of boys, still gasping for wind. After a few moments Margama speaks.

Margama: One of these days I am not going to drop the knife.

Wu-feng: *(Laughs)* You are such a stranger to yourself!

Margama: It is you who have become the stranger. You lean too heavily upon the friendships of boyhood. I tell you, one day, and perhaps soon, I will **not** drop the knife.

Wu-feng: You have no cause to hate me.

Margama: *(Sitting up)* No cause! I, Margama, son of Piong-shih. I, Margama, heir to the Chieftanship after Piong-shih.

B15

Wu-feng: *(Also sitting up and laughing)* Ah, there? You see, you forget. I saved you from that. I disinherited you. *(Lies back)* So relax, Margama, you are no longer heir to the Chieftanship after Piong-shih. Do you not remember?

Margama: Forgive me elder cousin Feng. I remember many things. I remember our boyhood here in the mountains. I remember our fathers exalted on rice wine bawling ribald songs into the spirit filled night. I remember them leaving for the last of the Ancient Rites and returning after the Act of Purification even more exalted than with wine. I remember the Emperor's men coming and you being taken away as a hostage and my heart breaking in the sunlight of a cold day. I remember Soldiers in the mountains and the years when we were no longer men. And you — You came back. An educated Chinese gentleman! You! *(Throws his head back and laughs)* And the Emperor's soldiers said if we would choose you as our Governor they would leave. And we did! *(Laughs again)* I remember how we thought cousin Wu-feng had fooled the Emperor. Now we could be men again! *(Darkens)* Only the Emperor was no fool. We were the fools. Elder cousin Feng was, indeed, Governor. Oh, yes. I remember it all. *(Leaping up)* But I do **not** remember requesting to be relieved of my rightful claim to the Chieftanship!

Wu-feng: True, you never have been grateful for that.

Margama: Grateful!

Wu-feng: Perhaps not as Margama, but as a tribesman you might have shown some small sign of appreciation.

Margama: At being disinherited!

Wu-feng: Consider — Piong-shih, on your behalf, gradually taking to himself more land, more goats, more rice for the Chief's granary, not for himself, mind you — for his son. For you. To protect the royal line. And you, being active, strong, and ambitious, doing the same. Not for yourself, mind you, but in turn for your son. To protect the royal line. No, no don't deny it. It is not a matter for shame nor a matter for denial. It is a matter of fact. That is the way hereditary power works. It must protect itself to survive. It must survive for the sake of the ruling family. But power should not be for the sake of the family. The family should rule for the sake of the people. Therefore power is for the people. Therefore I disinherited you.

Margama: But — but — to make that reptile! That scorpion! That grub! That worm! To make Tsai-yu heir to the Chieftanship in my place!

Wu-feng: You have a point there. But the idea was molded by theory, not the application. Let the power pass from the dead Chief to the son of the dead chief's sister. It is a system much favoured by certain islanders.

Margama: The minute my father becomes the dead Chief my life won't be worth a sesame seed.

Wu-feng: I admit you certainly are not an entrenched member of the establishment.

Margama: I'll need to fight, die, or flee!
Wu-feng: I question that.

Margama: You even gave Tsai-yu full authority over the Protectors.

Wu-feng: Ah ha — only to lose it when he becomes Chief. The Protectors will go to the son of Tsai-yu's sister. That's an embellishment I thought of by myself. If you ponder it you will see it helps maintain a delicate balance.
Margama: It is abominable.

Wu-feng: The old system was abominable. This one is merely bad.

Margama: You say that, and it was your doing?

Wu-feng: To make the abominable bad is an improvement.

Margama: You are laughing.

Wu-feng: Not at all. I am a realist. Next we make the bad bearable, then the bearable better. Who knows, on some future day you and I and the tribe may survey a system we have evolved and finally, honestly, be able to say — "ah ha! **This** is good!"

Margama: In the meantime, I'm in a damned delicate position. I still warn you, one day I may not drop the knife.

Wu-feng: (Cheerfully) Ah ha, see? When you came in you said "will not", now you say "may not". We are making progress.

Serenity enters in considerable agitation.

Serenity: The young nobleman has arrived.

Wu-feng: Are the noodles ready? No matter, no matter.

Serenity: But Father! He has been dragged here by Tsai-yu's men!

Wu-feng: (To Margama) Notice the way women exaggerate. They must always embellish simple facts. (To Serenity) My child, I am **pleased** they have escorted him here. An escort is a fine way to do simple honour to a scholar. It does Tsai-yu great credit.

The Stranger is propelled violently on stage by two of Tsai-yu's men. He stumbles to a heap at Wu-feng's feet.

Margama: If that is the way Tsai-yu's men escort the governor's guest I'd hate to be a criminal.

Wu-feng: They lack the ceremonial graces. (He raises the Stranger to his feet) Welcome to my most humble home. (To the Sgt.) Tell your master that the Governor believes his men should take further training in public etiquette.

Sgt.: Begging your pardon, sir, how's a man supposed t' be able to hold his own one minute down in the swamp section of town and then turn right around and be all polish and politeness up here in the pine grove? It's not etiquette we need, begging your pardon, sir, but crossbows.

Wu-feng: Tell me Sergeant, have you never beaten your children one moment and embraced your wife the next?

Sgt.: (Indignant) It's not the same thing at all as clobbering a thug one minute and being civilized and polite to an honest citizen the next.

Wu-feng: In what way is it not?

Sgt.: I beat my children, sir, but I love them. That's why I beat them!

Wu-feng: May I suggest, Sergeant, that you give some consideration to the idea of loving your children who live down by the swamp?

Sgt.: (Puzzled) My children down by the — (Comes inidgnantly to attention) Are you implying, sir, that I've been enjoying some extramarital activity down in the swamp section?

Wu-feng: No, no!

Sgt.: (Seeing the light) Ah-h-h. You mean I should go beat them up some for their own good!

Wu-feng: Certainly not!

Sgt.: Then I don't follow you, sir.

Wu-feng: (Wearily) Indeed, that is the crux of the problem.

Wu moves back to the Stranger and Margama. He takes the Stranger by the arm in a friendly fashion and presents him to Margama.

Wu-feng: This is my good friend and enemy Margama. I regret that I am unable to give you a name.

Stranger: The Master says, "Worry not that no one knows of you."

Wu-feng: (Stops him with a gesture, and takes over the quote) "Seek to be **worth** knowing."

They bow to each other.

Sgt.: Sir.

Wu-feng: (Surprised) You have permission to leave.

Sgt.: It's not that, sir. As Magistrate you were to tell us the disposition of the thief.

Wu-feng: Thief? (Looking around)

Sgt.: *(Indicating the Stranger)* Him, sir.

Wu-feng: *(To the Sgt.)* Do you mean my friend the scholar?

Sgt.: Said thief, your Honour, has already confessed.

Serenity: He is a nobleman. I am sure of it.

Margama: I know this young man. He is a visitor. Poor, without powerful friends, travelling alone in our mountains. He is interested in our music and dance and the ways of our culture. *(To Wu-feng)* He remains by invitation of Margama and Margama's friends.

Wu-feng: *(To Stranger)* This is so?

Stranger: I have been asked to participate in the upcoming festivities.

Wu-feng: *(Turns and looks at Margama)* The upcoming festivities, eh?

Sgt.: Sir, what of the thief?

Wu-feng: *(There is sudden anger in his voice)* Do not call a man a thief without first presenting evidence!

Sgt.: The evidence is in his mouth, sir. He has confessed.

Wu-feng: *(To the Stranger)* Well, what is it to be? Nobleman, scholar, anthropologist, or thief?

Stranger: *(Humbly)* I see no conflict in being all four.

Wu stares at him a moment, then laughs cheerfully and takes a turn around the stage. He stops in front of the Sergeant.

Wu-feng: Tell Tsai-yu that the magistrate and the prisoner are going to examine each other over a bowl of wine and a pot of noodles. *(Goes to Serenity)* My dear, we will enter presently.

Serenity exits.

Sgt.: But sir, he's dangerous! I know the type.

Wu-feng does not even look at the sergeant. The Governor merely slaps his hands resoundingly together and snaps a finger in a gesture that plainly says "Go". The Sgt. snaps to attention and exits.

Wu-feng: *(To the Stranger)* Come, let us go in.

Margama draws Wu-feng aside.

Margama: Watch him. He **may** be dangerous.

Wu-feng: Your concern touches me.

Margama: *(Sincerely)* Our hearts share many memories. I wish you no personal harm.

Wu-feng: Even though I disinherited you?

Margama: It was a miserable inheritance. One poor mountain tribe. As you say, I owe you appreciation.

Wu-feng: Good. *(Pats Margama's arm affectionately)*

Margama: *(Beaming)* Yes. You showed me the meanness of my tiny ambitions.

Wu-feng: *(Without enthusiasm)* Really. Well, you must excuse me. I had hoped to have a long talk with you, but hospitality calls.

Wu-feng and the Stranger exit together. Margama watches them go.

Margama: Poor, simple, trusting, generous, fool. Go and may the blessings of your ancestors go with you. Go to your noodles and the wine bowl and your intellectual orgy of Confucian quotations. We'll see what "the Master saith" about things afoot. Take your scholar to your table but Margama, too, is a scholar. Margama has been listening and learning. *(Shouting)* "Excellence does not remain alone; it is sure to attract neighbours." Thus saith the Master! But what is excellence? Is it that worm, Tsai-yu, with his perfume and Protectors? Is it my elder idiot Piong-shih with his abject grovelling, and his cultural amnesia? Is it little Governor Wu with his gentle heart stuffed so full of dreams for tomorrow that he forgets he is living today? No! No! No! *(Shouts off)* I, Margama, am True Man. **I** am excellent! It is **my** excellence that will attract neighbours, not yours.

Margama moves toward side of stage almost as though to follow Wu.

Margama: Do you hear that, little Governor Wu? I am excellent. Not you. I, Margama, am True Man!

Poolee hurries in, and stops just on stage.

Poolee: *(Calls)* Margama. Good news. Quickly.

Margama crosses to him.

Poolee: Remember this morning?

Margama: I remember.

Poolee: And the Counsellor who called out to us in the Elder Tongue?

Margama: *(Impatiently)* Yes, yes. The one we liberated from protector brutality. I remember.

Poolee: You recall we have given him safe sanctuary in a cave we know of, and —

Margama: I remember. I recall. My memory is excellent and functions in great detail. What I do not remember is the good news because it has not yet been told to me!

Poolee: But I am here, breathless from haste, perspiring with eagerness to tell you the tidings. The Counsellor of the Elder Tongue, overcome with gratitude . . .

Margama: Badly hurt?

Poolee: He will recover.

Margama: No marks?

Poolee: They will vanish.

Margama: About this "gratitude" —

Poolee: He has recalled where he has hidden his personal copy of the Manual of the Ancient Rites!

Margama: Quickly. Take me to him.

Wu-feng, the Stranger and Serenity enter with Servants as though passing through to dine. They have almost crossed when Margama swings briefly toward them.

Margama: Elder cousin, respected Governor, there is something you should know. Political power you have taken from me but I have authority neither you nor the Emperor can touch. By ancient custom established in the days of the waning flood by the ancestors of the five animals and the five sons, I, Margama, son of the Chief, am also to be High Priest of the tribe of Ali. Heir to the Chief I am not. This you have done. High Priest I will be. This you cannot undo.

Margama and Poolee exit.

Serenity: I am frightened. That did not sound like Margama your friend.

Wu-feng: No. That was Margama the High Priest.

Serenity: What does it mean?

Wu-feng: *(Darkly, looking off)* It means that Rebellion, having already raped Hunger, is now going to seduce Religion. *(Pulling himself with difficulty back to his guest)* Forgive me. My mind probes caverns my eyes cannot yet see.
They exit.

Scene Four

The children enter, walking backward as though spellbound by something they are watching. The something makes its first appearance in the person of a Chinese herald, or crier, who enters already proclaiming in full voice.

Herald: Han-sun comes! Free gifts for all at only half price! Buy with Confidence! Trade with Profit! Discount prices to celebrate the arrival of Han-sun's caravan! Special rates for the noble mountaineers! The annual event you have been talking of, dreaming about, waiting for! Special Introductory Offer on all good goods for the Good Life! Han-sun comes!

He exits, distributing handbills as he goes, but even as he goes the caravan enters and proceeds across stage. The principal point of interest is a large sedan chair carrying the large, rotund, al-most Buddha-like figure of Han-sun, a beaming Chinese merchant. The sedan chair is followed by several coolies bearing packing cases slung on carrying poles. The cases are all labelled, "Han-Sun Enterprises". The caravan crosses the stage and exits.

Scene Five

Some young village women enter. They are dressed in the Chinese manner, but a very simplified, peasant style. They seem excited, and the name "Margama" can be heard passing from one to the other. Some of Margama's young men come in. They too appear to be excited. Tsai-yu's sister, Tranquility, hurries in.

Tranquility: Is it true? I hear they have found it?

Youth: You'll not tell your brother Tsai-yu?

Tranquility: Tell the Protector! What do you take me for?

Youth: It's a religious matter, you know.

Tranquility: But have they really found a Manual? Are they really going to bring back the Ancient Rites?

Youth: Margama says our culture is the only thing that tells us who we are. It's like knowing your own name.

Tranquility: I know my own name.

Youth: It would be very difficult to maintain your self respect if you didn't.

Tranquility: But I do.

Youth: That's not the point.

Margama, Li-yu, and Poolee enter. The youths gather around them. Margama is carrying a small scroll, rolled up. He stops, dramatically, and raises the scroll high, in his clenched fist.

All eyes are raised to it, and a low, almost orgiastic sigh rises from the group.

Margama releases one end of the scroll while still holding it high. The scroll unrolls it's full three foot length, and he continues to hold it high.

The Youths, eyes on the scroll, all go down onto their knees.

Margama: The Manual of the Ancient Rites!

Voices: Read from it. Let's hear it. What's it say?

Margama swivels his wrist around so he can see the scroll himself, then rolls it up, and goes aside with Poolee and Li-yu.

Li-yu: Why are you doing that? Let's hear a bit of it. It'll be good publicity.

Margama: It's not enough that it's in the Elder Tongue, it was written by some idiot with the palsy. I can't make it out.

Youths: Margama, read to us! Let us hear the Ancient Rites!

Margama: *(To Poolee)* Bring old Ai-lee the scholar here.

Poolee: Ai-lee! He hasn't walked for ten years. He's been dying for five.

Margama: I didn't say walk him here, I said bring him here.

Poolee exits with Li-yu, and two others.

Youths: *(Various voices in turn)*
Read Margama, read.
Let us hear the old phrophecies.
Let us hear of the great days.
Tell us of greatness to be.
We are lost children of the tribe of Ali.
Where have we been?
From where have we come?
Where are we going?
Read, Margama.

Margama: Patience. Together we will unravel the mysteries of the Ancient Rites. Together we will learn to command our destiny. Together we will explore the trail to fulfillment. I am no different than you. I have no insight that you do not have. I have no power that you do not give me.

I, like you, am a lost child of the Tribe of Ali. I, like you, have a father who sold my birthright to the Emperor in Peking. Our fathers have forfeited our culture for security and our language for commerce. We few are hostages to the many, a generation stripped of its identity, forbidden to dream. *(Raising the scroll again)* But here, preserved in the scroll that entombs the rites of the ancient culture are the seeds that will grow into the tree of our liberation!

Poolee and Li-yu and the others enter carrying a simple sedan chair. In the sedan chair is an incredibly ancient and feeble old man. When the chair is put down the old man, Ai-lee the Scholar, makes no attempt to move out of it, for the simple reason that he does not have the strength.

Margama: *(To the youths)* I will not read the Mysteries to you. It is not fitting that I, who am your brother, should learn more of the Mysteries than you. It is more fitting that Ai-lee the Scholar who once spoke the Elder Tongue as a right, who himself has practised the Ancient Rituals, who was already an old man when the Emperor forbade the practice of the Act of Purification — it is most fitting that Ai-lee be the first to read.
Margama unrolls the scroll and holds it in front of old Ai-lee.

Youths: Read, Ai-lee! Read!
Ai-lee tries to do as bidden, but all that comes out is incoherent babble.

Youths: Read, Ai-lee! Read!

There is more babble. Margama turns away to Poolee.

Margama: His mind is no longer in his brain!

Poolee: Perhaps he can't see.

Li-yu: That's right! He went blind two years ago. *(To Margama)* I thought you knew.

Margama: How am I supposed to know. The old fool never stirs out. Well, I've heard some of it. Let's see what we can do.

Margama returns to Ai-lee and again holds the scroll for him.

Margama: Revered Ai-lee, scholar and custodian of many memories, do not strain to make yourself heard by all. Speak softly and I, Margama your servant, will be your voice. Read us the words of the Song of Purity.

Youths: Read, Ai-lee, read!

The old man begins to babble again, but this time Margama pretends to unscramble and project the words. With Poolee and Li-yu helping him out with the occasional improvisation, it goes like this:

Margama:
Oh mighty Pu-la-lu-wan
Whose name is unspoken
We raise our —

Poolee: Hearts?

Li-yu: Knives.

Margama: Good.
We raise our knives to thee
In adoration and —

Li-yu: Token.

Margama: — token.

Youths: *(In chorus)*
O Mighty Pu-la-lu-wan
Whose name is unspoken
We raise our knives to thee
In adoration and token!

Margama:
O Mighty Pu-la-lu-wan
Ruling ancestral mountains
We purify —

Poolee: Our souls?

Li-yu: Ourselves?

Margama:
We purify our hands for thee
In red flowing fountains!

Youths: *(In chorus)*
O Mighty Pu-la-lu-wan
Ruling ancestral mountains
We purify our hands for thee
In red flowing fountains.

Margama:
O Mighty Pu-la-lu-wan
The guardian of culture
We offer this head to thee —
(To Poolee)
Culture — culture.

Li-yu:
The body to vultures.

Poolee: That's a bit heavy.

Li-yu: Margama started it. Let him finish it!

Margama:
We offer this head to thee
The body to vultures.

Piong-shih and other Elders enter and listen.

Youths: *(Triumphant chorus)*
O Mighty Pu-la-lu-wan
The guardian of culture
We offer this head to thee
The body to vultures.

Piong-shih: Margama!

Piong-shih comes forward. He looks very angry as he confronts Margama.

Piong-shih: What desecration is this? What do you have there?

Margama: The Manual of the Ancient Rites. If it is desecration for the sons and daughters of the mountains to hear the words of the Song of Purity, then let there be desecration.

Piong-shih: *(Low)* You've not even got it right.

Margama: A mere updating. Just the words have been changed.

Piong-shih: The Emperor forbade the Ancient Rites.

Margama: The Emperor's soldiers forbade them. Margama, the Emperor's loyal subject, brings them back.

Piong-shih: Governor Wu will hear of this.

Margama: Good. Governor Wu will handle the problem by quoting the Master. (To Poolee, etc.) We will translate Confucius into the Elder Tongue for him, to facilitate his insight.

(Laughter)

Piong-shih: The Elder Tongue is a stream that fish no longer swim, useful only to dream over.

Margama: It alone conveys the true sound of native hearts. We will return to it, or die, lost in our own shapelessness, suffocated by our own silence.

Piong-shih: You talk nonsense. No doubt your brain is fevered by the hunger in your bellies. The famine has struck hard at us all.

Margama: We have an Elder in custody who grew fat on our hunger.

Piong-shih: Yes. We will speak of that later. But I have good news for all of you. Han-sun the merchant has come. But this time not to sell — to buy! It is rumoured he wishes to buy land from us — poor sterile land that is letting us starve. He will pay much gold. With it we can buy rice from the people of the plains — buy fish from the people of the sea — buy silks from the mainland —

Margama: For our land! Our **land**!

Piong-shih: It is merely another way to make our land support us! I, your Chief, would not —

Margama: You stand there in your Chinese robes, speaking the Chinese tongue, talking of Chinese gold! No! Not your land! My land! (Including the youths) Our land!

Youths: (Angry agreement)

Piong-shih: I overlook your arrogance. Leave now. Go to your homes before Governor Wu hears of this disrespect. I, your Chief, command it.

Margama: You are no Chief. The Emperor is Chief. Governor Wu is Chief. You are merely Chief fool.

Piong-shih: I am High Priest of the Tribe of Ali.

Margama: You abdicated when the Emperor banned the Ancient Rites and the old tribe died. I, Margama, am the High Priest who is about to preside over the rebirth of the Tribe of Ali.

Youth: Hail Margama! Hail High Priest of Ali!

Piong-shih: The mantle of High Priest passes only with death.

Margama: That can be arranged.

Piong-shih: (Almost tottering) Margama — Margama, my son — It is I, Piong-shih — your father.

Margama: (Almost sadly) I have been taught to have reverence and respect for my departed ancestors. The sooner you have the good sense to join them, the sooner will I be able to revere thee.

Laughter and applause from the Youths. They begin a dance of defiance in and out and around their elders. Tranquility runs off.

Tranquility: Brother Tsai-yu! Tsai-yu! Help — Protectors!

She exits.
The dance continues then Tsai-yu and Protectors run in. The Protectors stop, draw their daggers, and begin to move in.

Margama: Stop!

The dancers and the Protectors freeze.

Margama: Tsai-yu. It is only a dance.

Piong-shih: It is rebellion.

Margama: Let them dance. It will take their minds off hunger.

Piong-shih: He has the forbidden Manual of the Ancient Rites.

Margama: I have no manual.

Piong-shih: Seize him. He claims to be High Priest.

B24

Margama: My father lives. How can I be High Priest?

Piong-shih: Seize him.

Margama: You do not uphold the Chief, Tsai-yu, you uphold the law.

Tsai-yu: What law has been broken?

Piong-shih: He threatened me. He wished me dead.

Margama: I merely wished to be able to revere you. *(To Tsai-yu)* The wish for his death was the unfortunate corollary.

Tsai-yu takes a turn around the two opponents, then —

Tsai-yu: No law has been broken.

Piong-shih: I will pass one.

Margama: The Governor will not sign it.

Tsai-yu gestures to his men and they leave as smartly as they came.

Tsai-yu: *(To Margama)* You'd best take good care of him. When the old fool dies, I make the laws.

Tsai-yu exits and the dance begins with renewed vigour. After watching a moment, Margama moves to a girl who is dancing right in front of Piong-shih. In a gesture of defiance Margama tears her Chinese clothing from her and hurls it at Piong-shih's feet. All the youths get the idea and all their Chinese clothing gets torn off during the dance. They decorate old Scholar Ai-lee's sedan chair with the pieces, use others as streamers to ornament the dance, and generally go wild, to the point where they are all naked, both male and female, except for loin cloths. It is a somewhat savage but beautiful spectacle.

The youths dance off, carrying old Scholar Ai-lee with them in his decorated chair.

The Elders, including Piong-shih, are left huddled in one small area, on their knees, bowing forward, their hands firmly over their eyes.

They rise, slowly, and shuffle off, their heads still bowed, their eyes still covered.

Scene Six

The Stranger and Serenity enter together, laughing. They are running, almost like children at play. He slows down, trying to catch his breath.

Stranger: Wait. Hold on.

Serenity: We're almost there.

Stranger: I'm just an ox from the plains. How can I keep up with a mountain fawn.

She comes back to him, laughing.

Serenity: You don't like my mountain?

Stranger: I love it. Someday we'll climb it. Not today.

Serenity: *(Alarmed)* No, no. Never.

Stranger: Oh yes. Tomorrow, maybe. Or perhaps the day after.

Serenity: My people never go to the top.

Stranger: It might do them good.

Serenity: Pu-la-lu-wan lives there.

Stranger: Who is Pu-la-lu-wan?

She merely puts her fingers over his lips.

Serenity: I think we should go down now.

Stranger: I suppose so. Too bad, though. One should never go down.

He stands a moment, gazing upward.

Stranger: *(Quotes)*
Though the mountain is high
it's only a hill beneath the sky.
Here's the bottom, there's the peak,
the path to follow is the path you seek.
Why don't you climb, instead of sigh
and say, "The hill is high"?

Serenity: You're a poet!

Stranger: If you wish.

Serenity: *(Teasing)* You mean you are what I wish?

Stranger: *(Laughs)* Why not?

Serenity: I wish — I wish — that you were a handsome prince.

Stranger: That's a big wish. What do your eyes tell you?

Serenity: *(Slightly bashful)* That you are handsome.

Stranger: Then I tell you that I am a prince.

Serenity: But how do I know that is true?

Stranger: How do you know it is not true? If you have no proof one way or the other, why not believe what will make you happy?

Serenity: *(Laughs and makes a pretty obeisance)* Your highness. Another wish?

Stranger: *(Laughs)* If you dare.

Serenity: I wish you were a handsome prince come to carry me off to the palace at Peking.

Stranger: What a marvelous wish.

Serenity: Against my will, mind you.

They exit, both laughing.

Tsai-yu and the Sergeant come on stage as though they have been watching the young couple. They confer in whispers a moment, then the Protector quietly moves across stage and exits after Serenity and the Stranger. Tsai-yu looks smugly pleased and exits in another direction.

Scene Seven

Han-sun, the merchant, enters along with Wu-feng.

Han-sun: My dear Governor, I must protest. You're not considering the possibilities, the — the — advantages the scheme offers your people. *(Stops, amazed)* My word! What a magnificent garden. You do yourself proud. *(Returning to the subject in hand)* A company has already been formed — the Emperor's blessing, of course — all properly accredited, legally constituted, a charter from the Minister of Federal Development, you know — *(Gets sidetracked again by the apparently beautiful garden around him)* This stream is incredible. The Emperor's best men have not created a stream the equal of this. Who is your Environmental Architect?

Wu-feng: We call him Pu-la-lu-wan.

Han-sun: He can't be local. Where does he live?

Wu-feng: Up there.

Han-sun: *(Staring upward toward the mountain top)* How very odd. I must tell the Emperor. He'll no doubt call your Pu-la-lu-wan to Peking.

Wu-feng: I doubt he'd go.

Han-sun: Not go! I thought your headstrong tribesmen were learning some sense of proportion! Hasn't it dawned on them yet that it's not enough just to lean on the Emperor — that they've got responsibilities, too? That if they're asked to contribute their skills for the larger good, then they contribute?

Wu-feng: Are we talking of the Emperor's garden or of Han-sun's Company!

Han-sun: The principle is the same. Consider. You're a farsighted man. The Company buys the most useless portions of the land — rocky — vertical — broken by waterfalls — useless. *(Stranger and Serenity enter, but do not intrude.)* The Company re-develops it — there are gems here, mere baubles, but of value to the Court — good locations for secluded holiday homes for the nobility — none of this of any particular account to your people. For them, you see, we have gold. Real gold. Cash on the barrel head. What can they lose?

Wu-feng and Han-sun exit as Han-sun expounds.

Serenity draws the Stranger to a seat.

Serenity: Now, tell me about it.

Stranger: Not me, I don't have the words for it.

Serenity: But you've been to court. What have you seen?

The Stranger gets up and paces in mock exasperation.

Stranger: You can't just start in and describe something like that! It's just not — not — why I'd do as well trying to describe your father's garden to the Emperor. What could I say?

Serenity: What **could** you say?

Stranger: I could say, "Beloved Emperor, I have seen a mountain that is serene as you are serene, that is rooted to the earth as your authority is rooted in our hearts. A mountain whose head is wreathed in white as your head is wreathed in silver and which, like you, will endure to eternity. I have climbed peaks where the storm's rage is no less awful than your displeasure, O my Emperor, and trod valleys where the soft dew falls with no more gentleness than the caress of your own merciful forgiveness."

Serenity: *(Clapping with pleasure)* Go on.

Stranger: To his daughter I could say, "I hear the courtiers tell that you, Our Princess, are the most beautiful of all women, but I did not understand until I saw your beauty mirrored in the daughter of Wu-feng." *(Goes to Serenity)* I have not dared gaze directly into the eyes of the Princess but I have seen the eyes of the daughter of Wu-feng and know my mind could not comprehend any sight more lovely. I have heard the laughter of the Princess echoing through the halls and gardens of the palace but it was only when I heard the voice of the daughter of Wu-feng laughing with the hills and rills springing from beyond creation that I came to understand this truth — the palace of the Emperor is a cold golden fortress within which men attempt to imprison beauty, but the garden of Wu-feng is a warm nursery of love tenderly cultivating beauty as a wild vine to reach out and encircle the hearts of all men.

He is just reaching out gently to stroke her hair from the side of her face and they are drawing together.

The Sergeant enters.

Sgt.: Beg pardon, Miss.

He moves as though to take the Stranger by the arm.

Serenity: My father will be angry! He hasn't completed the examination.

Sgt.: *(Gestures at the Stranger)* You mean he hadn't completed the examination. Ah, hah! Eh, eh? *(He gives a gross wink at the Stranger, then relents)* You must forgive a humble man his little joke, Miss. One must spice a hard job with a little levity. Good humour kills more hatred than a quiver full of arrows, I always say. Did I ever tell you of the time I had to put the arm on one of the canyon lads who'd been into more rice wine than was good for him? Big fellow he was, and didn't want to come, even though I had an armlock on him. Great sense of humour he had, too. Threw pepper in my face. How I sneezed. Of course I didn't let go that armlock. First sneeze broke his arm. Every sneeze after that, well, you can just imagine. How we laughed. Why he laughed so hard he fainted right at my feet. *(To the Stranger)* I want a word with you.

The Sergeant takes the Stranger by the arm and propels him downstage, leaving Serenity by herself.

Sgt.: Just be a moment, Miss. *(Lowers his voice and talks to the Stranger)* It's come to the attention of some in high places that you show interest in the daughter of Wu-feng.

Stranger: I am aware of no crime.

Sgt.: It is merely an observation!

Stranger: Very well.

Sgt.: As you may know, things aren't all they might be in the mountains these days. In fact, there are those in high places who apprehend insurrection.

Stranger: What's that to do with me?

Sgt.: Nothing. That's why you can be useful.

Stranger: Oh? In what way?

Sgt.: By giving in to your natural inclinations as a gentleman, and to her natural inclinations as a female. Abduct her. Seize her. Carry her off. Do I make myself clear?

Stranger: Perfectly. But why?

Sgt.: The fact is, there are those in high places who are very fond of Miss Serenity. Who'd feel very broke up about it if the lid blew around here and she got hurt. Do you realize there might even be those who'd stoop to kidnapping her! After all, she is the Governor's daughter, you know.

Serenity: *(Calls)* If you're talking about me, it's unfair that I can't join in.

Sgt.: *(Ignores her)* There'd be those in high places who'd be mighty relieved to see her taken quietly safe out of here. For awhile.

Stranger: Why are you telling me? I'm a prisoner.

Sgt.: Not for anything that'll stick, you aren't. The Governor'll let you go. If he doesn't, we've got precious little time to waste guarding anyone these days. Got our hands full making arrests. You know how it is.

Serenity: *(Calls)* Are you still talking about me?

Sgt.: Only indirectly, Miss. *(To the Stranger)* You understand, then?

Stranger: Imperfectly.

Sgt.: Look at her. You'd not want her caught in the middle of a resurrection.

Stranger: Insurrection.

Sgt.: Either way a most mighty upheaval. *(Turns to Serenity)* It's all right, Miss. Just keep an eye on the prisoner here, until the law needs him.

Serenity: What will happen to him?

Sgt.: Now, now, don't worry. Unless he escapes, something suitably unpleasant, no doubt.

He winks at the Stranger, then moves across the stage to leave, but almost collides with Han-sun and Wu-feng, who enter.

Wu-feng: What is it now, Sergeant?

Sgt.: Beg pardon, sir. Commissioner's orders. Just making protective rounds.

Wu-feng: I see. Who are we protecting this time?

Sgt.: You, sir.

Wu-feng: From whom?

Sgt.: That criminal there, sir.

Wu-feng: *(Looks sadly at the Sergeant, then claps the Stranger on the shoulder while still talking to the Sergeant)* "When you see a man of the highest calibre, give thought to attaining his stature."

Stranger: *(Eyeing Han-sun)* "When you see one who is not, go home and conduct a self-examination."

Wu-feng laughs and turns to the Stranger. They bow.

Both: Thus saith the Master.

Wu-feng: *(To the Sergeant)* Tell Tsai-yu the Governor appeciates his concern but does not share it.

He gestures imperiously. The Sergeant snaps to attention, salutes, and exits.

Wu-feng nods to the Stranger and Serenity and the two of them happily exit on the run.

Wu-feng watches them go, a gentle smile on his face. He continues to watch even after they have gone, then begins to talk, the remains of the gentle smile in sharp contrast to the content of his words.

Wu-feng: I have listened to your most practical proposition. The concern of Han-sun the merchant for the plight of my people has touched me deeply.

Han-sun: You honour me too much.

Wu-feng: The Company of which you speak can move into these mountains —

Han-sun: Excellent!

Wu-feng: — when I and my children's children are dead and our spirits fled to the outer darkness.

Han-sun: The offer's for now! Immediate. Cash on the barrel head.

Wu-feng: Though my bones be crushed in my living body I will not give my permission for your Company to buy into this territory.

Han-sun: What? Surely — ha ha — you joke. What reason! Do you not trust me? Han-sun is a man of good faith. I am known throughout the Empire! My partners in this venture are men of honour — stature.

Wu-feng: We are not speaking of Han-sun, my Chinese brother. We are speaking of Han-sun's Chinese company.

Han-sun: There is no difference!

Wu-feng: Han-sun is a living man who believes in Buddha.

Han-sun: Of course! So.

Wu-feng: The Company is a figment of Han-sun's imagination and believes in Profit.

Han-sun: Oh come now, that's —

Wu-feng: When Han-sun makes a decision he leans on Buddha for guidance. When the Company makes a decision it leans on Greed for guidance.

Han-sun: I am the Company! I and my partners!

Wu-feng: Oh? Indeed? You will die. They will die. But the Company goes on for ever. No god but gold. No morality but profit. We men at least create our gods in our own image and ignore them at will, but Companies we halluci-nate into a reality more real than ourselves. Oh yes, when we have all gone raving off the precipice our Companies will be left to assess our demise as profit or loss, counting the total on an abacus made from the ivory of our own bones.

Han-sun: Then you'll not deal? Wu-feng rejects assistance? This is the message I take to my backers — to Peking? To the Emperor?

Wu-feng: The message you take is that Governor Wu-feng, speaking out of love and respect for his people and in fulfillment of the responsibilities laid upon him by the Emperor, Governor Wu-feng says the people of Ali will deal, bargain, confer, trade, with anything that comes in human form, with anything that can feel anger, fear, compassion, love, frustration, envy, hope, or even hate! Yes. But not with your hallucinatory unemotional ammoral corporate monster that comes under the guise of seeking our own good.

Han-sun: (Quiet, affable) Very well. We'll talk of it some other time.

Wu-feng: Certainly.

Han-sun: Yes. After all, it's almost harvest time, and there's no harvest.

Wu-feng: My dear Han-sun you never were a philosopher. The lack of a harvest doesn't alter the principle.

Han-sun: We'll see.

Han-sun goes to the edge of the stage and claps his hands and makes a gesture off. He returns to Wu-feng.

Han-sun: But you are right. So much for philosophy. I have the baubles you ordered. Perhaps you would care to inspect them?

Two Chinese coolees enter carrying an ornate packing case suspended between two poles. They put it down and wait.

Han-sun unlocks the packing case, talking while he does so.

Han-sun: A most unusual order this. It was not

at all easy to fill. The, ah, specifications, you know.

Wu-feng steps up and looks into the now opened case.

Wu-feng: Excellent. Well done.

Han-sun: Go ahead. They won't bite.

Wu picks a white human skull up out of the packing case and looks at it from all angles.

Wu-feng: You'd swear it was real.

Han-sun: The Emperor's own Master of Ceramics took a special interest in it. On his own time, of course.

Wu-feng: *(Abruptly)* How much?

Han-sun: Well now, that's a very difficult question.

Wu-feng: Surely you have the invoice?

Han-sun: There's the freight-rates, of course, overland from Peking, the channel, the caravan into these mountains —

Wu-feng: Yes, yes.

Han-sun: On the other hand, we realize that something of this nature, designed as a tourist bauble, must be priced to sell. *(Probing)* They are souvenirs? Devices to extract voluntary taxes from witless visitors?

Wu-feng: You know our history.

Han-sun: Precisely. *(Laughs)* Is life not marvellous! One generation, bloody head hunters, using human skulls for harvest rituals. The Emperor waves the sword of brotherhood! Lo, the next generation become gentle peasants slyly selling clay skulls to their more gullible Chinese brothers.

Wu-feng: *(Dryly)* It is most remarkable.

Han-sun: You see what commerce can do.

Wu-feng: How much?

Han-sun: How many? This first batch may seem unduly expensive. A first run. But, if you approve of them, and place a quantity order, the savings can be reflected immediately. On the other hand there was a suggestion that these might be too bare? Perhaps a little dried blood — a few illusory shreds of skin — even some hair. The grisly touch would be very big with your middle class visitor. If you cared to give Han-sun Enterprises an exclusive franchise we would consider doing some research among neighbouring tribes to learn the cranial characteristics of their deceased heroes and politicians. We could turn out a few carefully customized items that might well have adorned the shoulders of specific individuals among your people's enemies. The status implications are enormous. Of course that moves away from souvenirs, and into collectors' items. The price would have to reflect the attendant research and risk. The Company would want to do some market research on that before committing itself to a firm quote.

Wu-feng: I'm sure.

Han-sun: I fear you don't quite wrap your mind around the possibilities.

Wu-feng: The possibilities leave my mind quite limp.

Han-sun: The trouble with you philosophers is you have good brains but no imagination. Here you are, in a position of power, sitting on top of a cultural treasure chest and you have no more idea how to open it, or exploit it, than — than — *(He is finally, believe it or not, stymied for words.)*

Wu-feng: True. *(Puts the skull back in the case)* At the moment I find myself trying to keep that cultural treasure chest closed. *(Lets the lid drop shut)*

Han-sun: You see what I mean!

Wu claps for servants.

Wu-feng: Submit your invoice. It will be paid.

Han-sun: And future orders?

Wu-feng: There will be none. I had an idea, but

you have shown me it was a poor one. As you say, I lack imagination.

Servants come in and carry the skull case out.

Han-sun: *(Sadly)* My dear Wu-feng. You'll never make a businessman.

Another servant comes in and catches Wu-feng's attention.

Wu seems to know what his presence means.

Wu-feng: Forgive me, Han-sun. We've let our talk trespass into an hour reserved for some of the Emperor's most important tribesmen.

Han-sun: *(Bows)* Please convey the apologies of Han-sun the merchant. *(He moves off)*

Wu-feng nods to the servant, who exits.

Han-sun: *(Turning again to Wu-feng)* Tell them that Han-sun is ever at their service. If there is anything at all he can do for them — *(Spreads his hands expressively, and bows again)*

Wu-feng: *(Bows)*

Han-sun: Should your consultations enter an area within the experience of Han-sun, do not hesitate to call upon my humble expertise. *(Bows again)*

Wu-feng: *(Bows)*

Han-sun: The Emperor's influential tribesmen are like brothers to Han-sun. The Company could be persuaded to waive the usual consultative charges. *(Bows again)*

Wu-feng: *(Bows)*

Han-sun exits.

Wu-feng looks off in another direction.

Wu-feng: They come. And I'm unprepared. Unprepared! Quickly now, Governor. An idea. *(He seems agitated. Paces rapidly around as though hoping through sheer muscular activity to generate an idea. Suddenly —)* Ah ha. Freight rates! Shipping! Merchandize — That's it! Thank you, Han-sun.

Several Children run in. They all stop and they and the Governor confront each other. The children bow solemnly and Wu-feng returns the bow just as solemnly.

Then the children run forward and surround him, laughing.

He claps his hands and they fall silent.

Wu-feng: Line up.

They line up.

Wu-feng: Today we are all merchants.

Child: Like fat Han-sun?

Wu-feng: Like our honourable **guest** and **friend** Han-sun.

Wu-feng steps into the line at one end. The children all watch him. He recites:

Wu-feng:
My ship is in with a cargo of tea
And plenty of presents for you and me,
She's brought me a fan! Oh joy! Oh bliss!
I fan myself every day like this.

Wu-feng begins to fan himself with his left hand and continues to do so.

The children repeat the verse in chorus and at the end of it they too, begin fanning themselves with their left hands.

Wu-feng: *(Still fanning)*
My ship is in with a cargo of tea
And plenty of presents for you and me,
She's brought me a drum! Oh joy! Oh bliss!
I play my drum every day like this.

Still fanning, he begins to beat an imaginary drum with his right hand.

The children, still fanning, repeat the verse in chorus and at the end of it begin to drum with their right hands.

Child:
My ship is in with a cargo of tea

And plenty of presents for you and me,
She's brought me a ball! Oh joy! Oh bliss!
I roll my ball every day like this.

The Child, still fanning and drumming, begins to roll a large imaginary ball with his left foot.

The others, including Wu-feng, repeat the verse in chorus and add the ball rolling motion with their left feet.

2nd Child:
My ship is in with a cargo of tea
And plenty of presents for you and me,
She's brought me a clock! Oh joy! Oh bliss!
I watch my clock everyday like this.

Without dropping any of the other motions his head begins to wag back and forth like a pendulum.

The others, including Wu-feng, repeat the verse in chorus and add the clock motion to all the others.

3rd Child:
My ship is in with a cargo of tea
And plenty of presents for you and me,
She's brought me a pony! Oh joy! Oh bliss!
I ride my pony everyday like this.

While trying to keep the other motions all going, the child begins to hop on his right foot.

Wu-feng stops for a moment, looking horrified, but the others have carried gamely on into the last verse, so he starts up again, and embarks valiantly into the hopping.

With all parts in motion the children exit. Wu-feng is left behind. He has to abandon the hopping. He is very dizzy. Children run back in, laughing, and escort him off.

He exits swaying somewhat unsteadily.

Scene Eight

Serenity and the Stranger enter. Serenity is first, almost running. She pauses impatiently, waiting for the Stranger to catch up. He is almost out of breath again.

Serenity: Oh what a great adventure it would be! It is quite marvelous to think about.

She darts ahead again, but his voice brings her back.

Stranger: Slow down. Wait. You move too fast. I take one step, you take two. I think one thought, you think three. I say one word, you add four.

Serenity: Steps, thoughts, words, let us run with them, play with them, dance to them. Steps run, run thoughts, thoughts play, play words, words dance, dance steps — *(Her cheerful babble dissolves into a trill of laughter)*

Stranger: So now you're the poet.

Serenity: I merely feel good. It's just one of those nice-to-be-abducted days.

Stranger: Don't you think, however, that if I'm to be the abductor, I should at least go first?

Serenity: Oh. Is your pride hurt?

Stranger: I'm just not sure you understand the suggestion.

Serenity: I understand perfectly. You may abduct me as far as the waterfall in the lower garden.

Stranger: You're laughing at me.

Serenity: I'm not even smiling! *(Giggles)* You may carry me, if it will help.

Stranger: At least it's all downhill.

He picks her up in a fireman's lift and jogs around a few steps.

Serenity: Oh! Oh! Oh!

He stops.

Serenity: Your shoulder's so hard. This doesn't seem right at all. It's not at all what I imagined.

Stranger: Nothing ever is.

They exit, the Stranger carrying Serenity.

They are no sooner gone than the Sergeant appears as though from cover. He watches a moment, then gestures and is joined by two more Protectors.

Sergeant: You saw?

Protector: Yes, Sergeant.

Sergeant: All right. Arrest them.

Protector: But Sergeant. The Governor's daughter!

Sergeant: I know, but duty's duty.

Protector: The Commissioner will be very upset.

Sergeant: I'll report to him personally.

The two Protectors go off in the wake of the Stranger and Serenity, and the Sergeant exits another direction.

Scene Nine
Sound, off. The low sound of voices keening a ritual tune. No words, just the tune. It has oriental overtones to it but with a distinct Gregorian flavour.

Piong-shih and some Elders enter, hurrying.

Other Elders enter from another direction. They all meet.

Piong-shih: We must find the Governor before it's too late.

1st Elder: It was too late months ago.

Piong-shih: I even hear they've been drilling in the woods. Why doesn't somebody tell me these things!

They all hurry off together.

The Sound of the singing is coming nearer.

Several Servants cross the stage. They look frightened, and are almost running.

Han-sun enters with a Servant.

Han-sun: Give my respects to the Governor. Tell him I had intended to enjoy his hospitality for several days but that urgent business calls me —

He stops, downstage, looking off. The Singing is getting closer.

Han-sun does an about face and just as hurriedly exits back in the very direction from which he had come.

Wu-feng enters, with Tsai-yu.

Tsai-yu: I have just had the report. I feel this may be a case that should be heard at once.

Piong-shih and the Elders hurry in.

Piong-shih: Governor Wu. A matter of most urgent, most pressing, most painful importance.

Wu-feng: My dear Piong-shih. You're quite out of breath.

Tsai-yu: Consider this, sir. A man. A woman. Both unmarried, and he a foreigner. And what do my men find?

Piong-shih: How can I tell you this. Margama, my own son!

Tsai-yu: Open defiance of the Statute for the Preservation of Racial Purity!

Piong-shih: Defiance from Margama! My own son!

Wu-feng: Sit down, sit down. Let us hear about it, calmly.

Tsai-yu: There's only one way to put it, sir. Seizure and rape!

Piong-shih: They've been training in the woods!

Wu-feng: Softly. One at a time. *(Gestures for Tsai-yu to speak)*

Tsai-yu: A foreigner, sir, and a tribal woman. What's your wish?

Wu-feng: Who are they? What law did you say?

Tsai-yu: He was carrying her away, sir, in a

manner contrary to the Federal Statute for the Preservation of Racial Purity.

Piong-shih: That's what happens when there's a famine and no harvest.

Wu-feng: *(Darkly)* What happens is that one of our tribal prejudices, enshrined in a Federal cloak of respectability, turns intemperate enthusiasm into a crime. Bring them here.

Tsai-yu exits.

Wu-feng turns to Piong-shih. But the latter, instead of speaking, merely points off, trembling.

Han-sun enters from upstage.

Han-sun: Governor! Shelter! Protection! Sanctuary! *(He stops also looking off.)*

Margama and his half naked young men and women enter. They are chanting the liturgical music and are carrying torches and long knives.

The Elders, Han-sun, and Servants tend to clump together in a fearful group away from the newcomers, but Wu-feng claps his hands and gestures off. Servants enter carrying his throne chair, and so, as the singing, naked, torchlit procession of youths, led by Margama, comes to a dramatic halt, they are confronted by the Governor calmly seated on his chair of office. The singing stops and Margama approaches Wu-feng.

Wu-feng: It has been a long time, but I recognize the tune.

Margama: Then it tells you more than any words I could use.

Wu-feng: It tells me you are learning old folk songs.

Margama: We are throwing off ways that are not our ways.

Wu-feng: *(Coolly eyeing the group)* You are throwing off a great deal.

Margama: We come clothed in the cloak of Pu-la-lu-wan, and I am his High Priest.

Youths: Hail Margama! Hail the High Priest of Pu-la-lu-wan!

Margama: Our culture is dying, our rulers disinherited, the Elder Tongue unheard, the Ancient Rites unpracticed. The rice dies on the stalk, the millet rots in the root, breasts run dry and babies die in the womb. We are held down by swords and beaten with words until we have forgotten who and what we are. We are the brave, surrounded by cowards and immersed in pestilence and poverty.

Youths: Hail Margama! Hail the High Priest!

Wu-feng: *(Calmly)* The Master says, "He who is fond of bravery but complains of poverty is certain to create disorder."

Margama: We have listened to what the Master says until our heads spin. Let the Master's disciple hear what we say. Let the might of the Emperor provide food and comfort for the people of the mountains — let the laws here be **our** laws — let the language here be **our** language. If not —

Wu-feng: Ah. We come to it. If not?

Margama: If not, on the day of the Harvest Festival we return to the Ancient Rites — we turn our hearts to Pu-la-lu-wan — we return to the ritual hunt of our forefathers. We find a victim. We perform the Act of Purification. We take a head!

The Youths all raise their weapons high in the air. They utter a long drawn "Hi-yeee-ih-huh!" and on the last explosion of breath take a giant stride forward, striking downward with their weapons as they do so.

Wu-feng rises abruptly from his seat and everything goes to black except for a spot on Wu-feng. He stands motionless a moment, looking very angry, very defiant, then he seems to relax and sits down again.

Wu-feng: *(Calmly)* We will negotiate.

Blackout

End of Act One

B36

Act Two, Scene One

Enter Han-sun's Coolees carrying his packing cases, etc., on poles. They come from several directions as though they are getting organized to leave, rather than actually in the process of leaving.

Han-sun enters and inspects the preparations. Wu-feng enters accompanied by the usual children. But both he and they seem very subdued. Wu eyes the preparations.

Wu-feng: You are leaving? Perhaps it is as well.

Han-sun: You agree then! It **is** dangerous here!

Wu-feng: Not at all. But I would like to send a letter with you to the Emperor.

Han-sun: If it's troops you want I'll add my plea to yours. There's nothing the Emperor understands better than an eye witness.

Wu-feng: That's precisely what I wish to assure the Emperor. There has been nothing to witness.

Han-sun: You call that obscenity and sedition "nothing"!

Wu-feng: It will take more than a naked parade or two to topple the Empire.

Han-sun: I wish I shared your confidence.

Han-sun sees the case of skulls.

Han-sun: That shouldn't be here! After all you did pay for them.

He opens the case and looks in.

Han-sun: A pity. You wouldn't like to reconsider?

Closes the case and returns to Wu-feng.

Han-sun: You never did intend them as souvenirs!

Wu-feng: The Act of Purification is very complex. Our forefathers used the skull afterwards for the Harvest Libations. It ensured the continuous pleasure of the gods — of our Pu-la-lu-wan.

Han-sun: By all the bones of my ancestors! You saw famine coming, foresaw pressure to bring back the Harvest Libation, and decided to have a skull on hand! *(He is very impressed)*

Wu-feng: *(Dryly)* If it worked I would have had them on hand for ever after. A small compromise.

Han-sun: *(Musing)* One skull a year for ever

after. There's a specialty item of the first order!

Wu-feng: It was a cheap idea. I regret having it.

Han-sun: *(Suddenly irate)* You saw all this coming and you did nothing! No troops? No special laws? Nothing!

Wu-feng: I have been listening to the inner thoughts of Confucius instead of to the drum beat of my mountain blood. I was wrong.

Han-sun: A costly mistake.

Wu-feng: True man must always err on the side of hope.

Han-sun gestures to a couple of coolees and they take the skull case and put it to one side.

Han-sun: It was a **good** idea. I suggest you still try it. Buy time, if nothing else. In the meantime, I'd like safe conduct to the Plains.

Wu-feng: Certainly.

Han-sun: Better still, some of Tsai-yu's men as escort.

Wu-feng: You're in no personal danger!

Han-sun: I have seen the ceremonial knives.

Wu-feng: I promise you safe conduct.

Han-sun: You and your promises are here. I journey away from both.

Wu-feng: Tsai-yu's men are needed here.

Han-sun: Ah. So there is danger?

Wu-feng: *(Laughs)* There is always danger.

Han-sun: With your permission I will postpone my departure.

Gestures to the Coolees and they exit with everything except the skull case.

Han-sun: Somehow I feel safer under the protection of Wu-feng's near presence than the protection of Wu-feng's distant promise.

Both men bow politely to each other and Han-sun exits. Tsai-yu and some Protectors enter hurriedly.

Tsai-yu: Governor Wu. Margama is coming. Shall we arrest him?

Governor Wu gestures negatively.

Servants carry in the two throne chairs. Wu-feng sits on one.

Margama, Poolee, Li-yu and several Others enter. They are armed.
They stop and face Tsai-yu's men. Wu-feng is seated in the middle.

Wu-feng gestures imperiously to Tsai-yu.

Tsai-yu: But Governor! They're armed!

Wu-feng repeats the gesture. Tsai-yu and his men exit.

Wu-feng: Well Margama? I am armed only with words. You may choose knives if you must, but it will be a poor discussion.

Margama hands his knife to Poolee and gestures.

Margama's men all exit.

Wu-feng gestures to the other chair and Margama approaches but does not sit.

Margama: You offer me the Chief's chair. Does the Chieftanship go with it?

Wu-feng: I offer it to the High Priest.

Margama: So. You recognize me as High Priest?

Wu-feng: The people appear to do so. It is a matter of no concern to government.

Margama: I will sit in the chair as heir to the Chieftanship.

Wu-feng: I said I would negotiate, not capitulate.

Margama thinks this over, then nods pleasantly and sits down.

Margama: Very well. As High Priest, then.

They sit looking at each other a few moments.

Wu-feng: I congratulate you on a most spectacular uprising, but fail to see what more you can hope to gain.

Margama: Freedom.

Wu-feng: A beautiful word.

Margama: We are done with being forced to be what we are not.

Wu-feng: The tribe is merely being forced to live in peace.

Margama: You admit there is force?

Wu-feng: The outcome is not loss of liberty but achievement of self-discipline.

Margama: We have no desire to discipline ourselves into being something we are not!

Wu-feng: *(Annoyed)* What is this thing you are not which you seem to fear so greatly you will become?

Margama: You ask that! Clothed in your Chinese robes, speaking the Chinese tongue!

Wu-feng: *(Angry)* You mistake the clothing for the man, the language for the thought!

Margama: Forgive me. "Become" is too strong. You would merely have us lose ourselves within them.

Wu-feng: Only as a man loses himself in a woman, to merge the strength of one with the beauty of the other, to see what new child the gods will send!

Margama: An exciting thought, were it not for the fact that in the match you recommend we waste our seed between the fat thighs of a sterile whore.

Wu-feng: The seemingly sterile has been known to bloom under loving cultivation!

Margama: Very well then, let us, lovingly, plough the Imperial Whore more deeply. Let us present our conjugal demands with upstanding boldness. Re-instate the Elder Tongue, bring back the Ancient Rites, guarantee our freedom to be ourselves, ensure the food supply, and let the Chief's son be the Chief's heir. Does that stimulate the flow of productive juices?

Wu-feng takes a long moment to compose himself.

Wu-feng: Let us consider what we have in common. Item. Food supply. A most understandable and compassionate request. Problem. We are not the only corner of the Empire that has to live with a tight belt. The Emperor does not control famine and poverty with a wand. You understand?

Margama: But do not agree.

Wu-feng: Item. The Elder Tongue. The Elder Tongue preserves much that is beautiful. There are thoughts that grow out of it and ideas that hide within it. I am in favour of liberating beauty, thoughts, and ideas. Problem. A Tongue can be a prison within which one nurtures hate, fear, and suspicion. Therefore you and I must bend our genius to liberating the one without creating the other. Agreed?

Margama: Agreed.

Wu-feng: Item. Freedom to be yourselves. How can one object! Free to become True Man! Problem. The medal has two sides. All men must have the same freedom. Therefore, freedom we will strive for, but always within the bounds of freedom. Your freedom is controlled by my freedom, my freedom by yours. Agreed?

Margama: Yes. But to at least make an imperfect beginning somewhere, I would prefer to start with my freedom rather than yours.

Wu-feng: Item. Restore the Ancient Rites. An understandable request. Many of the Rites were mindless, but not harmful. A certain ritualistic release can at times be most beneficial. Problem. The Act of Purification is part of the Ancient Rites. Since it involves the removal of another person's head, it automatically violates the freedom principle on which we have already agreed. Therefore, The Ancient Rites — possibly. The Act of Purification. Absolutely not! Agreed?

Margama: No.

Wu-feng: Ah — but as you can see, my dear friend, we are very close together on most other points.

Margama: There is a small problem you have forgotten. I would overlook it, myself, but it affects the future of the tribe.

Wu-feng: Then let's reach agreement on our major points and discuss this smaller thing at our leisure.

Margama: It is this small matter of my disinheritance.

Wu-feng: You're still determined to be Chief? You're already High Priest!

Margama: The two go hand in hand. I dislike the break with tradition.

Wu-feng: *(Darkly)* I see.

Margama: I thought you would.

Wu-feng: *(Coldly)* The government is seldom impressed by moves for power.

Margama: True. The Act of Purification is much more impressive.

Wu-feng: You use the Old Culture like a club!

Margama: One cannot "use" it. One can only unleash it.

Wu-feng rises in exasperation and paces a moment. Stops in front of Margama.

Wu-feng: Your weapon is self-destructive.

Margama: I think not.

Wu-feng: I can call Federal troops.

Margama: You won't.

Wu-feng: I have the authority.

Margama: For Governor Wu-feng to negotiate with troops would be for Governor Wu-feng to admit his life's work has been a failure.

Wu-feng: It is no failure to use one's authority!

Margama: Quote: "When the Master wanted to live among the tribes, a courtier said, 'But they're so crude! ' 'Ah', said the Master, 'If only True Man were living amongst them, how could they be crude? His very presence would alter all that.' " End quote.

Wu-feng sits down wearily in his chair.

Wu-feng: You know me too well.

Margama: I warned you I would use the knife.

Wu-feng: I thought it would be steel.

They both say nothing for a moment, Wu-feng looking beaten, Margama watching him, smilingly. After a moment Margama rises.

Margama: Well, that's that. I'd suggest you issue a statement right away, while I can still cool things down.

Wu-feng: *(Firmly)* No Act of Purification. Never. Under no conditions.

Margama: Then re-instate me as heir to the Chieftanship and retire Piong-shih within the year.

Wu-feng rises and faces him.

Wu-feng: *(Incredulous)* You insist on absolute power!

Margama: I am the tribe. I can do no less.

Wu-feng: *(Angry)* You fool. Then there is nothing to negotiate. He who goes for absolute power must be opposed absolutely.

Margama: You force us to violence!

Wu-feng utters a sound of disgust and wheels away from Margama. He moves away and then

B41

stops. The Governor looks close to a fit of rage but seems to get himself under control. Margama is about to exit.

Wu-feng: One moment yet.

Wu-feng makes an effort, calms himself, and turns to face Margama again.

Wu-feng: Let us explore this problem of your thirst for power. I remind myself that I am partly to blame.

Margama: *(A harsh laugh)* Partly!

Wu-feng: I have been forgetting your reasonable feeling of insecurity when you contemplate Tsai-yu as next Chieftan.

Margama: Insecurity! I'm as good as dead!

Wu-feng gestures for him to simmer down.

Wu-feng: There is safety as High Priest.

Margama: It all depends who controls the Protectors, and you've sealed me off from that, too!

Wu-feng: Ah, but there you're wrong. As Governor I'll arrange for you to marry Tsai-yu's sister. When Tsai-yu inherits the Chieftanship, your son inherits the Protectors. Since he will be unborn, or but a child, it is an easy matter to make you — uh — Protector Commissioner Regent, shall we say? High Priest **and** Commissioner Regent — ah, ah, — no, no — I'm too generous. Margama, Margama — that's enough security and enough power to destroy even you.

Margama: Nevertheless, I will think about it.

Wu-feng: And we hear no more about the Act of Purification?

Margama: I will think about it.

Wu-feng: Very well. If you insist.

Wu claps.

Tsai-yu enters, followed by some Protectors.

Wu-feng: Safe passage for Margama, my friend.

Tsai-yu bows in acknowledgment, gestures to his men. They ceremoniously make way for Margama. Wu-feng bows politely to Margama who nods curtly to him.

Margama exits, being met just as he leaves by a swirl of his friends who exit with him, surrounding him like some celebrity. The Protectors exit a discreet distance behind, leaving Tsai-yu and Wu-feng.

Tsai-yu: Beloved Governor, Margama is not your friend.

Wu-feng: Then I will have to be content with being his.

Tsai-yu: Let me seize him. Make an example of him.

Wu-feng: There is no crime.

Tsai-yu: The Ancient Rites! The Act of Purification! Defiance!

Wu-feng: One must discriminate between the word and the deed.

Tsai-yu: Protective Custody!

Wu-feng: *(Angry)* Enough!

Wu-feng is about to exit.

Tsai-yu: There is another matter.

Wu-feng: Well, well. On with it.

Tsai-yu: The couple under arrest, sir.

Tsai-yu gestures off and his men bring in Serenity and the Stranger, but well back, up stage. Wu-feng is far downstage and so occupied their presence hardly registers.

Wu-feng: *(Exasperated)* Oh-h-h—

Tsai-yu: You said, sir —?

Wu-feng: I said good for them. More passion over women and less over power and the world would be a better place!

Tsai-yu: There's a law on the Statutes, sir.

Wu-feng: Take them to Piong-shih. Racial Purity is under him.

Tsai-yu: *(Very pleased)* Very good, sir. Just thought I should remind you.

Wu-feng: Of what?

Tsai-yu: The mandatory sentence, sir. Depending on Piong-shih's verdict, **you** pass sentence.

Wu-feng: *(Almost a growl)* Oh-h-h yes. That's true. *(Sadly)* Ah-h-h-h here. Let me look at them. But there's nothing I can do. Morality is out of my hands.

Wu-feng wearily walks over to Serenity and the Stranger. She is hanging her head. He confronts the Stranger first.

Wu-feng: You! *(To Tsai-yu)* You have proof?

Tsai-yu: Sworn witnesses. My own men.

Wu-feng: *(To the Stranger)* I am sorry. It's a Federal Statute but a Tribal crime. I am not the Judge.

Stranger: "In hearing cases you would be like anyone else."

Wu-feng: Yes. "The important thing is to see to it there are no cases."

Wu-feng moves on and raises Serenity's face. He steps back as though slapped. He and his daughter look at each other a long moment. Then Wu-feng turns away.

Wu-feng: Take them to Piong-shih.

Tsai-yu gestures and the police take the prisoners out, again leaving Wu-feng and Tsai-yu alone. Wu-feng looks very tired and suddenly much older.

Tsai-yu: For weeks now I've been making a proposal that no one will heed. With your permission, I put it forward again.

Wu-feng: Be brief.

Tsai-yu: If we're to maintain law and order, my men need better equipment. With your permission, sir — every man must have a cross-bow!

Wu-feng: Not granted.

Tsai-yu: I can't answer for the consequences.

Wu-feng: Agreed.

Tsai-yu: My men can't even protect themselves!

Wu-feng: I will not have the Protectors armed like soldiers!

Tsai-yu: *(Hurt)* You don't trust me?

Wu-feng: I trust no one who has the power to be violent!

Tsai-yu: Then I'm not responsible.

Wu-feng: No. **I'm** responsible!

Tsai-yu: But, sir —

Wu-feng: No more!

Wu-feng exits.

Tsai-yu watches him go, and Tsai-yu seems strangely pleased with himself.

Margama enters, along with Poolee and Li-yu.

Protectors come on to back Tsai-yu.

Tsai-yu: What is it this time?

Margama: The same as last time. I wish to talk to Governor Wu.

Tsai-yu gestures and his men move discreetly away.

Poolee and Li-yu also drop back.

Tsai-yu: I'll give him your message.

Margama: Tell him I'm inclined to be reasonable.

Tsai-yu: Don't be too reasonable.

Margama: Why?

Tsai-yu: He's starting to break.

Margama: Why are you telling me?

Tsai-yu: I'm a Tribesman.

Margama: So is Wu-feng.

Tsai-yu: The Chinese took our Pu-la-lu-wan out of him and put Confucius in. A poor exchange.

Margama: (Laughs) Suddenly Tsai-yu is a patriot.

Tsai-yu: (Darkly) My blood is your blood. My mountain is your mountain. I thought you understood that.

Margama: (Generously) I am sorry.

They touch the palms of their right hands together as though in a tribal handshake.

Tsai-yu exits, and the Protectors exit with him. Poolee, Li-yu, and Margama watch him go.

Margama: We're stronger than we knew. Too bad we're not trying for the lot.

Li-yu: With Tsai-yu on our side there's no need to stop short of the ultimate.

Margama: Nevertheless we shall.

Poolee: Everything is going to seem so incomplete!

Margama: (Laughs) You've known that all along. I doubt I could even do it.

Li-yu: It begins to seem cowardly to compromise. Now that we are winning, you know. Besides, Poolee and I may have known, but the others are expecting the Act of Purification.

Margama: I thought we all understood! It is essential that our elder idiots believe we desire the final step, but we don't have to believe it ourselves!

Poolee: I will feel so terribly unfulfilled.

Margama: Maybe so, but there is a point in politics where to threaten is wisdom but to act is madness.

Li-yu: If you back out now, Margama, you're even a bigger fool than your father.

Margama: (Laughs) But the Governor is mine! I hold him, so! — He is clay for us to mold. He is hair for us to braid. He is wood to be carved in our image. A fire to be fueled with our desires. He will not oppose us with force. His religion forbids it, his vanity prevents it. The mere threat of the Act of Purification makes us masters in our own mountains.

Poolee: Nevertheless, I still feel unfulfilled.

Margama: We compromise. I marry Tsai-yu's sister and soon control the Protectors. We compromise. A resurgence of the Old Culture makes the High Priest more powerful than the Chief. We compromise. The Elder Tongue is reinstated the better to glorify Pu-la-lu-wan and thus stave off the necessity of using the Act of Purification. (Laughs) But don't you see? Compromises are not ours. Only the victories are ours. The compromises are Wu-feng's. Poor elder cousin Wu. Kind, foolish, gentle cousin Wu.

Han-sun bustles in and is almost halfway across before he spots them. When he does he is almost paralyzed with fear.

Han-sun: (Suddenly) Help! Help!

He runs, or more correctly, waddles to exit, but his path is quickly blocked by Poolee and Li-yu who can't resist having some sport. They are brandishing their knives.

Poolee: You called for help?

Li-yu: We are here!

Poolee: Who dares frighten Han-sun?

Li-yu: Where? Who? What?

The two of them are turning and dodging and

B44

darting in and out around Han-sun, whirling and thrusting their knives in a vigorous mock hunt for imaginary assassins, making certain that every pass of the blades comes perilously close to Han-sun's person.

Margama watches, laughing. He laughs so much he sits down on the skull case which has never been moved. Finally —

Margama: Enough. Enough.

Poolee and Li-yu relent. Margama beckons the perspiring Han-sun to come closer.

Margama: Forgive them. *(Almost laughing outright while he talks)* We'd not want the Emperor to think we harbour disrespect for Chinese merchants.

Han-sun: *(Still very nervous. Panting)* Uh-uh-uh — certainly not. Tribal uh-uh-uh — customs.

Margama leaps up and whacks him cheerfully on the back.

Margama: How understanding! Tribal customs.

Han-sun: Certainly, a-a-a-a-greeting ceremony.

Margama: A greeting ceremony! How discerning. *(Takes a turn around Han-sun, eyeing him, but playing with his own knife with remarkable carelessness)* There is more to this Chinese gentleman than meets the eye. How well he understands us. How well he sees into the soul of our customs.

Poolee: How well indeed!

Margama: This man should be made honourary ambassador to Peking!

Poolee : Nominated.

Li-yu: Yea.

Margama: Elected. To explain the ways of the mountain people to their beloved Emperor. You would do that?

Han-sun: M-m-m-m-most honoured.

Margama: You understand the contradictions of mountain life?

Han-sun: M-m-m-m-most certainly.

Margama: The mountains are not high.

Han-sun: The mountains are not high.

Margama: It is merely that the valleys are deep.

Han-sun: Valleys are deep.

Margama: Our knives are not weapons.

Han-sun: No. Not weapons.

Margama: It is merely that some weapons are knives.

Han-sun: Some weapons are knives.

Margama: All life is but ritual.

Han-sun: Life is ritual. That is so.

Margama: Ritual is illusion.

Han-sun: Of course!

Margama: So all that you have witnessed here is illusion. You'll explain all that to the Emperor?

Han-sun: All that. All that, most honourable young sir.

Margama bows and he and his two friends back off a few paces as they bow.

Margama: May tears attend your departure and laughter your arrival.

Han-sun has finally regained his composure, and his nerve. He is about to go, but changes his mind.

Han-sun: An illusion, you say?

Margama: Yes.

Han-Sun: That — that Act of Purification?

Margama: A tribal memory. Nothing more.

Han-sun: And the — uh — the Harvest Libation?

Margama: (His turn to be puzzled) You know of that?

Han-sun: An interesting custom.

Han-sun stares at the skull case thoughtfully a moment, then, common sense overcome by greed, continues —

Han-sun: You're a very realistic young man. No illusions. No nonsense about you. (Laughs a little ponderously) Might almost say you know nonsense when you see it.

Margama: (Cooling slightly) Yes?

Han-sun: Now, take that Harvest Libation. Some sort of an offering to the gods out of an old skull. Right?

Margama: If you say so.

Han-sun: That's nonsense, right?

Margama: You say so.

Han-sun: But if your people believe it, it's not nonsense. Oh, I'm no philosopher like the Governor, but I can wrap my mind around that much.

Margama: (Beginning to sound dangerous) How very fortunate.

Han-sun: So there's hard times up here. No crops. Famine. All right! But you know what the problem is? Laziness. Plain, simple, unadorned laziness. No I'm wrong about that.

Poolee and Li-yu are all but sharpening their knives.

Han-sun: Despair, too. Hopelessness. That's where this Harvest Libation comes in. Now take my word for it, boys. Never mind the Act of Purification, but if you could have a real dragon popping fire-cracker of a Harvest Libation every so often, your people would get so juiced up with hope they'd work so hard you'd be able to hear the rice grow! There'd be millet practically popping out of the ground! Get these lazy mountaineers working and the world's your jewel box. I tell you this, and there's no consultation fee — the Harvest Libation. That's the secret!

With a grand gesture he lifts the lid of the skull box, reaches in, sweeps up a skull, and hands it to Margama.

Poolee and Li-yu fall to their knees. Margama looks suddenly most reverent. He takes the skull in an almost ceremonial fashion and holds it in front of him.

Margama: Who's is this?

Han-Sun: Mine. Yours! Oh, I see — (Laughs cheerfully) Whose? Why that's the joy of it. Whose dome would you like it to be? You name him — (Points at skull) That's him. You want one a year, one a month, one a week? I don't care. You go off on your ceremonial hunt, come back all smeared with pigs blood, tell any story you wish, but I'll see there's one of these here whenever you need it.

Margama: You mean — you — you would — (He makes a slicing gesture across his throat)

Han-sun: What! (Horrified) Not on your Pu-la-lu-wan I wouldn't.

Margama suddenly takes a much closer look at the skull in his hands.

Margama: (Suddenly angry) This is not real!

Han-sun : Of course it's not real. That's the whole point!

Margama: You mock the Ritual!

Han-sun: Don't mock it. Make it work for you.

Poolee: (Low) Kill him.

Margama: You would desecrate our culture!

Han-sun: Desecration nothing. Exploitation, boy.

Li-yu: (Low) Kill him.

B47

Han-sun: Eh? What's that?

Poolee: *(To Margama)* Kill him.

Li-yu: *(To Margama)* Kill him.

Han-sun begins to back off.

Poolee and Li-yu make a few ceremonial but deadly serious warm up gestures with their knives, and end up by blocking Han-sun from both sides.

Han-sun: *(Bellows)* Help! Assassins!

Margama, confronts him, still holding the skull.

Margama: When we kill it will not be for hate. When we kill it will not be for profit. When we take a head it will not be from a Chinese doll!

Margama smashes the skull at Han-sun's feet. Margama, Poolee and Li-yu exit, running.

Servants come running in, followed very closely by Wu-feng. They are entering before Margama and his friends have quite vanished.

Wu-feng: Who was that!

Han-sun: That High Priest of yours.

Wu-feng: Did he harm you?

Han-sun: I make a simple business proposition and they try to cut my throat.

Wu-feng: What did you do? What did you say?

Han-sun: Until these savages of yours —

Wu-feng: My brothers!

Han-sun: Well until your brothers learn some respect for commercial enterprise there's nothing more I can do for them. Do I get that escort to the plains? If not, I assure you mine will be the last caravan into this territory for many a long hungry moon.

Wu-feng: Another club!

Han-sun: What?

Wu-feng: An observation. I am a student of the art of persuasion.

Han-sun: Do I get my escort?

Wu-feng: *(Calming down)* Yes, my dear Han-sun.

Han-sun: Excellent. *(Comes close)* And that's a decision that can be turned to your advantage. I've been thinking about your problem here. *(Looks around at the servants)*

Wu-feng gestures and the servants take the skull case and thrones and exit, leaving Wu-feng and Han-sun alone.

Han-sun: As a friend. May I dare offer advice?

Wu-feng: I listen.

Han-sun: *(As though it is a great revelation)* You are underprotected here.

Wu-feng: Yes.

Han-sun: On my way out, let me advise the Governor of Chai-Y. He can send troops into the foothills.

Wu-feng: Troops are not protection. They're an aggravation.

Han-sun: Only into the foothills. No farther. But at least the foothills are closer than the Plains. Insurance.

Wu-feng thinks a moment, then —

Wu-feng: That's a dangerous game.

Han-sun: Tell me, if your — brothers — do go head hunting, are they likely to kill one of their own?

Wu-feng: They hold an Elder prisoner.

Han-sun: They would kill him?

Wu-feng: No.

Han-sun: Of course not. Some unfortunate from a neighbouring tribe. **That's a dangerous game!**

Wu-feng: It won't come to that.

Han-sun: If it does, you'll pray for troops in the foothills.

Wu-feng: This is a tribal problem. It will be solved amongst ourselves.

Han-sun: All right. All right. Then take **this** advice. Don't give in to Margama. Say "Do your worst. Take a head. Kill the Elder" as they are about to perform the Act, fall upon them. Seize, slay, imprison, execute. Force is the only language their kind understand, violence the only weapon. The Emperor didn't place you here to play with children. He placed you here to maintain law and order.

Wu-feng: Come. I'll arrange for your escort.

They exit.

Scene Two

Piong-shih enters, followed closely by other Elders, and by Tsai-yu's men who have Serenity and the Stranger with them as prisoners. Piong-shih is highly agitated.

Piong-shih: I know, I know. How could I not know. I heard the Protector's evidence. What has the evidence got to do with it?

1st Elder: The evidence proves the crime.

Piong-shih: Crime? The Governor's own daughter says it was all a misunderstanding.

1st Elder: Nevertheless, the evidence proves the crime.

Piong-shih: *(Low)* I don't believe the evidence.

1st Elder: *(Low)* Under the circumstances that is irrelevant.

The other Elders all seem to agree.

Piong-shih: How? Irrelevant!

1st Elder: The desire for Racial Purity is a legacy from the Old Culture.

Piong-shih: I know that. Why should I not know that?

1st Elder: This is no time to turn our backs on the Old Culture.

Piong-shih: This is no time to turn our backs on the Governor!

They all take a turn past the prisoners then huddle again.

Piong-shih: This is one of those quasi-morality cases that should never have gotten into law.

1st Elder: It **is** in the law. Our law.

Piong-shih : *(Inspiration)* Let the High Priest decide.

1st Elder: Next time it might be us.

Piong-shih: At our age!

Piong-shih breaks away, and gestures to the guards. The prisoners are marched forward.

Piong-shih points at the Stranger without really looking at him.

Piong-shih: Him. He's guilty. Take him to the Governor for sentencing.

He points at Serenity definitely without looking at her.

Piong-shih: Take her home to her father.

The prisoners are taken out. The Elders move off in another direction.

Piong-shih: I'm not very happy. That wasn't justice, you know.

1st Elder: Justice is poor comfort in hard times.

Piong-shih: I know, I know. You think I don't know?

They exit.

Scene Three

Servants carry in the Governor's chair. They seem to be excited.

Piong-shih and the Elders enter, and wait.

Protectors bring in Serenity and the Stranger.

Tsai-yu comes in and takes up his position behind the Governor's chair.

Wu-feng enters in a ceremonial robe.

Everyone present bows deeply to the Governor, who walks slowly past his daughter and the Stranger then takes his seat.

Only when he is seated do those present unbend.

Wu-feng: I wish to make it clear that the case before us involves a Tribal law that the Emperor was prevailed upon to retain out of respect for the Old Culture. In such a case the Governor does not Judge. In such a case the Governor passes sentence which is mandatory.

Everyone bows very low in acknowledgment.

Wu-feng: Let the accused approach.

Serenity and the Stranger come forward. Wu-feng draws Serenity close to him.

Wu-feng: My child, what led you to this indiscretion?

Serenity: Love, laughter, the song of birds, mountain streams, poetry, the breath of Pu-la-lu-wan, and — *(Looking shyly at the Stranger)* his presence.

Wu-feng: Human reasons. Worthy of my daughter.

Serenity: No law, my father, has been broken.

Wu-feng: We shall see. *(He turns his attention to the Stranger)* What led you to this?

Stranger: It was expected of me.

Wu-feng: Yes? *(Waits)*

Stranger: That is all.

Wu-feng: All? That is nothing! *(Outraged)* At least let us hear there was lust, desire, curiosity — something more than the expectations of others!

Stranger: There is never anything more.

Wu-feng: Who are you? What are you?

Stranger: I am whatever people wish me to be. *(Indicating Piong-shih)* He said I was a beggar. I became a beggar. *(To Wu)* You said I was a scholar. I became a scholar. *(To Serenity)* She said I was her lover. I became her lover.

Wu-feng: What madness is this?

Stranger: Madness? Is it madness to serve others? I abdicate my desires, my emotions, my needs, myself — all — everything — to the service of others.

Wu-feng: *(To Piong-shih)* What is your verdict?

Piong-shih: He is guilty.

Wu-feng: *(To the Stranger)* Do you know the penalty?

Stranger: I am told it is death. *(Bows)* I am honoured to be of service.

Wu-feng reaches out and takes Serenity by the hand. Draws her close, then turns to Piong-shih.

Wu-feng: What is your verdict?

Piong-shih: Not guilty.

Some of Han-sun's coolees and some battered looking Protectors run in. The coolees fall down, groveling. Protector kneels in front of Wu-feng.

Tsai-yu involuntarily comes forward to him.

Tsai-yu: Here, what's this. We're holding court.

Protector: Robbers, sir. Brigands! They fell upon us in the pass.

Wu-feng: Are many hurt? Where is Han-sun?

Protector: They seized him, sir. He is gone.

Tsai-yu: Who were they? What did they look like?

Wu-feng: Ah, we don't have to ask that, do we!

A Child runs in. He runs right up to the Governor who bends down. The child whispers something to him, pointing off. Wu-feng nods and the child runs out.

Wu-feng: Margama is coming.

The Protectors draw their short knives.

Wu-feng: I gave the child his safe conduct.

Tsai-yu: *(Strangely urgent)* Sir. The Judgment. Sentence must be passed.

Serenity: He is innocent. Father, it is as he said. It was I who wished for prince, poet, abductor — *(Bashfully)* lover.

Wu-feng: *(After a pensive pause)* Leave the prisoner in my custody.

Tsai-yu: The sentence.

Wu-feng: I reserve it. *(Looks at Piong-shih)* There's something amiss in the lower court.

Margama enters, flanked by Poolee and Li-yu. They confront Wu-feng.

Wu-feng: Margama my friend? Margama the High Priest? Or Margama the guardian of culture, the saviour of his people?

Margama: *(Bows)* I am worthy only to be known as the friend of Wu-feng who has been my teacher.

Wu-feng: I suspect your teacher is about to become your pupil.

Margama: True. We have come to the last lesson. All the demands of our people are to be met. The Elder Tongue, the Ancient Rites, — all are to be reinstated. Just as the mountain belongs to Pu-la-lu-wan, we belong to ourselves. This is our destiny and we will celebrate it in the Act of Purification.

Wu-feng: This cannot be.

Margama: It will be. If we are opposed along the path to destiny the first head offered in the Act will be that of Han-sun.

Tsai-yu gestures and his men rush forward but they are stopped by Wu-feng.

Wu-feng: They have my safe conduct!

Tsai-yu: They are brigands!

Wu-feng: *(To Margama)* Han-sun is not one of us. He is a visitor. A merchant. A friend of the Emperor's.

Margama: He is a fool.

Wu-feng: He is a man.

Margama: And a head is a head.

Wu-feng: The Federal troops will come. The mountains will stream blood. Our blood. Tribal blood.

Margama: Enact all other demands and we hold the Act of Purification in abeyance.

Wu-feng: I cannot.

Margama: *(To all)* Listen to our Chinese Governor. We ask for the right to be ourselves, to speak the Elder Tongue, to enjoy the Old Culture, to raise our children under the arms of Pu-la-lu-wan. Our Chinese Governor says he will not.

Wu-feng: I cannot.

Margama: We ask that our children should not starve, that our roofs should not leak, that our heads should not be bowed. Our Chinese Governor says he wills it not.

Wu-feng: That right is yours. My will cannot make it reality.

Margama: Yield to us and tell the Emperor it is good, or Han-sun dies.

Margama and Wu-feng confront each other for a moment in silence, then Piong-shih totters forward.

Piong-shih: Beloved Governor, Honourable Wu-feng, dear brother — yield to them. Do as they say. We wish the merchant no harm.

Wu-feng: *(To the elders)* This affects you more closely than you seem to know. Your days of tranquility are done.

Piong-shih: We are content.

Wu-feng: Where will it end? Next time the challenge may be issued over your head, or yours, or yours.

Piong-shih: There will be peace.

Wu-feng: If the rabbit, cowering motionless in the bracken, is at peace, there will be peace.

Margama's youths invade the theatre quietly, singing softly, dancing slowly, waving burning incense sticks.

Margama: You strangle yourselves in talk. We have done with talk. Already the incense sticks are burning, a new tribe is stirring in the womb of the old, a new people rise in the mountains swimming above corrupting cultures like the ancestral parents breasting the submerging floods. The children of the five animals and the five tribes are about to give birth to new man. To True Man.

The youthful dancers surge toward the stage, the smoking incense held high, their bodies inclined toward Margama. There is a cry of adulation, then the surge is reversed and they exit into the depths. Low, from the depths, we hear a soft chorus of voices.

Youths: Kill, kill, kill, kill — *(It softly fades away)*

Margama: *(Slowly turns to Wu-feng)* Soon it is unleashed. What is your answer?

Wu-feng takes a moment, then gestures to all.

Wu-feng: Leave me.

All bow and back off. The Elders begin to shoo the children away.

Wu-feng: The children may stay. I merely wish to think.

All now exit except Wu-feng and the children.

The children, however, much subdued by all that is happening, tend to keep quietly to themselves.

They play jacks in a corner of the stage while Wu-feng paces.

Tsai-yu enters.

Tsai-yu: *(Softly)* Governor.

Wu-feng: I am in no danger.

Tsai-yu: I wish to speak to you. I have a solution.

Wu-feng: I listen.

Tsai-yu: The situation is impossible.

Wu-feng: An accurate observation, but hardly comforting.

Tsai-yu: Margama has chosen the weapons we must use.

Wu-feng: If one is unskilled with all weapons it is pointless to use any.

Tsai-yu: That is what Margama will expect of you. So continue your role of stubborn passivity. Make no compromises. Call Margama's bluff.

Wu-feng: And give Margama no exit? That is bad diplomacy.

Tsai-yu: But good strategy.

Wu-feng: I have already been advised to follow this path. To fall upon them just before the Act. To slay, punish and imprison.

Tsai-yu: Brutal counsel!

Wu-feng: Oh? The path has a turning I did not see?

Tsai-yu: Consider the Stranger, sir. He is already under mandatory sentence of death. The fact that you hesitate to declare it is a mere technicality. I will have the suggestion quietly put to Margama that if he were to take the Stranger, he would be sacrificing a man who is already dead.

It would be an act that the government could be persuaded to view with leniency. You can remain adamant. Margama can save face. No one need suffer.

Wu-feng: I confess, that is a diplomatic exit that would not have occurred to me.

Tsai-yu: I present it only from Margama's point of view. There is more. Consider. They take the Stranger. I and my men, armed with cross-bows, lie in wait. You can picture the scene? The surround. The seizure. The ritual chant. The sacrificial blade singing downward —

Wu-feng: Enough. I will not have an innocent man killed!

Tsai-yu: It is not we who would kill him. Margama is the High Priest. Margama wields the ritual knife.

Wu-feng: We could prevent, and you would have us watch?

Tsai-yu: We could save one life and lose a hundred more.

Wu-feng: I fail to see security in your method.

Tsai-yu: Beloved teacher, you have not yet heard my proposal. At the moment of the Act, as the deed is done, as the head is severed, my men will rush from cover. Bloodied Margama will fall, an arrow through his heart.

Wu-feng: You would kill Margama.

Tsai-yu: A regretable accident.

Wu-feng: And what do you have in mind for the others?

Tsai-yu: They will be arrested but not harmed. One must consider the future. There would be, for instance, your report to the Emperor. But this way nothing need be witheld. There has been a rebellion. A criminal has been executed by the rebels. A murderous rebel leader has been slain by the Protectors. All others have received compassionate pardon in the Emperor's name, and once again there is peace among the Ali people, under the gentle Wu-feng.

Wu-feng: No mention of Tsai-yu?

Tsai-yu: My reward will lie in your permission for your humble servant to perform yet another service for his beloved Governor.

Wu-feng: Your beloved Governor's obligations to his humble servant show signs of being more than my conscience can bear.

Tsai-yu: You yourself have taught us that Great Man must lead the people through example. I merely propose to do what my duty dictates.

Wu-feng: The teacher listens while the pupil rephrases the lesson.

Tsai-yu: The purity of the daughter of the Governor has been made suspect by the Stranger.

Wu-feng: In whose eyes?

Tsai-yu: In the eyes of any man seeking an unflawed gem in the marriage mart. We have discussed a way for the Stranger to pay the penalty.

Wu-feng: Indeed we have.

Tsai-yu: But as a public gesture acknowledging the criminal's full atonement for his crime and to demonstrate the Tribe's loyalty to our beloved Governor, I, Tsai-yu, your servant, willingly abase myself to offer your daughter my hand, my name, and my bed.

Wu-feng: You overwhelm me.

Tsai-yu: It is a gesture of magnanimity that will not be lost upon the Emperor.

Wu-feng: That is true.

Tsai-yu: Your servant Tsai-yu stands as living proof that Wu-feng's instruction has not fallen on hard clay.

Youths: (*Off in the depths. A low, swelling, chant*) Kill, kill, kill, kill, kill — (*It fades even as it comes, like a dim memory*)

Wu-feng: You may leave me now. With my

teaching bearing such remarkable fruit on every branch I feel a need for quiet self-examination.

Tsai-yu: You will consider my advice then?

Wu-feng: I will think about it.

Tsai-yu exits.

Wu-feng: I will think about it as one thinks about black pestilence, wondering what miscalculation in the natural scheme could account for such an abhorrent aberration from the master Plan.

And yet — only two lives. (*In deep anguish*) What other route can a practical man follow?

Wu-feng paces slowly around. He moves in among the children, hardly aware of them. They try to entice him into a game. One of them starts the merchant game from Act 1, but Wu-feng moves away and the game dies almost unborn. The children move together for comfort, and watch from a distance.

Again we hear the chant from beyond.

Youths: (*Off. Low*) Kill, kill, kill, kill —

Margama enters. He is hurrying and looks worried. He is accompanied by Li-yu.

Margama: I come for your answer.

Wu-feng: More time.

Margama: (*Alarmed*) It is not mine to give. (*Looks nervously away*)

Wu-feng: Delay.

Margama: I cannot!

Wu-feng now becomes aware of the children. He moves to them and looks down upon them as they almost huddle together.

He returns to Margama.

Wu-feng: You have won. Bring me Han-sun. Unharmed.

Margama: *(Frightened)* It has gone too far. I cannot draw back. They demand the Act of Purification.

Wu-feng: You promised me Han-sun! His life was our condition.

Margama nods to Li-yu who exits.

Margama: *(He sounds desperate)* You can have Han-sun but it has gone too far. You took too long! My people crave the supreme moment.

Wu-feng: You destroy us all!

Margama: It is not my doing! It is in our blood, it springs from our loins! It is not my fault!

Wu-feng: Bah!

Wu paces angrily a moment, then glares at Margama.

Wu-feng: He who unleashes a dragon should wear asbestos!

Youths: *(Off. Low)* Kill, kill, kill, kill —

Wu-feng: When does it climax?

Margama: Tonight.

Wu-feng: Who will you have?

Margama: The Elder?

Wu-feng: Ah. The man you "rescued".

Margama: You forget. He was diverting relief food into his own belly.

Wu-feng: You forget. He called out in the Elder Tongue.

Margama: His kind betray us all.

Wu-feng: The ultimate betrayal is the Act of Purification.

Youths: *(Off. Low)* Kill, kill, kill, kill —

Wu-feng: Very well. They may have their moment. **You** may have your moment.

Margama: I don't want it.

Wu-feng: Nevertheless you have it. However, to contain this tragedy, to keep, as it were, the explosion within the bamboo, and give it some controlled direction, **I** will designate the place and the victim. Do you concur?

Margama: Most humbly.

Wu-feng: One condition.

Margama: It is granted.

Wu-feng: All your personal claims to power are dropped.

Margama kneels in front of him.

Margama: My shame lies deep as the waters of the great sea.

Wu-feng lifts him up.

Youths: *(Off. A distant, liturgical chanting)*

Wu-feng: Tonight, at the tenth hour, a stranger will pass out through the gate of my upper garden. Take him, but let it be done speedily.

Margama: *(Aside)* The Stranger! At last, and too late. Much scheming has finally brought me, fruitlessly, to the victim of our first choice.

Li-yu enters with Han-sun.

Wu-feng: My good friend. You are safe.

Han-sun: But not well! The Emperor's going to hear of this I can assure you!

Wu-feng claps his hands and servants enter to help Han-sun away. He goes, still complaining.

Han-sun: "Wu-feng's simple people", that's what they call them in Peking! "Gentle savages". "Noble mountaineers! " Savages all right. Barbarians more like it. A man tries to bring a little civilization and prosperity to them and what does he get for it!

He exits.

Margama: How are we to know the — victim?

Wu-feng: He will be wearing a red cloak.

Margama bows and he and Li-yu exit.

The sound of chanting rises and becomes a constant.

Wu-feng, looking defeated and tired, stands alone, lost in weary thought.

The children come to him, hesitantly, and surround him, looking up at him. He appears not to see them.

Suddenly he gestures impatiently and speaks aloud, to no one in particular, unless to himself.

Wu-feng: No, no, no!

The children scatter.

Wu-feng: There is only one way left.

Wu-feng signals and some servants enter solemnly. With them they bring Han-sun, the Stranger, and Serenity.

The last servant is carrying a red cloak.

Wu-feng gestures and all the servants, except the one with the cloak, exit. The one with the cloak stands beside the Governor and follows him now wherever he moves.

Wu-feng goes to Han-sun. He looks at him thoughtfully.

Wu-feng: What is your fondest wish?

Han-sun: Right now I'd like to be shut of that noise.

Wu-feng: The people are singing.

Han-sun: Well they've no right to be singing. Not at this hour. Not after all the turmoil I've been through.

B57

Wu-feng: Turmoil is not in the market place, nor quiet in the hill, but in the hearts of men. *(Sadly)* You may go.

Han-sun exits.

Wu-feng moves on to the Stranger.

Wu-feng: What is your fondest wish?

Stranger: *(Bows)* To be of service.

Wu-feng: How?

Stranger: By accepting all insults, by absorbing all blows, by admitting all guilt.

Wu-feng: Why should the innocent plead guilty?

Stranger: But I am not innocent. Without wealth there would be no poverty, without knowledge there would be no ignorance, without masters there would be no servitude. Since I was born at once wealthy and noble, and was educated to suit, it follows that I am guilty of perpetuating poverty, ignorance, and servitude.

Wu-feng: Who are you?

Stranger: I have forgotten.

Wu-feng: You have surrendered your personality. You have nothing more to offer.

Stranger: My life.

Wu-feng: *(Aside)* A life without personality is a purse without coins. It carries no weight in the market, and can be taken without being missed. Perhaps this is an offer that should be accepted. On the other hand, he who takes an empty purse may in turn feel victimized. The cheater cheated becomes self-righteous. Self-righteousness is not exactly the emotion I wish to instill in Margama's rebels.

Besides, Governor, when you come right down to it, a simile is a simile, but a man is a man. *(He returns to the Stranger)* You have sentenced yourself to live as a shadow cast by others. I can impose no penalty greater than that. You are free to go.

Wu-feng gives a half bow and the Stranger exits.

Wu-feng confronts Serenity. They look at each other for a moment, then Wu-feng takes the red cloak from the servant.

The servant exits.

Wu-feng, Serenity, and the children are now alone on the stage.

The offstage chanting is getting louder.

Wu holds the cloak out to Serenity. She takes it. They look at each other a moment, then Wu turns around and Serenity places the cloak over his shoulders. He turns toward her again. She throws herself into his arms. He holds her a moment, then kisses her tenderly.

Serenity exits, running.

Wu-feng turns, looks at the children, then smiles and holds his hands out. They run to him, seizing his hands and the corners of his red cloak. They laugh with relief to find the Governor is smiling again.

Wu-feng exits, surrounded by happy children.

Scene Four
A torchlit procession of almost naked youths moves across the stage. They are chanting a wordless processional and are carrying incense and ceremonial knives. They exit.

Scene Five
Wu-feng and the Children enter. They are playing. Wu-feng stops them and mimes for them to place their hands over their eyes. Each child does so. The Governor turns each child around a few times to disorient them. While Wu-feng does this, he soliloquizes.

Wu-feng: How can I leave them now just when I am needed most?
Who will teach them?
And what?

Shall Piong-shih school them in the cowardice of age?
Shall Tsai-yu impart the scheming ways of the unintelligent?
Shall Margama instill the stunted dreams of the short-sighted?
Han-sun implant the greed of possession?

Or am I the Greedy one, wanting the
immortality of martyrdom?
Am I the Coward, afraid to use armed
authority?
Am I the Unintelligent one who will not scheme
to survive?
Am I the Short-sighted one who, with myopic
eyes fixed in terror on the fly looming large on
the end of his nose, screams that a monster has
occupied the entire visible world!

But one in authority must lead through
example.
One must "be" what one teaches.

Will they see only the example of a foolish man
going to a foolish end?

Yet Father Confucius described the path to
excellence and if I will not follow through a
little darkness then I have no faith in the Wisest
of the Wise.

"Excellence will attract excellence."
Since that is what I believe,
what I must do I will do.

*Wu-feng moves quietly away from the children
who are still obediently keeping their eyes covered. He pauses and stretches out his arms to
them.*

Wu-feng: Play with them — somebody.

*Wu-feng raises the hood of the red cloak over his
head, and exits.*

*The Children uncover their eyes, look around,
and, laughing, exit searching for him in another
direction.*

Scene Six
Piong-shih and the Elders enter, fearfully.

1st Elder: I am afraid to be here and afraid not
to be here.

Piong-shih: I think there is little danger.

1st Elder: Little danger! The Emperor won't
have to send troops. His rage will destroy us.

Piong-shih: Margama is no fool. He is using some
criminal sent out to him by the Governor.

1st Elder: The Governor approves?

Piong-shih: He knows rebellion would be worse.
Hush. I hear them coming.

1st Elder: Just the same, I'm nervous.

Piong-shih: We're not participating.

1st Elder: I'd not want my presence to be mis-
understood.

Piong-shih: Or your absence. Ah-h-h listen.
Listen. The heart begins to beat.

1st Elder: Indeed, indeed. The old song makes
the blood sing.

Piong-shih: I know. You think I don't know?

1st Elder: Then why am I frightened?

Piong-shih: Let us enjoy it. Our hands are clean.

*The Elders withdraw discreetly to one side as
the first procession returns. This time it forms
onstage to await the arrival of yet another procession. This second one consists of Poolee and
Li-yu carrying the scroll of the Manual of the
Ancient Rites. They are followed by Margama.
He is followed by bearers carrying the sedan
chair of old Ai-lee the Scholar. The chair is so
festooned and draped with ornamental cloth
that only the fact that one arm is hanging in
view tells us that the old man is indeed inside.*

*This entire ceremony is driven by the pulse and
the beat of the chant, illuminated by the flicker
of the torches, wreathed in the smoke of incense, and has a sense of primitive power and
savage naked beauty. It is choreographed to climax as Wu-feng enters, the hood of his red cloak
raised over his head. He is seized, brought un-
resistingly to a kneeling position, and, the action
partially masked by choreography, Margama de-
livers the fatal ceremonial stroke. Margama remains standing as the group kneels in a circle
around him and the victim, and words rise out
of the chant. They are words we have heard
before, being improvised, but now they sound
firmly rooted in ritual.*

B60

Chant:
O Mighty Pu-la-luwan
Whose name is unspoken,
We raise our knives to thee
In adoration and token.

O Mighty Pu-la-luwan
Ruling Ancestral Mountains,
We purify ourselves for thee
In red flowing fountains.

O Mighty Pu-la-lu-wan
The guardian of culture,
We offer this head to thee,
The body to vultures.

Margama stoops and stands again, raising the head.

As he rises the group rises with him, their hands stretching forward as though to touch the sacred object. There is an almost orgiastic sigh as they do so. Then they freeze. Margama drops the head.

With a tremendous gasp the entire ring leaps backward, expanding the circle outward from Margama and the body at his feet.

There is a low group moan and each person subsides into what is almost a fetal position. Margama goes to his knees and bends low until his forehead is resting on the ground. The Elders huddle, rather than kneel, to one side. For a long moment there is no sound and no movement.

One of the girls slowly crawls out of the central group and just as slowly rises and turns away. She stops, acutely aware of her nakedness. Others begin to move. Others become aware of their nakedness. A gentle singing begins, but it wails and is full of tears. The youths dance slowly, and as they do so they strip the ornamental cloths from old Ai-lee's sedan chair and twine themselves in the fabric to hide their nakedness.

Poolee and Li-yu raise Margama to a kneeling position.

Li-yu: Margama, come.

Poolee: You must leave. You must hide.

Margama: *(Slowly, softly)* I can hide from Piong-shih, or Tsai-yu, or even from the Emperor, but where is the canyon in which I can hide from me?

Poolee: Margama, you have killed Governor Wu!

Margama: *(In anguish)* I have assassinated Excellence. I have murdered True Man. Where is the cave dark enough to hide Margama from Margama!

Only now do the Elders stir. They come forward hesitantly, as though not knowing whether to approach the kneeling Margama or old Ai-lee in his sedan chair. Ai-lee is now completely exposed to view. He is absolutely motionless, as he has been throughout the entire scene. He is pasty white, as he has been throughout the scene. He is quite dead, as he has been throughout the entire scene.

1st Elder: He's dead. Old Ai-lee the Scholar is dead.

Piong-shih: I know. You think I don't know?

1st Elder: You should have told somebody. What do we do now?

Piong-shih: We should bury him. It might be a good idea to have a state funeral.

1st Elder: That's true. Ai-lee was very very old.

The Elders raise Ai-lee's sedan chair and begin to shuffle off stage, carrying it. They stop and look back at Margama still kneeling beside Wu-feng.

1st Elder: The Governor is dead, too.

Piong-shih: Oh we don't know anything about that. We wait until we get Tsai-yu's official report. Besides, you never can tell.

The Elders exit, carrying Ai-lee's body in the sedan chair.

Margama remains motionless beside Wu-feng.

The children enter, and run across the stage.

馬笑如

B62

They are oblivious of both Margama and the body. They are laughing and skipping and chanting Wu-feng's game.

Children:
My ship is in with a cargo of tea
And plenty of presents for you and me,
She's brought me a fan! Oh joy! Oh bliss!
I fan myself every day like this.

The children exit.

Margama remains motionless beside the body of Wu-feng, and the lights slowly fade to blackout.

The End

Only it is not quite the end. As the audience leaves the theatre they find some booths in the lobby. The booths bear the name "Han-sun Enterprises" and are manned by Han-sun's servants. They are selling small plastic skulls for fifty cents apiece. These souvenirs are advertized as "Wu-feng's skull. Authentic miniaturizations of the true skull. Real plastic bone."

That is the end.

Love Mouse
Meyer's Room

Sheldon Rosen

Sheldon Rosen has a Bachelor's degree in Psychology and a Master's degree in Film and Television Production. After graduation, Mr. Rosen worked in educational television for a year and one-half and then spent another two years producing and directing television commercials.

Love Mouse and Meyer's Room are Sheldon Rosen's first two theatre pieces. They were produced at the Poor Alex Theatre in Toronto during August, 1971, and received unanimous critical acclaim.

"If Franz Kafka were alive and writing comedy for the contemporary stage, it would probably look very like the two Sheldon Rosen one-act plays which opened a three-week run last night at the newly air-conditioned Poor Alex Theatre, — Love Mouse and Meyer's Room. Mr. Rosen is a writer of imagination and real skill and these first produced plays of his surely bode well for the future." (Don Rubin, Toronto Star)

"Sheldon Rosen. Remember that name. He might be one of our great American inheritances, at least if his first two plays are anything to base a judgement upon." (Bernadette Andrews, Toronto Telegram)

"That Sheldon Rosen is a playwright with a bright gift for using the stage is confirmed in the program offered at the Poor Alex last night." (Herbert Whittaker, Globe & Mail)

"Love Mouse" was first performed at the Learning Resources Centre of the Toronto Public Libraries; staged and directed by Geoffrey Read. It was subsequently performed together with "Meyer's Room", at the Poor Alex Theatre in Toronto; designed, staged and directed by Geoffrey Read.

© Sheldon Rosen 1974

Love Mouse

Sheldon Rosen

Photographs by Paul Appleby.

Love Mouse

The action of the play takes place in the kitchen of a medium-size apartment. The kitchen is divided from the dining room by two pillars set roughly centre stage. The proverbial four walls of the room are created by styrofoam blocks suspended in the air. One kitchen chair is required, plus a small number of hand props.

The only additional setting is in the area upstage of the pillars and to the right and left of the styrofoam "walls". Geometric patterns of all shapes and sizes, flashing lights and anything that will create a "goldfish-bowl" effect with the cyclorama which encloses all of this is lit from the rear.

Cast of characters

There are three characters. A man and wife, a couple in their mid-thirties. And a third character who plays all the other parts. The third character interpreted as a mime in white-face. As the wolf, the mime communicates through a recorder that hangs around his neck.

The play begins with a prologue; a frenetic account of their first eleven years of marriage.

Act One

Sheila and Harry are situated between "walls" down stage right and up stage right, and down stage left and up stage left respectively. The man in whiteface is upstage between pillars. They are both wearing straw hats and canes. They begin to tap dance. *

He: Gee you look awfully familiar. I'm sure we've met before.

She: Do you love children as much as I do?

He: I think love is my whole reason for being. *(Music begins and they tango)*

The tango ends with Sheila and Harry facing the Reverend upstage. During the following speech the Reverend hands Sheila a bouquet of flowers (unseen by the audience)

Mime as Reverend: Do you Harold Jacobs hereafter to be known as the party of the first part take this woman Sheila to be your lawfully wedded wife, to cherish and honour her through sickness and health through good times or bad through rain or shine on weekends and weekdays, on all major holidays no matter what her mother thinks of you . . .

He: *(to audience)* Her mother can shove it as far as I . . .

Reverend: And do you Sheila, hereafter to be known as the party of the second part promise to adhere to regulations two through seventy-four of the marriage by-laws from today ad infinitum . . .

She: *(to audience)* I thought he liked my mother . . .

Reverend: If you will now both reach out and touch one another and repeat after me 'you're it'. *(They kiss)* I now declare you . . . *(Wedding March)*

Sheila and Harry turn and march down the "church aisle" to the edge of the stage, both making contact with their "friends" in the audience as if outside church . . .

*Author's addition since production. (All such "suggested improvements" will be footnoted)

Man: Congratulations you old sonuvagun you . . . *(he tosses some rice and leaves with Harry off left)*

Sheila is alone but not undaunted, carries on with the ritual — throwing the bouquet of flowers to anyone in the audience. She leaves right.

While the Wedding March is fading with the lights, Sheila and Harry must age 11 years. When they re-enter, Sheila is wearing an old housecoat and floppy slippers with her hair in curlers. Harry is down to an old T-shirt and slippers.

Sheila takes the broom and starts sweeping up the rice while Harry finishes up the floor in the other room.

Voice: And now a word from our sponsor.

He: *(from the other room)* Why am I waxing the floor again?

She: Because it needs it again. Our floor doesn't glisten like it once did. I don't know why you're complaining. We've stopped using that other floor wax. This new wax takes 30% less time and is gentle to your hands as well.

He: You're a fanatic, you know that? You've been a fanatic since our wedding day.

She: Whattya mean? Because I like a clean house, I'm a fanatic?

He: When I get up in the middle of the night to go to the bathroom, I come back and my half of the bed is made.

She: You're exaggerating.

He: An armed robber couldn't come in unless he promised to take off his shoes.

She: Oh come on now, I'm not that bad . . . am I?

He: Who else puts slipcovers on the ashtrays? *(He comes into the kitchen to wash his hands)*

She: Aha, you missed a spot.

C6

He: Where?

She: There.

He: Where?

She: The-r-e-e!

He: There?

She: Where?

He: There.

She: I don't know . . . I can't see it any more.

He: *(back to handwashing downstage right)* It's finished.

She: See, it does make a difference. It looks like a brand new floor.

He: After all that, it better look like a new floor.

She: Poor baby worked so hard on the floorie-poo.

He: You think waxing the floor was a picnic?

She: Did I say anything?

He: It wasn't my idea.

She takes chair from behind down left "wall" and places it centre stage.

She: Don't be such a grouch. Sit down. I'll make you some coffee and you can read your news-paper. *(She moves to stove up right)*

He: The paper is in the other room.

She: Turn on the radio and listen to the news.

He: Who wants the news? I just want to read the newspaper.

She: How bad do you want coffee?

He: Whattya mean?

She: The burners won't go on. We've got a power failure.

He: It's a gas stove, Einstein. The only power failure is between your ears.

She: Okay, genius, let's see you get them going. *(She sits in chair and starts a crossword puzzle)*

He: They don't work. You don't have to be a genius to see that. We'll have to call in a specialist. Damn kitchen. Next thing you know, the whole damn thing will fall apart *(Pause)* So what are we going to do for two hours?

She: We could talk a little.

He: Talk? I talk all day at the office. You think I come home to talk?

She: I'm sorry I even mentioned it.

He: *(after a pause)* So whattya want to talk about?

She: Nothing . . .

Defeated by feminine logic he moves stage left to refrigerator to get a beer (the fridge is located in the space between "walls" up left and down right) . . . As Harry moves to the fridge area, the Mime who is behind the up left "wall" thrusts out his hand on which the beer can stands.

She: You don't care about me any more.

He: We made love on a weekday this week, didn't we? That must mean something.

By the end of this speech Harry realizes he has just been handed a beer by a Mouse. During the next few speeches Harry and Mime engage in a game of hide-and-seek in and out of the hanging walls.

She: It was a holiday. Holidays don't count as weekdays . . . what are you looking for?

He: Didn't I wax the floor for you? You know how I hate to wax floors. Now that must mean something.

She: No it doesn't. It doesn't prove anything. You know why you did it? You didn't do it because you care about me . . . **You did it so I'd stop yelling . . . and goddammit what are you looking for?**

He: *(appearing from behind a "wall")* I can't tell you. You'll get upset.

She: Upset! What do you think I'm being right this minute? You want to see upset? If you don't tell me what you're looking for I'm going to step all over your floor! *(She moves towards the dining room but is stopped by the next line)*

He: I'm looking for that mouse that I saw.

She: *(turns on him)* There never has been and never will be a mouse in my kitchen.

He: *(Sits in chair)* You're right. There's no mouse in the kitchen. *(They hear a scratching noise from inside the "wall", created by the Mime using only the mouthpiece of his recorder)*

She: What's that noise?

He: It sounds like a small mouse-like animal.

She: I do not want to see a mouse in my kitchen. Make it go away.

He: Go away, mousie.

She: Go away, mousie! Is that you're idea of doing something? Well, I'm telling you, you better do something quick, before that thing has babies.

He: Babies? Why it's no bigger than a baby itself.

She: *(more sound from mouse)* O-hh, there it goes. We're living in a slum.

He: Now take it easy. It's only a small mouse.

She: Don't tell me to take it easy. I will not take it easy with a sewer rat running around my kitchen. *(She grabs the broom and hands it to him)* Here.

He: What am I supposed to do with this broom?

She: I want you to sweep the floor so the mouse won't get his feet dirty. **I want you to get that mouse!**

He: You mean mash the little bugger?

She: *(wincing)* No, you better not do that. Not on the kitchen floor . . . who'd clean it up?

He: You want me to kill it and clean it up too? Now that's not fair. What makes you think I would enjoy getting down next to a mashed mouse? *(Handing the broom back)* I'm not cleaning it up.

She: Well . . . then I'm going to call up Mrs. Camise and tell her there's a mouse in her building. *(She goes to telephone up left)*

He: What good is that going to do?

She: I'm sure she's had more experience with mice. She'll know what we should do.

He: How would she know? She's not going to tell you anything different than what I'd do. Just leave it to me. You're not going to call someone and let them know that I can't handle

a mouse. As long as I'm alive and healthy you're not going to have someone else coming in here and taking care of your mice. *(She motions to give him back the broom)* As soon as the wax on the floor dries, I'll go out and get some traps. We can use that godawful cheese you got stinking up the refrigerator.

She: Well I'm telling you that I'm not staying in this kitchen with a sewer rat.

He: And I'll be damned if you're going out there and tramp up the floor after I've just spent an hour on my knees washing and waxing it! Dammit, it's just a little mouse. I'm sorry I even mentioned it. If I'd known you were going to get so hysterical, I'd never have brought it up. Sewer rat. Next thing you know you'll be calling it a timber wolf. Just do your crossword and forget about it.

She: I can't play games with things crawling all around.

He: It bothers you that much, eh?

She: Yes it bothers me that much.

He: Then give me back the broom.

She: You're going to do it then?

He: I'm going to do it.

She: Then I better not watch.

He: No, you better not watch. *(He takes the broom and slowly raises it over his head)*

She: *(turning her head away from him)* Can you do it without scaring it?

He: How am I going to kill it without scaring it?

She: If you scare it, it will leave droppings all over. Animals are like that when they're nervous. My beautician told me.

He: Oh my god... *(general lighting comes down a little and a tight spot picks up the white face of the Mime upstage centre)* ... Oh my god!

C10

She: What, what?

He: It is a sewer rat.

She: Cut that out. You're just trying to scare me.

He: Well I'm scaring me too, because that thing is a sewer rat. I could have sworn it was just a mouse ... my eyes must be going bad after breathing in all that floor wax.

She: *(not looking)* Is it still there?

He: It's just standing there and staring ... now don't you make any sudden moves. I'm going to get that cocker. *(He slowly rises, raising the broom)* Say your prayers, pal, because the end is near. *(He swings the broom. There is a loud crash and everything goes dark)* **Goddammit!**

She: Now you've done it. How many times have I told you to watch out for that light. I told you

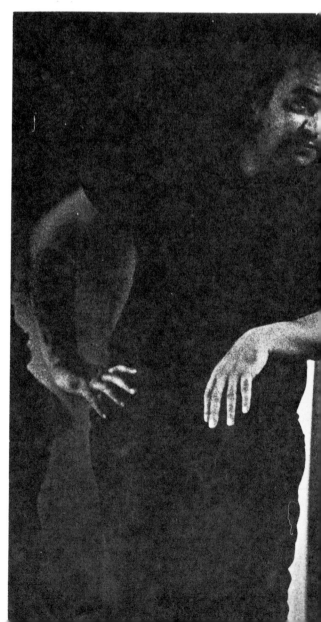

not to go swinging things in the kitchen. *(She jumps)* Oo-ooo! He brushed his whiskers against my foot!

Lights come up slowly on the back of cyclorama (blue gell). This leaves Harry and Sheila in silhouette and most of the action now takes place between the two pillars. During the blackout the Mime moves and sits on the top of the chair down left.

He: It wasn't his whiskers, it was just the broom. I don't see him any more.

She: I don't care if you see him or not. He can see us, Harry, I really don't like being here in the dark with a rat.

He: All right. Hold your horses. I'll get a new bulb.

She: I'm going with you.

He: I'm just going into the next room . . . I'll phone you when I get there.

She: *(taking him by the arm)* I'm serious, Harry. I'm . . .

He: Will you stop shaking my arm? How can I light a match with you shaking my arm? If you . . . Dammit *(drops the matches. There is a gentle splash)* . . . Did you hear that?

She: What? . . . You mean the splash. What did you do, drop the matches in the sink?

He: No.

She: No?

He: They fell on the dining room floor.

She: *(Loudly)* But how can the dining room floor splash?

He: I don't know. *(He gets down on his hands and knees. He swirls his hand through what used to be the dining room floor. It is now a major body of water)* . . . Feel my arm.

She: It's wet.

He: Did you leave the bathtub running?

She: I don't think so. How deep is the water?

He: Deeper than my elbow . . . Give me the broom. *(Lowers the broom into the water)* . . . And it's deeper than my elbow plus the broom. Sheila, there's no dining room floor out there. I don't know how or why but our kitchen is on top of water.

She: But that's impossible! *(She also kneels)*

He: Did I say it was possible? I just said it was there.

She: That means we're trapped in the kitchen with a mouse that's now a rat and no light. What are we going to do?

He: I suppose we could swim for it.

She: Harry, you know I can't swim.

Suddenly there is the howl of a wolf quite near by

She: Let's swim for it!

He: You can't swim!

She: But that was a wolf!

He: I told you you'd be calling it a wolf next!

She: Harry, **Stop fooling around!**

He: For God's sake, it's not a wolf. There's no wolf in our kitchen.

She: Thank God for that.

He: It's a coyote.

She: This is supposed to be good news! You couldn't tell me it was my imagination?

He: Maybe it is a wolf . . .

She: . . . Or a hoarse pussycat . . .

He: I think you only find coyotes out West . . .

She: . . . no, you had to tell me it was a coyote!

He: You're right, it's a wolf.

She: *(beginning to cry)* Oh Harry, what's happening here? . . . Are we on some kind of a trip or something?

He: How can we be on a trip? You won't even put oregano in the spaghetti sauce.

She: I don't know . . . maybe some foreign power put LSD in the drinking water.

He: Do you think so? Holy shit, what an idea . . . maybe I better turn on the radio and find out what's going on.

Harry moves downstage, feeling his way in the dark. The wolf allows him to take two or three steps then howls in his left ear.

He: I gotta watch those sudden movements. I certainly don't want to make him nervous.

She: Don't worry about making it nervous. If it makes droppings I'll clean it up.

The wolf moves round to the right side and howls in Harry's right ear.

He: Whatareyakidding! *(reeling back between the pillars)* You think I'm worried about it crapping on the floor? **I am worried about it jumping up and biting me.**

She: There you go again making me hysterical . . . oh where are my pills?

He: Forget your pills. They're all up in the medicine cabinet. And who knows where that is now? Pills? Since when did you start taking pills? What kind of pills?

She: Dramamine.

He: Car sick pills? You take car sick pills for your nerves?

She: No, I take them when I don't want to get seasick.

He: **Sea sick.** You worried about getting seasick? How the hell can you get seasick in your kitchen?

She: How am I going to get seasick? *(Rising hysteria)* How am I going to have a wild wolf in my kitchen? How is my tiny dining room going to become a major body of water? You answer me that and I'll tell you how I'm going to get seasick in the kitchen!

He: I'm sorry I asked. *(Blackout)*

As the lights come up (blue eye and some moonlight) Harry and Sheila are sitting back to back facing offstage right and left. Some time has passed. The wolf is sitting back on the chair down left. He begins to howl through the recorder during the blackout.

They do not feel threatened by the howl anymore. It is a sad and lonely cry, as they each turn inward to try to figure out what has happened and who is responsible. They let the cry reflect their own feelings.

C12

He: Listen to him howl. He probably doesn't know any better than we do what's going on here. I wonder how long before this stuff wears off?

The howl develops into the melody of "By The Sea". *The wolf is acting as a catalyst here, trying to unite Harry and Sheila through music. After the first few bars of* "By The Sea", *Sheila slowly and hesitatingly picks up the refrain.*

She: "By the sea, by the sea, by the beautiful sea. You and me. You and me. Oh how happy we'll be."

He: *(Joins in after the first stanza. Together they sing a short quiet round)* "By the sea, by the sea, by the beautiful sea. You and me, you and me. Oh how happy we'll be" . . . It's funny, I was thinking about that same song just before you started singing it.

She: I don't even know where I remember it from. It just came into my head. I guess that's where we are, though . . . down by the sea.

He: It even looks like the moon is out there rising . . . Sheila, look out there. It's really kind of nice. Tell me what you see out there?

She: My purse. *(She sees her purse which is hanging on the hook of a long fishing line off right)*

He: Your purse?

She: Thank God. *(She quickly gets up, leaving Harry sprawling on the floor)*

He: What's the big deal with your purse?

She: I keep my dramamine in my purse . . . and my knitting. Great. Now I'll have something to do.

The wolf starts to growl

She: Now what's he growling about?

He: How should I know? . . . I think I can reach it with the broom.

She: You'll get him angry.

He: Not him, dummy, the purse.

She: Oh could you, that would be fantastic. *(He takes the broom and starts fishing for the purse)*

He: It's just out of reach . . . Ohhh, I almost had it that time.

Harry is leaning as far as he can between the "walls" down right and up left but the purse is just out of reach. Sheila takes Harry's left hand with her right. She feels around for something to grab onto with her left hand and finds the hand of the wolf who has moved his chair centre stage to get a better look and is now standing on it.

She: Can't you stretch a little more?

He: Couldn't your purse come a little closer? . . . Do we have any string or rope or anything?

She: I have some yarn.

He: Good. That will be perfect. Where is it?

She: It's in my purse.

He: *(addressing audience — moves down centre as lights come up on him)* Christ! **World, I wanna tell you something. Behind every successful man there is an idiot!** In curlers. *(To her)* For what reason did you think I wanted the yarn? Did she think I was going to take time out to knit us life preservers? *(Lights on Harry fade. He returns to Sheila)* I tell you what: you go out there and get me the yarn from your purse, and I'll tie it to the broom and then I'll be able to fish in your purse to get the yarn to fish in your purse.

She: How was I supposed to know that's what you wanted the yarn for? Are you going to stand around yelling or are you going to get the purse?

He: I can't reach the purse!

She: Try again, maybe it's closer now. *(The wolf jumps off chair and moves around to push fishing line in closer to Harry)*

He: Yeah, it moved in closer so it could hear what we're saying about it. *(He repeats the fishing operation. This time he gets the purse with no difficulty)*

She: Ya got it, ya got it! How did you do it? *(She takes purse)*

He: *(somewhat subdued)* It moved in closer.

She: It's all wet.

He: I'll throw it back and see if I can get a dry one.

She: If you'd spend less time making jokes and more time figuring out what's going on here, we'd all be in better shape. *(She moves to chair and sits. She is looking in purse for her pills)*

He: You mean you think there's a logical explanation for all this? Well, I know one thing . . .

She: What's that?

He: I don't know what's going on here. I could spend the rest of my life figuring, and I still wouldn't understand what's going on — someone could come in here with a briefcase and explain everything right here in my own kitchen and I wouldn't understand it . . .

She: That's it!

He: What's it?

She: We're dead! That's what all this is, we're dead.

He: You mean death is a floating kitchen?

She: No, it's spending the rest of your life figuring out where you are.

He: You don't have to be dead to do that.

She: Well, if we were alive we would know where we were . . .

He: But you have to die to be dead, and I don't remember dying.

She: Do you remember being born? You have to be born to be alive, and I don't remember being born.

He: Holy shit. I must have gotten a heart attack from waxing your damn floor. I told you I shouldn't have given blood last week.

She: Well what about me. I was just doing a crossword. How could I die from a crossword puzzle? I never heard of a 36-year-old woman dying of a crossword puzzle.

He: Maybe we're not dead then.

She: Of course we're dead.

He: What difference does it make. Alive or dead, we're here, and if you hadn't gotten the brainstorm to wax the floor, we wouldn't be here in this mess.

She: Oh really? Exactly where is it we'd be, then?

He: If I didn't have to wax the floor we could have gone to a movie, or bowling or something . . .

She: A movie or bowling or something! I don't even remember the last time you took me to a movie — or something. You don't even drive me to the drycleaners any more.

He: That's right. It's my fault now. God is punishing me because I didn't drive you to the drycleaners.

She finds the dramamine and takes out a couple of tablets.

She: Would you reach me a glass, please.

He gets a glass from off left and hands it to her. She goes over to the sink down right for water. She turns on the faucet, but no water comes out.

She: The water doesn't work. There's no water.

He: It's all out in the dining room. *(giving her the cup)*

She: How am I going to take my pills?

He: Use some of the water from the other room. *(Sits in chair)*

She: I can't use that water.

He: Why not?

She: It's probably filthy.

He: Gimme the glass. *(He takes the glass and scoops up some water from the former living room. He holds it up to the moonlight. Then he smells it and finally tastes it)* Hey, this tastes pretty good. *(He takes another mouthful and passes glass to her)* It tastes fresher than the water out of the tap. *(She sips a little)* What do you think?

She: It's not bad . . . it tastes a little like floor wax, don't you think?

He: Floor wax? Come on now. You've never had water that good. You just take your pills like a good girl. *(She takes the pills and finishes all the water. He sits)*

The wolf howls again

She: *(beginning to crack again)* How long is this going to go on?

He: I don't know, but I don't think that wolf is just going to sit and watch forever.

She: You think he'd attack us?

He: You never know with wild animals. I wish it weren't so dark so I could see the bugger.

She: You mean you haven't seen it either?

He: I told you it was too dark.

She: But you saw the mouse . . .

He: Yes.

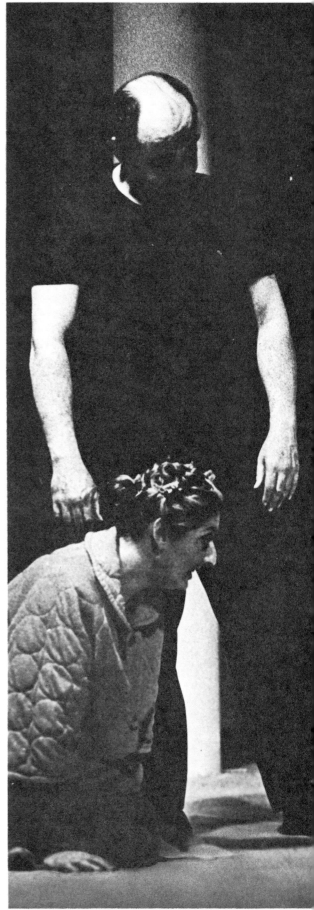

C16

She: . . . and the rat.

He: Of course I saw the rat. What did you think I was swinging the broom at?

She: But you haven't seen the wolf?

He: What are you trying to tell me?

She: Maybe there really isn't a wolf there.

He: If there was a mouse there and a rat there, why wouldn't there be a wolf there too?

She: I just don't think it's really there.

He: Well then that mouse-rat has some set of vocal cords. It wasn't too dark to **hear** a wolf. And boy, did I hear a wolf howl!

She: That was just the power of suggestion.

He: Who suggested that I hear a wolf?

She: Don't you remember? You said, "Next thing you know, you'll be calling it a wolf." Well, that's when it happened.

He: It's a good thing I didn't say wild elephant.

She: Don't say things like that.

He: Well if there is no wolf, why am I afraid to go over to the refrigerator and turn on the radio?

She: Because your imagination has made the wolf a real thing to you.

He: The wolf is not a real thing to you?

She: No it's not a real thing to me . . . I realize that it is just my imagination reacting to the power of suggestion.

He: Is this something else your beautician told you?

She: *(Icily)* **I do more during the day than do crosswords and go to the beauty parlour** *(She returns her cup and purse to right)* I do read **Cosmopolitan** you know. I refuse to let my mind go to waste.

He: And because of some magazine article, I'm supposed to walk up to a wild wolf and turn on the radio.

She: There is no wolf over there.

He: Then why don't you go over and turn on the radio?

She: You'd let me go over there?

He: All right, I'll go turn the radio on.

She: *(Just as he is gingerly getting up)* Maybe we should call the police.

He: *(Sits again)* Sure. We'll tell them someone took our dining room floor and that we're trapped by a vicious wolf that we're positive is not there.

She: I really think we should call someone.

He: Who would you call?

She: My sister. *(She moves up left to telephone)* She owes me a favour from the time I went over and took care of the baby.

He: What are you going to tell her?

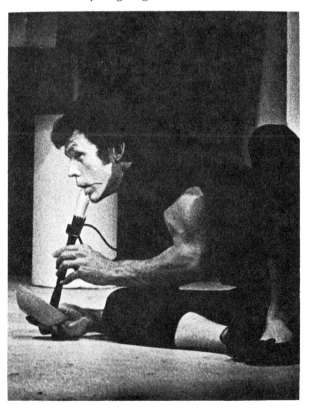

She: I'll tell her that we're both desperately ill in bed and could she come right over with a rubber raft and give us some help.

He: You don't think she's going to ask about the rubber raft?

She: When I'm sick in bed, you think **my sister** is going to waste time asking questions? *(She clicks the cradle several times)* There's no dial tone.

He: *(Getting up quickly)* How can there be no dial tone? Let me see that. *(He takes the receiver and clicks the cradle several times)* There's no dial tone!

She: No kidding.

He: Okay, okay, that's it. Give me that broom. I am going over there and turn on the radio and find out once and for all what is going on here. *(He takes the broom and moves slowly in the dark towards the refrigerator. Yes it is dark but by this time their eyes have adjusted to it and they are familiar with the kitchen, so they can function)* There is no wolf here . . . There is no wolf here.

The wolf growls menacingly

She: Harry, be careful.

He: *(A little louder)* There is no wolf here . . . There better not be a wolf here . . .

Wolf growls a little louder

He: Oh, there is a wolf there. *(He holds the broom out between himself and the wolf)* Now easy there, fella, I'm not going to hurt you. *(The wolf is now one continuous ominous rumble) (Harry begins stepping back as wolf becomes more menacing)* Damn wolf! You'd think it was his kitchen. Next thing you know he'll be asking us to prepare a meal for him.

Wolf: Prepare a meal for me.

She: Harry, are you out of your mind? You must be if you think I'm going to cook you a meal now.

He: Sheila, that was not me asking for a meal.

She: There are only two of us here and I know that it wasn't me.

He: There are three of us.

She: Now wait a minute. You're not expecting me to believe it was the wolf that asked for the meal.

He: I'm not asking you to believe anything. I'm just telling you that it wasn't me who said it. Next thing you know, you'll be saying it was my idea to wax the floor.

She: It was your idea to wax the floor.

He: Whattya mean it was my idea to . . . *(He stops dead)* . . . did you hear what you just said?

She: I think I said it was your idea to wax the floor. But I know it was my idea to wax the floor. Why would I say that?

He: *(Almost dazed by his new awareness)* Next thing you know, the phone will ring. *(the phone rings. Sheila answers it)*

She: There's no one there . . .

He: The next thing you know, the radio will come on. *(The radio does come on, but there is only static)* The next thing you know, the radio static will clear up and we will hear the news. *(The static gets louder. Sheila is mesmerized by what he is doing. And a little frightened. He commands again; this time louder)* **The next thing you know, the radio static will clear up and we will hear the news.**

This whole section of telephone, radio static can be pre-edited on audiotape. Instead of news we hear horse racing, a "post time" trumpet followed by the starter's bell and the sound of the starting gates open with the commentator's "they're off and running". During the following exchanges and until Sheila says "I just wish this would all stop", we hear the constant commentary of a horse race. But the words of the actors must not be lost. Physically, Sheila, Harry and

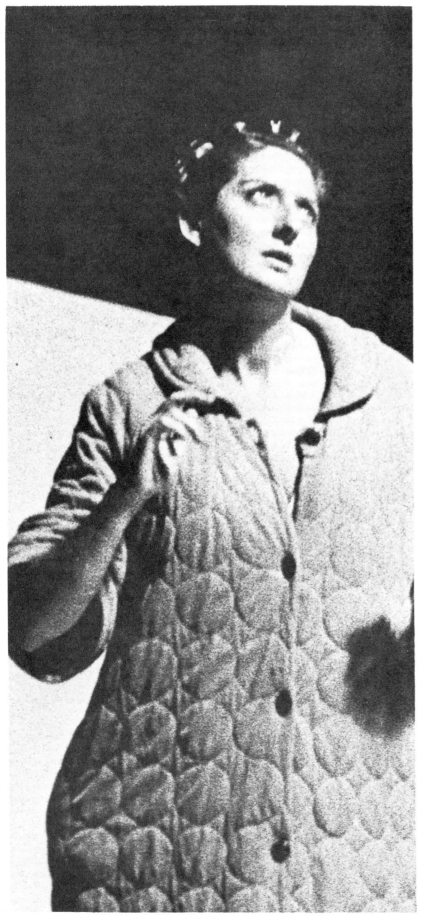

the wolf are also moving wildly around the room as if the floor was undulating.

She: We're moving!

Wolf howls

He: *(Shouting)* Next thing you know we will stop moving. *(Movement continues)* Goddammit, stop I said. **Stop!** I thought I had it. I thought I had control of it. I thought I had it . . .

She: Maybe if you apologized . . .

He: Apologized! For what? To who?

She: I don't know. I just wish this would all stop.

Everything stops. We hear a plane passing overhead. As it disappears there is an H-blast which fades with the lights to blackout. Harry, Sheila and the wolf have all been frozen with rivetted attention during this ultimate folly.

Blackout. The lights come up (general lighting as in Scene I) and it is morning. The wolf is lying on his side, he is breathing through the recorder which is still in his mouth. Harry and Sheila are asleep in each other's arms.

Harry is resting on the chair which is upside down and Sheila is lying across him. Harry wakes up first, and then Sheila. They both feel much better.

She: Did you ever mail that letter to Diefenbaker?

He: Mail a letter to Diefenbaker? Why would I want to do that? You were probably just remembering something from a dream.

She: No, no, you remember . . . it was years ago. You were steamed up about exhaust fumes. You were going to write Diefenbaker a letter and straighten the whole thing out. You were ahead of your time.

He: What on earth made you remember that?

She: I don't know. *(They are silent for a while.*

Each remembers something) How were you able to sleep last night with me lying all over you?

He: *(Not yet ready to say he enjoyed it)* Oh I managed. You're really not that heavy.

She: Am I as light as I was when we were first married?

He: Sophia Loren isn't as light as she was when she was first married . . . Hey, are you hungry?

She: I'm going on a diet. But you go ahead.

He: I'm hungry enough so that wolf better watch his step.

She: Did you see him? Look at him just lying there. The poor thing looks half dead.

He: Let's hope he stays that way. Maybe I can get over to the refrigerator and get us some food. *(Gets up)*

She: What do you think is the matter with him?

He: How should I know, I'm not a veterinarian . . . maybe he's seasick. *(Moving carefully to refrigerator)*

She: You think so?

He: I was only kidding.

She: No . . . I really think you're right. I think the poor thing is seasick.

He: Today he's a poor thing? Yesterday you were ready to jump overboard.

She: I think I'll give him some of my pills. Get me some milk *(they look at each other)* . . . please.

He: Yes indeedy, Miss Nightingale. Milk coming right up. *(He takes some milk out of the refrigerator)* The milk is warm. Looks like the refrigerator is out too. *(She is grinding some pills in a small bowl)* Are you the lady that ordered the milk? *(She smiles)* Well sign for it right here. *(He indicates his lips, and she responds with a gentle kiss)*

She: Thank you. *(He pours a little into the bowl)*

He: Will that be all?

She: Yes, that should do it . . . well, maybe there's one other thing.

He: What's that?

She: If you're not too busy . . .

He: Always looking for new business . . .

She: Maybe you could come around again tonight and hold me when I try to go to sleep.

He: *(Looks at her face for a while before answering in a much softer voice)* Sure, lady, sure. I think I can arrange that. Yeah, you can count on it.

She takes the bowl to the wolf.

He: Hey now, you better be careful. Seasick or not, that's a wild animal.

She approaches the wolf carefully. Not knowing exactly how to feed milk to a wolf, she lifts the other end of the recorder — his snout — and places it in the bowl of milk and steps back. The wolf, who is breathing through the instrument, cannot help but ingest some of the milk which has the effect of waking him and reviving him at the same time.

She: Do you think he'd like some raw hamburger?

He: If he's as hungry as I am he would.

She: I'm sorry, what would you like for breakfast?

He: What can I have with nothing working?

She: How about a peanut butter sandwich and some warm milk?

He: Sure, that'll be fine.

She goes to the fridge

She: The fish thawed all over the peanut butter, but the bread's still good. What are we going to do with the fish?

He: Throw it back in the dining room. *(Harry rights the chair and sits)* This is some vacation cruise. No running water, the refrigerator is hot, the stove is cold, our food is going bad, we got a sick wolf to take care of. The next thing you know we'll spring a leak . . . **Oh no, I didn't mean that!** *(it is too late; water starts coming from everywhere. This can be achieved with lights and sound. To Sheila:)* How quick do you think you can learn to swim? Now how come it worked that time? When I said the radio would work, nothing happened. I talk about a leak, and boom there it is.

She: Maybe you can make the leak go away.

He: You think so?

She: It's worth a try.

He: Okay.

He: *(Closes his eyes and clenches his fists — recites slowly)* The next thing you know, the leak will stop. *There is a sudden silence.*

She: You did it! You really did it!

He: And now I'm going to get rid of that wolf before he remembers how hungry he is.

She: I don't think you should do that. *(She defends the wolf who is now cowering behind her legs)*

He: Just because he's not bothering us now doesn't mean he's not going to attack later. We're lucky he didn't grab us last night while we were sleeping.

She: Harry, I really don't think . . .

He: *(Ignoring her, recites quickly)* The next thing you know, the wolf will go away.

The wolf begins to stir. He struggles to his feet. He looks up at Sheila almost as if pleading. He then walks between the pillars right into the water. He begins to whimper and struggle. He still hasn't the strength to swim for very long and there really isn't anywhere to swim.

She: You're not going to leave him out there, are you?

He: What am I supposed to do? I thought he'd just disappear.

She: Well he didn't.

He: If I try to bring him back, he might attack me.

She: Then I'll do it. *(Makes a dash for the water)*

He: All right, all right, I'll bring him back. Just to stop that damn whimpering. The next thing you know the wolf will come back. *(The wolf struggles harder but he can't make it. Harry looks up to heaven to deliver his next line)* You had to send me a wolf who couldn't swim. *(The wolf increases his crying)* All right, I'm coming.

He then, incredibly enough, dives into the water. Sheila gets down on her knees at the edge of the dining room lake to help pull them aboard. After much grunting and groaning and shoving and pulling they get everyone on board.

She: *(Cradling the wolf)* You poor thing.

He: *(Angrily)* That poor thing is a man-eating monster.

She: He's shaking.

He: Probably because he knows he's being held by a lunatic. *(She begins to dry the wolf with a hanky)* Would you like me better if I were shaking? I mean, I did jump in after him. I was in the same water he was in.

She: *(Nicely, not sarcastically) (Smiling at him)* Come here, hero, I'll dry you too. *(She dries him off)*

He: That wolf is going to have to earn his keep here.

She: Yeah, he can chop wood and milk the cows.

He: I'm serious, Sheila. It's not good for a wild creature to be pampered.

She: You're the boss, Harry.

He: *(Becoming the boss)* Today's lesson is sitting. Sit, wolf.

He: *(to wolf)* You want to go back in the water? Well, sit. How am I going to teach you to fetch the paper if you're not willing to learn the basics first? Look, watch this. *(He kneels down on the floor and then makes a big show of rewarding himself with a big piece of meat)* Oh, that's good. Mmmmm. That's good. And all I had to do was sit. What kind of big deal is that? Sheila, we have a wolf with a zero I.Q. *(getting up)*

She: Leave him alone before you make him neurotic.

He: It's your turn now to learn some tricks. *(Advancing on Sheila)*

She: Do I have to eat that awful hamburger.

He: Only if you don't learn the tricks.

She: I've never learned tricks in my kitchen before. Especially with an audience. *(Making like the coy virgin)*

He: But the show must go on.

She: And my pills were washed away at sea.

He: Sometimes you gotta live dangerously.

She: May I quote you on that, doctor?

His answer is to kiss her in a way he hasn't kissed her in a long, long time. They are going to make love with more feeling than they've felt, while sober, for a long time.
Blackout

Harry is fishing. He is using the broom as a rod. Sheila is doing exercises and eating potato chips. There is a small pile of wood for a fire.

She: Isn't there anything out there besides fish to catch? Another fish dinner and I'll be able to breathe under water.

He: Another complaint and you may have to. Call room service, maybe they can send something up.

She: Have we been out here 40 days and nights yet?

He: Yeah, we're a regular Adam and Eve.

She: I'm serious, Harry. Maybe the world has ended.

He: So welcome to Harry's Ark. Does that mean that I have been chosen to repopulate the world? Right now I haven't even got the strength to play pingpong.

She: Harry, believe me, you're doing fine. If you don't watch out I'm going to write to Dr. Kinsey about you.

He: I'm doing okay, huh? *(Starts whistling)*

She: Rock Hudson wouldn't do better.

Fade out

Fade in

Scene opens with the sound of a foghorn in the distance. It gets slowly closer and closer until the line "it looks like it's getting closer", then it fades and is out by "why is it you're the one that always gets to go places?"

It is nighttime. The sea is quiet and they are all asleep: the wolf sprawled down left, Harry slouched in the chair, Sheila crouched on the floor with her head on Harry's knee. The wolf awakens suddenly after the second or third blast of the foghorn. He is instantly alert. He moves carefully up to between the pillars and starts to bay sympathetically to the sound. This wakes Harry and Sheila.

She: What's the matter?

He: I don't know.

She: You think someone's trying to break in?

He: Who's going to break into a kitchen floating in the middle of nowhere?

She: Pirates.

He: Don't worry about it. We got a trained ferocious watch-wolf to protect us.

She: Well why is he growling?

He: I don't know. I think there's something floating out there. *(Getting up)*

She: Where?

He: *(Pointing)* Over there. Sight along my arm.

She: Yeah, I think I see it. What do you think it is?

He: I can't tell from here.

She: It looks like it's getting closer.

He: Maybe I'll go out and take a look.

She: It's too dark to go swimming out there alone.

He: It might be some driftwood. We can't afford to lose good wood.

She: But you could drown out there.

He: An old butterfly man like me? Just have yourself a sit and I'll be right back.

She: Why is it you're the one who always gets to go places? I never get to go anyplace.

He: Whattaya talking about? We go everywhere together.

She: You're always going off swimming somewhere.

He: You think I enjoy being wet?

She: You think I enjoy sitting in this dumb kitchen?

He: Is it my fault that you can't swim?

She: Harry . . .

He: What?

She: Why is this happening to us?

He: I don't know. Why does anything happen to anybody?

She: I don't want to spend the rest of my life in the kitchen.

He: But we're seeing the world.

She: It's not the same when you do it in a kitchen.

He: Look, I can't stand around talking. I have to find out what's out there.

She: Sure, leave me behind. Can I help it if I'm not as exciting as a piece of driftwood?

He: *(Soothing her)* Now cut that out. Of course you're as exciting as a piece of driftwood. I threw your underwear overboard, didn't I? How much more exciting can you be? For the first time in a helluva long time I am with a woman who really makes me feel like a man. Don't you realize that for the first time in God knows how long, being together means something? *(They embrace)*

She: Harry, you can stop all of this . . . you know you can.

He: I'm not so sure.

She: You stopped the leak.

He: This is bigger than a leak.

She: The kitchen is no place to raise a family.

He: *(Looking at her and then standing firm)* The next thing you know . . . *(The storm breaks loose)* I haven't said anything yet! *(The action is violent. Harry and the wolf slip and slide all over. Harry is lost at sea. Wolf disappears)*

She: Harry! *(There is a sudden crash and everything goes silent)* Wolf! Here Wolf! Wolf? *(She sits down lost. There is a pause and then Harry appears)* Harry! *(They embrace)* Oh, Harry!

He: I slid all the way into the bathroom.

She: Bathroom? *(She looks out through the doorway)* We're back! *(The phone rings)* It's the telephone! I wonder who it is? *(There is a knock on the door)*

He: It's probably the people downstairs wondering where all the water in their living room suddenly came from. *(He opens the door and lets a briefcase-carrying insurance man* into the apartment. From this point all the dialogues and cross-conversations occur almost simultaneously)*

She: *(Picks up the receiver)* Hello. Yes I am. Just a second . . .

Man: Hi, I'm Jerry Donovan. I'd like to help you take care of the difficult years ahead. *(He walks right in)* . . .

She: *(Putting her hand over the receiver)* Harry, we've won a prize. I just have to answer the question. *(Back to the receiver)* Yes. Just a second . . . *(to Harry, her hand over the receiver, whispering)* which Great Lake are we on?

Man: I'm a firm believer in the old adage "a stitch in time saves nine". And I'm sure you are too. After all, it's never too early to worry about your future . . .

He: *(To Sheila)* Who are you talking to?

Man: Now, I don't mean to alarm you, but tomorrow you could get crushed in an elevator,

God forbid, or maimed or crippled or lost in a natural disaster, and then where will you be? . . .

She: Miss McMaster. *(Into the receiver)* Just a minute, Miss McMaster. *(To Harry)* I don't know who she is, but if we get the question right, we win a prize.

He: If you hear the word magazine, hang up.

Man: If you sign here, you will never have to worry about your wife and family again. You can forget about your future.

He: If I give up riding elevators, will you go away? *(He rests his hand on one of the stove burners)* Ow! That damn thing is hot!

She: Harry, what lake is it?

Man: I have another plan that covers contingencies. Now here's something I'm sure you'll be interested in. *(Starts following Harry around)*

He: *(Opens the refrigerator and sticks his hand inside)* Oh, that's cold, beautiful cold!

Sheila in the meantime has tried the water and it works.

She: Harry, the water's back.

He: Good, that means we can shower afterwards.

Harry chases Sheila offstage . . .

Man: Come back here. You have responsibilities. You're adults, not children. What about your retirement?

He follows them

Telephone: *I'm afraid I can only give you another 30 seconds to tell us which of the Great Lakes you are located on . . .*

Blackout   **The End**

*played by the Mime

Meyer's Room
Sheldon Rosen

Meyer's Room

The action of the play takes place in a room that has only an armchair and small bed for furniture. The only other set required is two large doors hung between the pillars on double swing hinges.

Cast of characters

There are three characters in the play — all men.

Madeline, young, well-dressed, intellectual and a bit on the nervous side
Rock Hudson, again young but dressed in a cowboy outfit complete with Stetson and toy six-shooters; he is intellectual but extremely physical
Meyer, dressed in the uniform of a blind beggar — dark glasses, old hat and coat, cane and cap

This is Meyer's room and only he can move freely in and out of the room. The other two have great difficulty leaving the room.

Act One

Madeline enters gingerly through doors. The lighting is subdued. He surveys the room and finally, as if waiting for someone or something, sits in chair.

Just as he sits, we have the faint noise of footsteps running. The footsteps gradually get closer and louder. Madeline rises from chair and goes to door. Just as he reaches the door Rock Hudson comes bursting in, squashing Madeline between the right door and pillar.

By the time the doors come to rest Hudson realizes he is not alone. He draws his gun and turns suddenly on Madeline.

Rock: Don't move. I've got you covered.

Mad: My father who art in heaven . . .

Rock: Shut up.

Mad: *(Looking up)* I'll talk to you later.

Rock: I said shut up! *(He is slightly hysterical)* One more word from you and you're dead.

Mad: *(Whispering)* Can't we discuss this? *(Rock cocks the hammer)* If you shoot that thing they'll hear you for miles.

Rock: I have nothing to lose.

Mad: *(Breaking out of his whisper)* Then why were you running?

Rock: Because they were after me.

Mad: Whattaya mean "they"? Who is "they"?

Rock: *(Slight pause)* I don't know.

Mad: How do you know they were chasing you?

Rock: Because I was running. How do I know you're not one of them?

Mad: My God, do you think so? You don't suppose I was chasing you, do you? If I was, I'm sorry. I certainly didn't mean to.

Rock: Well I'm definitely going to have to keep my eye on you.

Mad: Do you have any idea where we are?

Rock: Maybe.

Mad: Where are we?

Rock: Ask me no questions and I'll tell you no lies.

Mad: Did you make that up?

Rock: It's none of your business where we are.

Mad: Why don't you come out and admit you don't know where we are?

Rock: Get off my back.

Mad: Are you ashamed of not knowing where you are?

Rock: No!

Mad: Then tell me where we are.

Rock: You know, you're beginning to get on my nerves with all your goddam questions.

Mad: Am I?

Rock: You wise-ass bastard. *(Strangles him on bed) (Suddenly the sound of Meyer's stick causes Rock to stop)* Sshh! Someone's coming.

He pulls out his gun and moves to the right pillar next to the door. Madeline stays in place. The door opens and Meyer enters. Lights up. He is wearing shabby clothes and dark glasses and carrying a cane and a cup. He hangs his cane on Rock's gun and gives his cup to Madeline. He kisses Madeline on the forehead and turns on the TV down stage. The TV is carrying the news.

Meyer: *(Sits in chair)* Is dinner ready?

Mad: Not yet. *(Moves to right of Meyer)* Did you have a good day, daddy?

Meyer: Bloody kids kept lighting matches in front of my eyes.

Mad: The little farts.

Rock: (Whispering to Madeline) Do you know him?

Meyer: Who's this?

Rock: Who are you?

Meyer: Who am I? **Who am I!** This is Meyer's room, isn't it? (Looking around) Of course it's Meyer's room. Well then, I must be Meyer. (Said uncertainly)

Rock: Aren't you sure?

Meyer: What difference does it make? Whatever I am, being called Meyer isn't going to change it. And whom are youm?

Rock: Rock Hudson.

Meyer: I've seen all your movies.

Mad: Dinner's ready.

Meyer: Wonderful. Come join us, Rock. Madeline, will you say grace?

Mad: Perhaps our guest would like to say grace tonight.

Rock: Fuck you.

Meyer: Good. Let's eat now.

Rock: There's nothing here to eat.

Meyer: What?

Rock: There's nothing here.

Meyer: Madeline, what are we eating?

Mad: Kidney pie.

Meyer: Then how come there's no kidney pie in front of me?

Mad: I was wondering the same thing. Maybe we've finished eating.

Meyer: Of course. Rock and I shall retire to the other room while you do the dishes. (Turns off TV and makes to exit)

Rock: You two are insane.

Meyer: What's that?

Rock: You two are nuts.

Mad: Two out of three are insane and one of us is normal? It's the minority that's abnormal. You're the one who's insane.

Rock: I'll kill you, you bastard, that will make me sane.

Meyer: Children, please . . .

Mad: Don't worry, daddy, Rock is just recreating one of his roles. Why don't you read your paper. (He does as instructed)

The newspaper should be present in Meyer's pocket so that it can be pulled out into a reading position in one flourish. Madeline goes to Rock and relieves him of the cane.

Mad: You're going to blow the whole thing if you don't watch out.

Rock: What are you talking about?

Mad: As long as we're in here, we're safe. And as long as we go along with Meyer, he'll let us stay here.

Rock: But he can't put us out — I have a gun.

Mad: But you can't use the gun because the noise will bring them in.

Meyer: You young people seem to be hitting it off beautifully. You really are a lovely couple.

Mad: Oh daddy.

Meyer: Well, I'm sure you young people have a lot to talk about, so I shall turn in for the evening and leave you to yourselves. (Chuckling, he falls asleep standing up)

Rock: Is he asleep?

Mad: I think so.

Rock: Well what are we supposed to do?

Mad: Just play along.

Rock: But how?

Mad: Just keep pretending that you're Rock Hudson.

Rock: But I am Rock Hudson.

Mad: Yes . . . of course . . . well that should make it easy enough.

Rock: But who are you supposed to be?

Mad: I'm Meyer's daughter.

Rock: But who are you *really?*

Mad: What?

Meyer: Aaggghhh! (Waking from a nightmare)

Mad: (Shaking him) Wake up, wake up . . . it's only a bad dream . . . it's all right . . .

Meyer: Well, I think I'll go to bed now and leave you two alone.

Rock: But what about your nightmare?

Meyer: My nightmare? I haven't gone to sleep yet.

Rock: You were just standing there asleep.

Mad: Rock . . . honey . . .

Meyer: Nobody sleeps standing up. (Exits)

Mad: Say goodnight, Rock.

Rock: Goodnight. Well, now what do we do?

Mad: We hope that he never wakes up again.

Rock: (Pacing) I hate rooms. I hate having nothing to do. I hate being trapped like this. Goddammit, I hate hating rooms, I hate hating having nothing to do, I hate . . .

Mad: Hey . . .

On "hey" Rock has reached the door in a tremendous effort to escape. He is stopped by the sound of men who were chasing them returning.

The lighting also changes from general lighting to just the eye lit in bright red. Madeline doesn't see or hear any of this. When the music starts in addition to the red eye can be introduced a sound organ coupled to the amp. to create the psychedelic effect.

Mad: I can't find the light switch.

Rock runs around the walls searching for the switch. Suddenly there is a pounding at the door and he freezes.

Rock: We've got to turn out the light, if we turn out the light they'll go away.

The pounding continues and the doorknob is frantically turned from outside as if the door were locked.

Rock: Help me push the chair against the door.

Madeline is still motionless. Rock tries to push the chair but it won't move. He is nearly frantic. The pounding increases to a crescendo. He runs to the doors in a desperate attempt to prevent them opening, but is met by hard rock music which pushes him tumbling downstage. The music is "Higher" by Sly & the Family Stone. The first and second section of this music is repetitious. At first he enjoys the music and is carried away by it into a fantastic dance ritual. The second time through he does not enjoy it but goes through the ritual because he has to. After the second repetition the music stops and the lights return to normal but he keeps dancing his ritual like a never-ending series of drug trips. It takes Madeline to shake him out of it.

Mad: Wake up, wake up . . . it's only a bad dream . . . it's all right. *(Coaxing Rock into chair)*

Meyer: I heard you screaming . . .

Rock: But I wasn't sleeping. *(To Madeline)* Don't you remember not being able to turn out the light?

Mad: You were dreaming.

Rock: But they were chasing us. They were right at the door.

Mad: Who was chasing us?

Rock: I don't know. I don't know.

Mad: (Stroking his head) There, there now, it was just a bad dream.

Rock: But I didn't go to sleep.

Meyer: Of course you did, no one dreams while they're awake.

Rock: *(Breaks away from their grasp to downstage)* Something's going on here and I don't like it.

Meyer: What do you mean "something's going on here"?

Mad: The poor boy is just overtired. He's been playing hard all day. He really should go to bed. *(Advancing on Rock)*

Meyer: Yes, of course.

Rock: I don't want to go to bed.

Mad: You're getting awfully cranky. *(Still advancing)*

Rock: Why do I have to be the one to go to bed? Why don't you go to bed?

Mad: You're really being unreasonable.

Meyer: Listen to Madeline.

Mad: Would you go to bed if I told you a story?

Rock: What kind of story?

Mad: It is a true and real story and quite meaningful *(guiding him to bed)*

Rock: Is it scary?

Mad: Only if you think about it. *(Laying Rock on bed)*

Meyer: May I listen too?

Mad: If you don't interrupt.

Meyer: I promise. *(Sits in chair)*

Mad: This story was told to me years and years ago by one of the Sisters from Holy Mother.

Meyer: I thought you said it was a true story?

Mad: I thought you said you wouldn't interrupt?

Meyer: I'm sorry.

Mad: There was a childless couple who lived in one of the poorer sections of town. They reached a point in their life when all they felt they needed to make them happy was a child of their own. But no matter how hard they tried she could never get pregnant. And then suddenly one day the curse was lifted and she became pregnant. And new meaning and purpose came into their life. And they were incredibly happy and finally the child came and it was a wonderfully healthy little boy and they were all wonderfully happy together.

Rock: It sounds like a kid's fairy tale. I thought you were going to tell me Dracula or something.

Mad: Wait a second now. I haven't gotten to the good part yet. Well one day the little boy was

C34

chasing his ball in the street and he got hit by a car. He was hurt quite seriously and the mother nearly went into shock and the doctors said that they didn't think he had any chance of surviving and rather than curse her fate the mother poured her grief into prayer and promised the heavens that she would be a fervent keeper of the faith if only her child would be spared. And for seven days and nights she kept up her vigil and her prayer and the boy did survive and they said it was a miracle. But the hospital bills put them deeply in debt and things did not go well for them but the boy lived and grew to young manhood and when he was about seventeen or eighteen he killed three people.

Rock: How did he kill them? *(Pressing Madeline for an answer)*

Mad: I don't know . . . it's not important.

Rock: Whattaya mean, it's not important? *(Pressing)*

Mad: He smashed their heads in with a baseball bat.

Rock: Really? How come?

Mad: *(Spills the beans)* Because they were walking too slowly and he had an important baseball game to go to.

Rock: Far out.

Slight pause

Meyer: Is that the end of the story?

Mad: No . . . he was found guilty and sentenced to death by hanging . . .

Rock: But they were blocking his way on the sidewalk *(to Meyer)*

Mad: . . . and his mother learned the meaning of prayer.

Meyer: I don't think the story put him to sleep.

Mad: *(Rises)* You have the understanding of a watermelon rind.

Rock: Was it a Louisville Slugger?

Mad: What?

Rock: The baseball bat.

Mad: I only wish I had a baseball bat with me now. *(Moves down left)*

Rock: I have a gun.

Mad: *(Wearily)* Yes, you've mentioned it.

Meyer: You're both becoming rather tedious, you know.

Mad: What do you mean, tedious? You find your own flesh and blood tedious?

Meyer: You're not my flesh and blood.

Mad: But I'm your daughter.

Meyer: You're not my daughter. You're not even a woman.

Mad: *(Short panic)* I think the jig is up.

Rock: What are you talking about? What's happening here?

Meyer: What's happening here is that I am not as stupid as you think I am. *(Advances on Rock)*

Mad: *(Picks up Meyer's cue and advances on Rock from other side of bed)* We're just doing this so you won't put us out.

Meyer: There are monsters out there waiting for us.

Mad: Hooded vermin waiting to chew our guts into little pieces.

Meyer: Long-legged liver lovers.

Mad: And if you don't let us stay here we'll tell them that you're here. *(Rock falls asleep suddenly)*

Mad: Children do love a good spooky story.

Meyer: I don't know why, it just gives me nightmares. Well, it really is time for me to turn in. I have a busy day ahead of me.

Mad: Goodnight, daddy.

Meyer: *(Kissing Madeline on the forehead)* Goodnight, dear. Try not to stay up too late. *(He leaves)*

Madeline wanders about the room. He is obviously restless. He would like to escape in sleep, but he can't. He sits down. He stands up. He finally rushes over to the window and whispers at the top of his lungs "I hate you, you bastards". . . . The sound echoes several times. The red eye comes up. He sinks down in fear.

Mad: Whattaya need me for? I don't bother anybody . . . look, let's talk about this . . . I can give you a boy . . . a young healthy boy . . . someone worth having . . . I can arrange it . . . *(softer)* I can arrange it. *(He goes over to Rock, gently brushes the hair out of his eyes. He then begins to bind Rock in the sheet he is lying on. Rock begins to struggle)* . . . Take it easy, you don't want to hatch prematurely.

Rock: What are you doing? Let go of me.

Mad: But it's time now.

Rock: Time for what . . . I said let go of me.

Mad: Didn't they tell you?

Rock: Cut out the shit and let me go.

Mad: Time to enter your cocoon.

Rock: Let me go, I'm no goddamn butterfly.

Mad: But you will be.

Rock: Me . . . a butterfly.

Mad: It's really quite an honour.

Rock: A real fly-through-the-air butterfly?

Mad: With painted wings. You'll be able to soar as high as you want to. To dive to float to sleep in the sun and smell the blossoms.

Rock: I can be a dive bomber.

Mad: You can be a dive bomber.

Rock: I can hide behind a leaf.

Mad: Yes, you can.

Rock: What do I have to do?

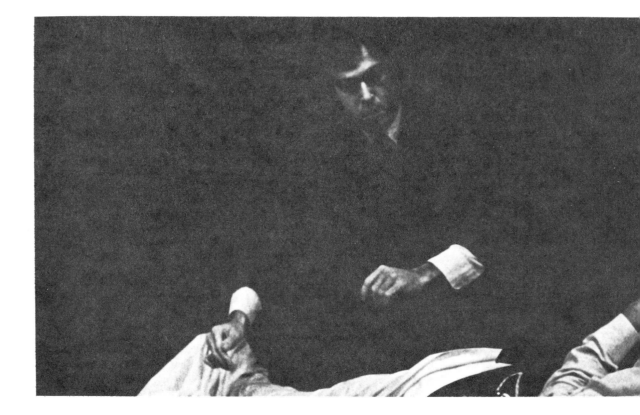

Mad: Just let me wrap you up in the cocoon and then all you do is wait. When the cocoon is unwrapped, you will be a butterfly.

Rock: Will it take long?

Mad: Not too long.

Rock: Then let's do it. *(They stand. Madeline finishes wrapping Rock in the "cocoon". Meyer enters just as Madeline is wrapping Rock's head. He goes over to intercede)*

Meyer: What are you doing?

Mad: Well, you see . . . I'm . . . I'm . . .

Rock: He's wrapping me in a cocoon.

Meyer: In a cocoon?

Rock: A butterfly cocoon. I'm going to become a butterfly.

Meyer: *(To Madeline)* Is he really going to become a butterfly?

Mad: *(Almost a verbal double-take)* Is he going to become a butterfly? Of course he's going to

become a butterfly. Why would I be wrapping him in a cocoon if he weren't going to become a butterfly?

Meyer: May I watch?

Mad: If you don't interrupt.

Meyer: I promise. *(Madeline finishes the wrapping as Meyer sits and observes)*

Mad: Help me carry him to the window. *(They do so. He is still standing)*

Meyer: Are you sure he can breathe? Better a live caterpillar than a dead butterfly.

Mad: Sshh, he'll hear you. Help me get him on the window ledge.

Meyer: On the window ledge?

Mad: He needs the sunlight to hatch.

Meyer: But he might fall off.

Mad: Yes, wouldn't that be a shame.

Rock: *(From inside the sheet)* I think I'm ready to hatch now.

Mad: No, you're not. It's too early.

Meyer: Don't you think he would know better when he's ready to hatch?

Mad: I thought you weren't going to interrupt.

Rock: My wings are growing.

Mad: It's just your imagination.

Meyer: You really are being unreasonable, don't you think?

Rock: It's too dark to see what colour they are.

Meyer: *(Speaking into the sheet)* We'll be right in.

Mad: *(Speaking into the sheet)* No we won't.

Rock: They're very strong wings.

Meyer: Let him out.

Mad: Let him out. There's no room to fly in here. Where's he going to fly in here? *(He sees the window and something suddenly occurs to him)*

Mad: Yes, you're right of course. *(He speaks into the sheet again)* Are you ready?

Rock: *(Impatiently)* Yesss!

Mad: Close your eyes. *(They turn him to face front and begin unwrapping him. Meyer joins in. Rock is unwrapped and his arms are crunched tight to his chest. His eyes are still closed. He is very anxious.)*

Rock: *(Hesitatingly)* Are my wings colourful?

Mad: Yes, they're quite nice.

Meyer: They are absolutely beautiful. I can see splashes of gold and brown and orange and extraordinary black markings.

Rock: Are they big?

Mad: They're good-sized.

Meyer: They're huge and powerful. You'll be able to fly to the heavens.

Rock: Can I look now?

Mad: I guess now is as good a time as any.

At the same time as Rock opens his eyes "butterfly music" begins. There are a few bars of this as he breaks free of the cocoon. As he begins to fly, the music increases. It builds up to the point where Sousa carries on with "The Stars and Stripes Forever" and we are into the circus with all the acrobatic tricks. Cartwheels, handstands, front flips off chairback, flips off bed, etc. As the march ends, Rock does a complete front flip.

Rock: I don't go very high, do I?

Meyer: You need practice.

Mad: What you really need is more room to fly.

Rock: Really? Is that it? *(Excited)*

Mad: I'm certain of it.

Rock: Maybe we can move the furniture. *(He tries to move bed)*

Meyer: I'll have the carpenter in to knock out a wall.

Mad: May I point out the obvious?

Rock: Sure.

Meyer: Please do.

Mad: Butterflies are not meant to be in rooms.

Meyer: What are you getting at?

Mad: Butterflies are free spirits. They fly "outside" of rooms.

Rock: I can't go out there.

Mad: Nonsense.

Meyer: Don't listen to him, boy. (They both advance on Rock)

Rock: They'll chase me again.

Mad: They can't catch a butterfly. You'll make fools of them.

Meyer: You're so beautiful.

Mad: What's the point of being a butterfly if you aren't going to fly?

Meyer: Then become a boy again.

Rock: But I feel good being a butterfly.

Mad: Then be a butterfly? Opportunity is fleeting.

Rock: What'll I do? (to Madeline)

Mad: You can be a dive bomber if you want.

Rock: I can hide behind a leaf.

Meyer: You can soar to the heavens . . . and we'll never see each other again.

Rock: But you have to understand. . . . I'm a butterfly.

Meyer: And you're the most beautiful thing in my life. I've never had anything like you before.

Mad: (Drags Rock to the door — and steps back) He's made up his mind. There's nothing you can say.

Rock is facing doors. He slowly begins to open them. As they open we hear the sound of the throb of machinery as if it will swallow up anything that steps inside it. The volume increases and the eye comes up as the door widens. Meyer is in great torment; he is struggling with himself.

Meyer: Wait! You bloody fool! (Rock collapses and the doors shut. Sound stops and lights

go to normal) You're no butterfly. You're just an ignorant, ineffectual nonentity . . . just like the rest of us . . . look at your arms. That's right, your arms, not your wings. You're more likely to find needle holes than feathers. *(Mocking him)* "I don't go very high, do I?" *(As Rock begins to react to what Meyer is saying, we see the impact of his defeat overwhelm Madeline and he sits down as his hope flies out the window). . . .* You should have seen yourself flapping around . . . *(Meyer is practically in tears)* . . . It was the most ludicrous thing I've ever seen in my entire life. *(By this time Rock has physically collapsed)*

Rock: (To Madeline) Why did you tell me I'd be a butterfly?

Mad: I just wanted to be able to leave this room. They don't need the likes of me. They need someone with a future. You could have made fools of them.

Rock: I've got a gun.

Meyer: (To Madeline) You selfish bastard.

Mad: You wanted to pin him to the wall like a goddam piece of art.

Meyer: He was so beautiful. . . .

Rock: Was I really? (He begins to daydream)

Mad: I just wanted to take a little walk. Just to be away from walls for a little while.

Meyer: Is that all you wanted?

Mad: All I wanted? Don't you realize. . . . (Rising to Meyer)

Meyer: You just want to go out there for a bit of a walk?

Mad: More than anything.

Meyer: Then do it. (Madeline leaps on Meyer and begins to strangle him)

Mad: Don't play games with me, you sonovabitch.

Meyer: Help!

Mad: Then do it, he says.

Meyer: He's killing me.

Mad: Just walk out the bloody door.

Meyer: Wear glasses.

Mad: Wear glasses, he says. . . . Wear glasses ? *(He stops fighting)*

Rock: Were you guys really fighting?

Mad: What did you mean when you said wear glasses?

Meyer: If you'd get off me I could tell you.

Rock: It was really a good fight.

Mad: *(Jumps off him)* You better not be playing around.

Meyer: I swear I'm telling the truth.

Rock: Are you guys going to fight again?

Meyer: Put on my dark glasses.

From here down to "walk" Meyer dresses Madeline in glasses, hat, overcoat, cane and cup. Underneath that shabby exterior, Meyer is immaculately dressed.

Mad: What's that going to do?

Meyer: If they think you can't see them, they won't see you.

Mad: Are you sure?

Meyer: I do it all the time. But it's not as easy as it sounds. You have to prepare yourself.

Mad: What do I have to do?

Meyer: They're always testing you.

Rock: I guess you guys aren't going to fight.

Meyer: They'll pass matches in front of your eyes. They'll stick their feet out to trip you. You'll have to learn how to fall. But most important, you'll have to learn how to see without looking.

Mad: I can't learn all that.

Meyer: Sure you can. I'll teach you. Don't close your eyes. You have to do this with your eyes open.

Mad: What do I do?

Rock: Is he really blind?

Meyer: Walk. *(Madeline begins to walk)* You're looking. You can't look.

Mad: How do I not look?

Meyer: You have to make your mind think of nothing and then you won't look and you'll see everything.

Mad: I can't do it. Things keep flooding into my mind.

Meyer: Try harder.

Rock: I don't believe he's really blind. *(He goes over and lights a match and holds it in front of Madeline's eyes)*

Mad: My eyes are burning.

Meyer: Feel the light, not the heat.

Mad: It burns!

Meyer: Think of nothing.

Mad: I can't think of. . . .

Meyer: Shut up! Do it! *(Madeline slowly walks towards the audience. The lights go out on the other characters. There is only a light on Madeline. He must make the audience feel that he is blind. They have to really worry about whether he's going to fall off the end of the stage or not. Meyer speaks from the darkness)*

Meyer: And you must learn a song. A song that will make them think you're a lighthearted fellow.

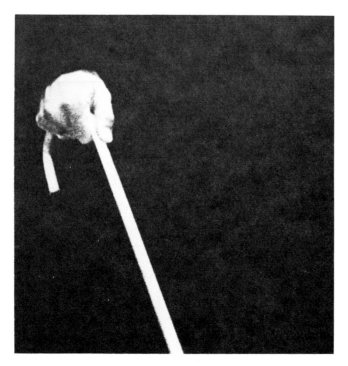

Mad: *(To the audience, rattling his cup)* Ai, Ai, Ai. . . .
In China they do it for Chile
So here's another verse
That's worse than the other verse
So waltz me around again Willy.

(He rattles his cup. Nothing happens, so he continues)

There once was a young man from Boston
Who drove around town in an Austin
The roadway was hard
His floorboard was weak
And his balls hung so low
That he lost 'em.
Ai, Ai, Ai . . .
In China they do it for Chile
So here's another verse
That's worse than the other verse
So waltz me around again Willy.

Meyer: *(Still in darkness)* Or you could try a dirty joke.

Mad: And there was the time that the young mother came out of the house and saw her little Sheldon playing with himself in the sandbox. "You mustn't do that" she told him. And Sheldon asked why and she told him that little boys who do that go blind. And Sheldon said "well can I do it until I need glasses?

Meyer: Sometimes they respond to social satire. But make it safe. If you get them riled, it'll be worse than poking a hornets' nest.

Mad: This is a science fiction piece. It begins out on some destitute stretch of land. There's no one around but an occasional couple messing around in the back seat of a car or some kids from a nearby farmhouse. Suddenly the peaceful darkness is shattered by the landing of a giant chicken from outer space. You can see it landing like this *(moves his hands appropriately)* with all the burning propellant flaming all around it. And finally it lands. And even though the guy in the car has to have his chick home by midnight, he stops what he's doing and watches the chicken. And then just as suddenly the chicken takes off again. But it leaves behind a giant egg. The small handful of witnesses run off to tell other people. No one believes them at first, but finally the sheriff goes out there, sees the egg, and ropes off the area and thousands of people come to see the egg and they throw stones at it and hiss and some even sneak past the guards and kick it. And the army shoots it, because everything out of the ordinary is considered hostile. But nothing affects it until finally they drop a nuclear bomb on it and the heat of the bomb causes the egg to start hatching and as we see the egg slowly cracking open in the distance other chickens begin to land and leave eggs. Finally the egg opens completely and reveals a huge Cadillac apartment building.

(Madeline wanders away from the audience and returns to Meyer and Rock Hudson. Their lights come up.)

Meyer: How was it?

Mad: It was marvellous. Difficult, but marvellous.

Rock: Weren't you scared?

Mad: Terrified.

Rock: Would you do it again?

Mad: I think so . . . yes, I'd do it again.

Rock: I want to do it.

Meyer: You can't.

Rock: Why not?

Meyer: You're not ready yet.

Rock: I'm as ready as anyone else here.

Mad: It's not an easy thing to do.

Rock: I know it's not, but I want to do it.

Meyer: If you do it, you'll ruin it for all of us.

Rock: I will not.

Meyer: How do you think it's going to look if three different people come out of here with dark glasses, cane and cup? They'd guess right off the bat what's going on here.

C44

Rock: How come you let him go?

Meyer: I got carried away.

Mad: What does that mean?

Meyer: That means that I can't let you out there again, either.

Rock: How you going to stop us?

Meyer: Take my word for it.

Mad: Your word? You're not going to stop me with your word.

Meyer: How quickly they forget. Don't you remember how you came here? You think I can't stop you? I don't have to stop you. *(He goes over and opens one of the doors. We hear a riot)*

(Rock is terrified. He clutches his ears and cringes. Madeline is struggling with himself)

Mad: It's not like that, it's not like that . . . it's not like that. . . . I saw it myself.

Meyer: You saw nothing. You saw with the eyes of a blind man. You saw what was in this room, not what was out there.

Mad: You're lying to me.

Meyer: My friend, I am not lying. . . . *(Kicks door shut. Sound dies)*

Rock: He's lying, he must be lying.

Mad: He is lying.

Rock: Show me that he's lying.

Meyer: You fool . . . the door is there. It's right there where it's always been.

Mad: You think I'm afraid to go out that door?

Meyer: You're petrified.

Rock: You said he's lying . . . show me he's lying.

Meyer: If you go out that door, you can never come back in here.

Mad: Bullshit.

Meyer: You'll see.

Mad: I can see without looking. . . . I have nothing to be afraid of. *(He follows his verbal momentum right out the door)*

Rock: He didn't take the glasses.

Meyer: I suppose you want to leave too?

Rock: You can't keep me here . . . he showed me you were just lying. You have no power over me.

Meyer: *(Laughs sadly and sits)* Yes, I have no power. . . . I never had any power. But I know that if you go out there, they'll make mincemeat out of you.

Rock: How do you know that?

Meyer: How? You've come to Meyer's room, that's how.

Rock: I don't remember coming here.

Meyer: No one ever does.

Rock: I only remember being here. . . . I don't want to be here any more. *(he sits)*

Meyer: You're just tired.

Rock: I'm not tired.

Meyer: We'll redecorate . . . we'll paint the walls; put in air conditioning. *(He eases glasses from Rock's hands)*

Rock: What else will you do?

Meyer: What else do you want me to do?

Rock: Take away all the walls. *(He moves away from Meyer)*

Meyer: I can't do that.

Rock: You're lying to me again . . . you're always lying to me.

Meyer: Please, just get some rest.

Rock: You're just trying to spoil everything for me. *(He gets up to leave)* I'm going out there to soar to the heavens, to hide behind a leaf . . . to become the world's greatest dive bomber ever . . . and you can't stop me.

Meyer: Please, listen to me. *(Grabs Rock by the arm)* Please!

Rock: Let go of me old man.

Meyer: You can't leave me.

Rock: I've got a gun.

Meyer: I'll do anything you ask.

Rock: Let go of me! *(Pulls out his gun)* I said let go of me! *(He shoots Meyer. It is a real gunshot)*

Rock: I told you and told you and told you to let go of me. You wouldn't listen.

The lights start to fade down to the level they were at when Rock first came into the room. He is scared. He notices gun in his hand — drops it. He finally makes a run for the door. It won't move. Madeline is pushing from the other side. The eye comes up to illuminate the two conflicting figures.

Rock: Let me out! Let me out!

Mad: Let me in! Let me in!

The End

Colour the Flesh the Colour of Dust

Michael Cook

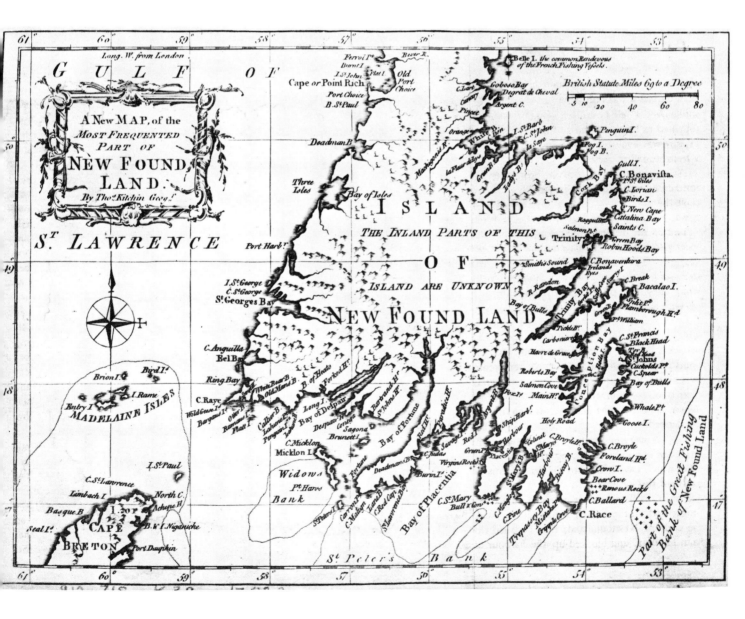

Newfoundland writer **Michael Cook** came to Canada a few years ago via Ireland and England, after a twelve-year stint in the British Army followed by a three-year course in Drama at Nottingham University College of Education. Since coming to Canada, Mr. Cook worked for three years as Drama Specialist with Memorial University's Extension Department, as well as a lecturer in English.

Mr. Cook has an impressive number of drama credits to his name. During the past five years he has written ten hour-long dramas for such CBC series as Midweek Theatre, CBC Stage, Summer Stage, etc., among them The Concubine, The Truck, A Walk in the Rain, A Seal at the Bottom of the Garden, Or The Wheel Broken and To Inhabit the Earth Is Not Enough.

He has also scripted and hosted a six-part Creative Drama series for television and, in collaboration with his wife, scripted and hosted a twenty-six-week series Our Man Friday, a weekly satirical review for the CBC.

Mr. Cook also lists among his current activities the Artistic Directorship of the Newfoundland Summer Festival of the Arts and a weekly column of dramatic criticism for the St. John's Evening Telegram.

We are very grateful for the assistance given us by the Librarians in the Baldwin Room of the Central Reference Library, Toronto, in helping find period Newfoundland illustrations. Map on page D1, courtesy Metropolitan Toronto Central Library. All other illustrations courtesy, the J. Ross Robertson Collection, Metropolitan Toronto Central Library.

D3

Cast of characters

Soldier 1
Soldier 2
Lieutenant Mannon
Marie, 'Woman' or 'Girl'
Old Woman 1
Old Woman 2
The Merchant Tupper
Boy
Mrs. McDonald
The Magistrate Neal
Three Urchins
The Spokesman
Captain Gross
Gert, a prostitute
Two Fishermen
Two French Officers
A Man and Woman in the crowd
English Officer
Extras in crowd scene; other soldiers

D4

Act One

Gibbet Hill, St. John's. The time Spring 1762. A dim, cold moonlight rises slowly on the cyclorama. Against it a gallows. From the gallows — a corpse. Two of the soldiers are huddled in fog, forestage — one drinks from a bottle, drains it, throws it across the stage in a movement of extreme violence. He staggers backstage and gives the corpse a shove. It swings — swings —

Soldier 1: Dance you bugger, dance.

Soldier 2: He was an Irishman. He liked to dance.

Soldier 1: He's dancing on air now *(Laughs)* Christ. It's cold —

Soldier 2: When is it anything else in this god forsaken hole — Here. Warm your gut *(Passes a bottle)*

A woman enters from left. Stands silently by the swinging corpse. She is shawled.

Soldier 2: Who's that?

Soldier 1: Rest easy. It's his whore.

Soldier 2: Which one?

Soldier 1: How should I know — one whore's the same as another. All look the same to me after twenty years.

Soldier 2: All feel the same, you mean — pst — someone's coming — Officer of the Watch.

Soldier 1: So what. He's as drunk as we are. He couldn't care less.

Officer of the Watch enters. He stands looking at the men. Reluctantly, they rise — do not salute — sullen — indifferent — a slight shrug indicates his acceptance of this indifference to discipline — he joins them.

Lieutenant: Well my lads, a cold night.

Soldier 1: The same as any other.

Soldier 2: Some colder than others.

Lieutenant: It'll be spring soon. Time for relief.

Soldier 1: Relief. *(Spits)* How many years — Sir *(it is exaggerated)* have you been saying that to us.

Lieutenant: Quite a few, I suppose — yes. Quite a few.

Soldier 2: Be a few extra kids born of a miraculous conception by the now.

D5

Soldier 1: That's something His Majesty doesn't take into account when he considers a pension.

Lieutenant: Now lads, that's mutinous talk.

Soldier 1: Nothing mutinous about the truth, Sir, is there? *(Produces bottle)* Care for a swallow?

Lieutenant: Well — yes. Why not — *(He squats. The soldiers resume their sitting positions)* Who is that woman?

Soldier 2: His whore, Sir.

Lieutenant: Faithful. Some of these creatures — you'd think —

Soldier 1: You'd think, Sir, wouldn't you that a legal married wife, no matter how long you were away serving your country, could behave a little like that. Is that what you were thinking?

Lieutenant: Yes. I suppose I was. *(Rises suddenly)* God. How I hate this country.

Soldier 2: She would have been young when you left.

Lieutenant: Twenty-two.

Soldier 2: I'll bet she was a looker too, eh. *(Passes bottle)* Why I remember when you got here; when was that, Ben?

Soldier 1: Seven — or was it eight years ago.

Soldier 2: Spit and polish. Well set up. Why — all the lads said — the Lieutenant — he won't tolerate any slacking, they said. He'll prove a right bastard — if you'll forgive the word, Sir.

Soldier 1: Well set up too. Sat a horse like a ramrod. No belly to speak of.

Lieutenant: For God's sake.

Soldier 1: No offence, Sir. Happens to us all, see. I mean — we know that our lives and yours run on two different levels so to speak — but when it comes to loving and hating, and owing, and breeding bastards while we're away, well — there's not too much to separate us, is there — I

mean — a woman now — she can be presented in court in the afternoon and be laid down with a galley boy at night if she's a mind. We haven't got that kind of — freedom, you might say.

Lieutenant: She was young — it's a long time.

Soldier 2: We was all young — That's the trouble — But we'll die here. Among the fogs and the stink of fish and the curses of the damned Irish — we've been here twenty years, Sir — or is it twenty-one?

A loud wail from the woman.

Soldier 1: Shut your mouth, you whore, or I'll —

Lieutenant: That's enough. *(An attempt at authority)* She's a woman. We haven't taken leave of our senses to the extent we'll assault a woman — God forbid.

Soldier 2: I tell you — you can't trust any of 'em. They say the Pope sent twenty here with the French disease. To get rid of us.

Soldier 1: Aye. And there was young Jim Clusky stabbed as he was athwart one.

Soldier 2: They say they're in the pay of the French. That the French are coming. Any day now. The houses are full of it.

Soldier 1: It's rumoured that the Captain caught the magistrate reading — a French book. Is that true, Sir?

Lieutenant: Who knows what's true and what isn't true.

Soldier 1: But the French are coming.

Lieutenant: That's what they say.

Soldier 2: What'll we do?

Lieutenant: Fight, of course. It's our duty.

Soldier 2: Fight! With what? With what, Sir? *(Rising. Agitated)* Not a gun in order. All rusty. Poking their rusty snouts over the narrows as useless as the King's codpiece.

A wail from the woman.

Soldier 1: I told ye to shut up. *(Runs across to her — smacks her across the head. She falls — makes no sound)*

Soldier 2: I tell ye something, Sir. If they come in, we go out.

Lieutenant: *(Tired)* That's mutiny again. We'll double the grog ration and you'll fight like heroes.

Soldier 2: But I'm not a hero. I never was a hero. And the grog ration been doubled every night for twenty years. You'll have to do better than that.

Lieutenant: He fought. *(Nodding towards the corpse)*

Soldier 1: Oh yes. He got mixed up in a brawl and killed a mate of mine. He fought. But he hates you, see. He hates us. But I don't hate him. Not really. I just hate this place. And you don't fight for something you hate. You fight against it — Right. Right. *(Holds bottle to Lieutenant)*

Lieutenant: *(Rises slowly. Refuses bottle)* I'll be leaving now. It'll soon be dawn — Cut him down at daybreak.

Suddenly, clear — like a bell — the woman.

Marie: May I have him, please?

Soldier 2: Fer Christ's sake. Can you hear her? Look at us, Sir. Look at us. Is he Jesus Christ? Are we the Romans? Is she Mary?

Marie: Please let me have him. He's nothing to you now.

Lieutenant: Cut him down.

Soldier 1: But —

Lieutenant: *(Authority returned)* Cut him down —

(They go backstage and cut the corpse down. The woman sinks down, cradling the corpse in her arms — the light is growing all the time — the mist rolls)

Lieutenant: Get to your beds. There's nothing to guard against anymore. Get to your beds. *(The Soldiers leave — He walks across to the woman)* I'm sorry. *(No reaction)* I'm sorry. It's just the way things are. We don't ask for them to be that way. *(No reaction)* He did kill someone. *(No reaction)* And we are the law. *(The woman laughs. High-pitched hysterical laughter)* Yes — I agree with you. It is funny. Very funny. *(Exits right)*

SONG OF THE WOMAN

I loved your brown body
I loved your brown hands
but look now at the neck of you . . .
bent like a broken bird's . . .

I sold my body
as woman must
sure what's a body
it's only dust
but I gave it you
and what's the gain
the weight of a corpse
an ounce of pain

I sold my body
rich and warm
to poor fishy creatures
fleeing the storm
But to you I gave,
As give I must
to colour the flesh
the colour of dust

Ach, stupid wild creature. What will I do with you now? Wrap you in canvas and drop you into the dark sea. Look at that hand that once played with my breast as tender as a child playing with a handful of earth. Will I like it if I put it in my mouth? *(Laughs)* You were nothing to anyone but me and your mother. Now you're dead. And she's dead. And there's only me left. What shall I do with you —

Swing by the neck,
hang by the toes
from birth to death
the swinging goes
But it's a fool
Who doesn't trust
to give himself
because he must . . .

D8

D9

D10

Two old women enter.

Woman 1: Marie. Marie. Bring him down now. Bring him down. They're all waiting.

Marie: All.

Woman 1: His friends — they're all waiting.

Marie: He had no friends.

Woman 1: Sure now he's dead, he's got a thousand. They're warming the grog for the wake. Come.

Woman 2: We must hurry. They say the French are coming.

Marie: And what's that to me? And what's that to him?

Woman 1: You know these Frenchmen, my dear. If they get here before we've done him properly, they'll take all the liquor.

Woman 2: And before you've done with one grief, they'll be slipping in another — You take the head.

Woman 1: And I'll take the legs.

Woman 2: And to show a proper respect, Marie — you can walk by the middle — Sure *(Bending down to feel the dead man's parts)* They're worth mourning. *(The three exit — the light full)*

End of Scene One

Scene Two ⸻⸻⸻⸻

On cyclorama — projection of Signal Hill silhouette.

Lights on platform stage right — extends into auditorium. It's a mess of casks, nets, twine; filthy — old chair and desk. It is the office of the Merchant. An oily, smooth, villainous, gratuitous man who would rob his grandmother if she was blind, paralysed and afflicted with syphilis. He is stock-taking, assisted by a boy.

Merchant: Flour — seventy-five barrels — mph — that's not enough to go round them all. This stupid war and the blockade will ruin us all — boy — where's the sawdust?

Boy: Sawdust, Sir?

Merchant: *(Mimicking)* Sawdust, sawdust — ach, when you were born, the good God left your brains in heaven. *(Fetching him a cuff)* The sawdust, you snot-faced brat.

Boy: Yes, Sir, I'll find it, Sir. *(Scrabbles frantically around the barrels and the mess — comes up with a sack of sawdust as big as himself)* There it is, Sir — The bag's full of it, Sir.

Merchant: What do you expect it to be. Empty of it. Now, take four scoops from each flour barrel and mix in four scoops of sawdust — get to it.

Boy: Yes, Sir. Does sawdust make good bread, Sir.

Merchant: It makes more flour that's what it does, which makes more bread, yes. *(Chuckles)* You could say that sawdust makes good bread.

A woman enters timidly.

Merchant: The drunken swine of soldiers couldn't tell the difference anyway. And the fishermen are too stupid to notice. *(Notices woman)* Mrs. McDonald. What can I do for you today?

Mrs. McDonald: I wonder, Sir, if you could let us have a bag of flour — I know we're down for a good deal.

Merchant scuttles across to ledger.

Merchant: McDonald — three flour, one sack sugar, twine, molasses — is he working yet, Mrs. McDonald?

Mrs. McDonald: It's his hand, Sir — you know, try as he can, he can't bend his fingers since that time in the ice storm.

Merchant: These are hard times, Mrs. McDonald. Why, there's not been a ship in here for six weeks since all that scare about the French — I've hardly enough to feed meself.

Mrs. McDonald: It's not for me, Sir. It's the children, you see — There's Susan now.

Merchant: How old is Susan, Mrs. McDonald.

Mrs. McDonald: Twelve, Sir; coming on thirteen.

Merchant: She'll soon be looking at the young fellers who come in during the summer.

Mrs. McDonald: God forbid, Sir. A life like that.

Merchant: Well — it's the world's oldest profession, Mrs. McDonald, if not the most respectable. And it does mean a bit of money coming into the house. If your man doesn't —

Mrs. McDonald: He'll be alright soon, Sir. I knows. There's an Irish woman says she can cure him with the juice of the dogberry — a few ounces of flour is all.

Merchant: I don't think so, Mrs. McDonald — It wouldn't be right now, for me to give you something and you worrying about whether you'd ever pay it back. I know you for an honest woman. That's rare. Very rare. But it's a terrible thing in these times to have a working conscience, Mrs. McDonald; and I'm afraid yours will drive you to the grave.

Mrs. McDonald: Just half a bag, Sir. Half a bag then — it's the youngest, ye see, Sir. Cries all the time — and I can't look after him properly — having to go out to chop the wood, ye see; and catch a bit of flat fish in the harbour — since —

Merchant: Well — Come back when your man's working, Mrs. McDonald.

Mrs. McDonald: Cries all the time, Sir. It's pitiful. And coughs — If only you could hear him.

Merchant: Where's your husband's boat, Mrs. McDonald — and his gear.

Mrs. McDonald: Oh! It's well cared for, Sir. It's out of the water — and the gear is all stowed in a shed at the back of the house.

Merchant: I'll tell you what I'll do. Now — you already owe me (To ledger) twenty-three pounds fourteen shillings and seven pence three farthings. I'll give you a sack of flour (The boy all the time has been exchanging flour for sawdust) and you in return will sign this note — Can you read?

Mrs. McDonald: No, Sir.

Merchant: Well — make your mark then (Busies himself writing) And it says — let me see — I agree that my husband's boat and fishing gear being worth twenty-four pounds —

Mrs. McDonald: Oh! It's much more than that, Sir.

Merchant: Just a technicality, Mrs. McDonald, to let me give you the flour — this being the amount I owe James Tupper, Merchant of Bristol and St. John's will be forfeit if this debt is not paid in full in cash or kind within thirty days — There.

Mrs. McDonald: Thirty days — A month, ye mean.

Merchant: A day more or less makes no difference, you see. It just helps me to get more flour, ye see. Satisfies the people to whom I owe money. Believe me, Mrs. McDonald — I have to pay cash for everything. In advance. Now, I'm sure he'll be working soon — just a thumbprint there — Boy! Get Mrs. McDonald a bag of flour — one of those you've been making up this morning — that's it.

Mrs. McDonald: Ye're sure it's alright, Sir — about the flour then.

Merchant: Of course, Mrs. McDonald — There — Boy — help Mrs. McDonald to get her flour on to a cart — and hurry back in here — ye.

Boy: Yes, Sir — (Mrs. McDonald and boy exit)

Merchant: He'll never work. Frostbite. Die most probably — Gangrene — That Susan — pretty young thing — she'll do well before the pox gets her — must keep her in mind —

(Magistrate Neal enters. He looks like an expen-

sive cadaver — he is carrying a handful of flour/ sawdust — Tupper, busy about his books again doesn't observe his coming. The Magistrate spills the flour very slowly across the ledger)

Merchant: Oh, Magistrate — I didn't hear you coming.

Magistrate: Don't ever sell me sawdust, Tupper — or I'll hang you.

Merchant: Now would I — where did you get that.

Magistrate: Not only have you given her sawdust, but there's a hole in the sack. The sack's rotten.

Merchant: It's the rats — everywhere they are. These stupid people littering the street with excrement, offal.

Magistrate: You don't have to excuse yourself to me, Tupper. I know you. And I suppose — in your own warped way, you know me. *(He dusts off a cask and sits)* Doesn't a man get a drink here anymore? Are times that hard.

Merchant: Of course, Magistrate, of course. *(Finds a corner containing a cask — breaks open a bottle)* A particularly good port *(Chuckles)* the soldiers stole the port from the officers in return for a little rum.

Magistrate: *(Bleak)* Watered, of course.

Merchant: *(Slyly)* Of course. It's for their benefit. In the long run. *(Pours) (Magistrate drinks)*

Magistrate: *(Suddenly)* The French have landed at Bay Bulls.

Merchant: What — What — Good God — They'll steal.

Magistrate: They won't steal anything, Tupper. That's what I wanted to see you about. We've got to surrender the city.

Merchant: But the garrison.

Magistrate: The garrison! A bunch of dissolute and debauched idiots who burst into tears at the mention of home — Whatever courage they had has been drowned in self-pity years ago.

Merchant: Captain Gross is —

Magistrate: Captain Gross is a middle-aged failure. The fortifications are in disrepair. The men mutinous and undisciplined. No — There's only the marine lieutenant — but he's junior in rank — But there's a chance they might do something stupid enough to annoy the French — And you know what that would mean, Tupper.

Merchant: Fire!

Magistrate: Fire. And the soldiers given licence to run wild — How many Irishmen do you have on your books, Tupper.

Merchant: Oh, a few; quite a few.

Magistrate: They'd like to burn those books I suspect. It is good port. *(Merchant hurries to refill)* As I see it, fight or no fight, the French will capture the city. News of it will reach the slow-thinking clods of the admiralty in Halifax in a week or so; and six weeks later, it will reach England. An expedition will be mounted and within six months, the English will re-take the city. We have to ensure, Tupper, that we are here to witness the defeat and are also here to witness the victory — We must encourage the British to capitulate. We must welcome the French with open arms and agree to their every term. The Irish have joined them, Tupper — as every landlord in Bay Bulls can testify — if they're alive.

Merchant: What should we do — what do you want me to do — anything — of course.

Magistrate: Get a petition at once, signed by every merchant in the city. Plead poverty, ignorance, fear, loss of life. Anything. Point out that if burning takes place, there'd be no possibility of placating the French with provisions. It's our trump card. In my turn, I've already sent an envoy to the French — I'll guarantee the oath of allegiance to the French King of every citizen of consequence. I'll guarantee their provisioning, under fair trade terms. That means they'll buy your stock instead of looting it, Tupper — but I'd dispense with sawdust for a week or two — If

Quidi Vidi Lake near St. John's, Newfoundland

D14

we don't do that, the rabble Irish will smash and burn and steal anyway — This way, we'll ensure law, order, and the continuance of trade — trade — wars may come and wars may go, Tupper — but trade —

Merchant: The backbone of empire.

Magistrate: And who cares which one — eh? Now — I have a ship arriving from the Indies within a few days. If all works as planned, there should be no obstruction. You may dispose of the stock for me in accordance with our usual terms — Of course *(Sound of a rabble and gunfire — Increasing)* The news has arrived at last. Lock and bolt your door, Tupper. *(Turns, turns back)* By the way, didn't I see you at the hanging last night?

Merchant: Black devil that he was. I'd have substituted for Jack Ketch myself — I couldn't understand.

Magistrate: Why I didn't hang him when he robbed your store? Because I, in turn, would have been strung up by the mob, Tupper. Besides, it was obvious that he'd kill a soldier one day — the decision wasn't ours then — But I must say — I almost admired him when I saw him giving your flour away.

Merchant: Admired him. Why, the man was a cheap crook. Threatening to kill me. Throwing my stock to the people.

Magistrate: These Catholics, Tupper — take their religion very seriously at times. Particularly when they're drunk — Get working now — There isn't much time.

Merchant: At once, Magistrate. At once. *(The boy enters, crosses the Merchant. He is dishevelled and breathless)* Where the hell have you been?

Boy: It was the flour, Sir, spilling all over the road it was. And someone came to help Mrs. McDonald get it all up and they found the sawdust in it. And they were going to throw me in the harbour, Sir — begging your pardon, Sir.

Magistrate: *(In doorway)* Why didn't they, boy?

Boy: Because I said that Mr. Tupper only put the best sawdust in, Sir. And it was to get a fine crust on it — And they began to argue about whether sawdust made a good crust or not and when they began to fight, I slipped away.

Magistrate: *(Laughing faintly)* Get to work on the petition, Tupper. Quickly. They're arguing about the crust now, but wait until they put their teeth into it. *(Exits)*

Merchant: *(A pause. He looking at boy. Boy looking at him)* My God. The flour. Boy — get the sawdust out of the flour.

Boy: How do I do that, Sir — it's all mixed.

Merchant: Sift it all, you blockhead — sift it all out — I'll be ruined else. The French have dainty manners I'm told. Get it out. I've got to go out now. Have it done by the time I get back. If it takes you all night. *(Exits hurriedly. The boy takes stock — goes to doorway — checks to make sure the coast is clear — goes back to a flour barrel, tips it out onto the floor — there's a soft knock — an urchin pokes his head round the door — followed by another and another — boy motions them in. They all carry shawls — without a sound they begin to scrape the flour into the shawls as crossfade — cyc lights only — blue. Small figures in black scurrying to and fro with bags, sacks, parcels.*

THE BALLAD OF MAKING ENDS MEET

Me mam's in the whorehouse,
Fathers on the rum
I've got to steal
from friend and foe
for death is on the run
Young Jimmy died of fever
And Alice of the pox
We threw 'em into Dead Man's Pond
It's cheaper than a box
And who's to care about the dead
and who's to share a tear
we're crying for the price of bread
and not the price of fear
On Sunday all the church bells ring
But they can ring forever
For the god the merchants worship
sent Jimmy of his fever,
And the God of the great magistrate
runs whimpering at his toes
For we know he screwed Alice
And God knows what she knows . . .
Steal and lie and murder
we learn that in the crib
know that the cord that gave us life
is the rope that swings from the jib
and the book that tallies what we owe
to merchant and to God
is written by the merchant
and don't you think that odd
that Heaven is a place of trade
and Hell a place of paupers
so every whimpering kid that's here
is a christ in worn diapers
who'll hang between two other thieves
if he lives that long that is . . .

Blackout.

A mob. Rising from the audience — from the wings — drunken, hirsute, dissolute, Irish. Improvised sentences. Shouts. Howls. Kill the English. Burn the Garrison. The Garrison in outline on the cyc. On platform overlooking — two soldiers. Silent sentinels. Spokesman rises — mounts platform.

Spokesman: Alright lads. The French will be here by dawn. *(Cheers and shouts)* The question is — do we wait for them?

From The Crowd: No. Let's burn the bastards out. Hang them. *(Above the crowd noise, the voice of the Lieutenant — very clear)*

Lieutenant: The first man to move is dead. *(A silence — he repeats)* The first man to move is dead.

A Voice From The Crowd: He's bluffing.

And Another: They've lost and they know it.

And Another: There's a hundred casks of rum in there, boys.

And Another: And flour.

And Another: And sugar and tea.

Another: Who cares about tea.

Laughter

Another Voice: They're all drunk anyway — couldn't shoot if their breeches were about their knees and the women begging.

Laughter. Crowd noise picking up again. Mob courage.

Remember Sean.

Picked Up and Echoed.

Yes — remember Sean — Remember Sean — defended himself — swinging.

Cries getting more vociferous — improvisation — spokesman.

Spokesman: Lads — I don't think it matter whether we have a go at them to-night or not.

A Murmur

The French will get them anyway.

Cheers — protests.

And if we play our cards right, we'll get what's left — to do what we like with.

Murmur of Approval.

D16

No chance of a bullet or two — just a length of rope, boys and that bastard there and others like him — all the time of the day to swing like Sean.

A Voice From the Crowd: And the merchants.

And Another Voice: And the Magistrate.

Spokesman: We can trust the French. Already, our fellers are with them and they've let them burn out Bay Bulls.

Loud Cheers: The English are running anywhere — to Halifax — back to England — in every scallop they can find. *(More Cheers)* The French will be with us — We'll meet them as they enter — They'll give us the freedom of the city.

A Voice: I owe my life to the devil Gaden.

A Voice: She cried all night, my woman, overdue now by a month and too weak to contract at all.

Spokesman: Just wait till tomorrow. We'll meet them.

A Voice: Will they fight.

Spokesman: The English. The fight left them twenty years ago. All they can bully is women and children.

Lieutenant: *(Above all)* — Come up here. *(A silence)* Come up here — You want to fight. Come up here. *(Uneasy silence)*

Spokesman: Come down here. If you want to fight, meet me on my own ground, you red and white pigeon you — Come down here.

Lieutenant: Alright. I'll come down.

Spokesman: No musket.

The Crowd: No musket.

1st Soldier: You're out of your bloody mind.

2nd Soldier: So what's it matter. We're all dead tomorrow anyway.

1st Soldier: Not likely. We'll surrender. Prisoners of War. Be exchanged for Frenchies, that's what. We'll get relieved at last, by the French. My God.

Lieutenant: Cover me.

1st Soldier: Now don't be foolish, Sir — Cover's not what you want. It's an army.

2nd Soldier: If you don't mind Sir, we'll just watch. *(Lieutenant disappears — emerges — walks through crowd to spokesman)*

Lieutenant: I'm here.

Spokesman: I can see that. *(Laughter)*

Lieutenant: Swords?

Spokesman: No. No, you don't catch me with that.

Lieutenant: Fists then. Clubs.

Crowd: Hang him — A life for a life — Let's run him to the Hill. *(They surge forward)*

Lieutenant: I came down here to face you with honour.

Crowd: Honour? Whats honour?

A Voice: It's like virginity, and that's no bloody use.

Spokesman: Well, Sir, honour's a fine word with gentlemen; but with us, ye see, it doesn't hold too much water. You need time and money to uphold honour. And you need to think of yourself as being someone with a place in life, as having a station, you see. But us now — we're scum. I think ye'd call us that now, wouldn't ye?

Lieutenant: I think I might have done. I'm not too sure.

Spokesman: Oh, don't just think it, Sir. That's what we are. It's your word for us and ye've made us that, ye see. And ye want me to act with honour in a hand-to-hand combat — because that's the way you gentlemen proceed with your quarrels. But we, Sir — we —

Lieutenant: Yes. I want to know about you.

Spokesman: Well, Sir, we proceed with the pain and the knowledge and the denial of our responsibilities — kids starving, women whoring with your soldiers for a penny or two, merchants selling us gear against not this year's fish but the next and the next — we don't have no honour, Sir. And what we need every now and again is a circus — a good hanging perhaps — one of yours instead of ours — or a good fight when the odds is with us.

Voice: "I'll lay 10-1 the Lieut loses" *(Voice)* and I'll lay anyone for free *(Laughter)*

Spokesman: Humour we have in plenty, Sir — The thing that you lack.

Crowd: Take him — Give him here. *(A man leaps onto the platform with a length of rope)*

Spokesman: Ye see, Sir — give us a good laugh every now and again — a good drunk — and ye can do what ye like with us — we're like cattle — No leaders, ye see — but lot's of humour. And ye — well, ye've lot's of leaders but no humour — It'll be the death of ye — OK, lads.

A surge from the crowd — the Lieutenant is pinioned — the rope put about his neck — above — the two soldiers look on impassively — one spits — they turn their backs — the woman enters — looks silently — business about the stage with the Lieutenant dragged about like a dog — the rope as collar — kicking and laughter — suddenly the woman.

Woman: Wait *(And again)* Wait.

Spokesman: Sean's widow — what do you want with us.

Woman: I want that man. *(A silence)*

Spokesman: Sean's woman. And you want an Englishman — An officer — The one who hung him.

Woman: I want him.

Spokesman: But why, woman? Why?

Woman: Because you do. Because he is the law. You are, aren't you. *(The Lieutenant bedraggled, bloody, bruised, roped)* Tell me again. *(She walks to him)* You are the law.

Lieutenant: I represent law.

Woman: No. No, that's not why I want you. You are the law — you said.

Lieutenant: *(Angered)* Alright. I am the law.

Woman: And as the law you hung Sean.

Lieutenant: I hung him.

Woman: Give him to me.

Spokesman: But —

Woman: Give him to me — He's mine. He killed my flesh. What was Sean to you?

Spokesman: He spoke for all of us. *(Crowd. Assent. Improvisation)* He led us. He spoke for us, etc.

Woman: But what did you do for him. When the fight came — and the soldiers came to fetch him — you drank more ale and you cried more tears and you made a hero of the fool and you didn't lift a finger — Jesus Christ, isn't that Ireland all over — To make heroes of fools and every fool a hero — Give me the Lieutenant — He's mine. He owes me.

Crowd Muttering: She's right. He owes her — She's best to take care of him — The French will if she doesn't, etc.

Spokesman: He's not run as much to seed as the rest. Perhaps it's him you fancy next, in your warm nest, to breed another generation of martyrs.

Woman: Who knows.

Spokesman: Come on, lads. Let's leave the whore with a new candidate for the gallows — by the time the French have done with him *(Laughter — coarse words, etc. Crowd slowly disperse — the stage is emptied except for the Lieutenant on his knees, neck roped, the woman holding the rope — the silhouettes of the two soldiers on the battlements — lights flare up on the cyclorama — sound of distant gunfire — During the following the woman helps the Lieutenant free of his ropes — but keeps one coil — like a lead. There is a strange almost fatal attraction between them. Its the physical attraction occasioned by bloodshed, danger. Hate. It was seen — a flash only — during their first meeting. Now it grows — unreasoning — urgent)*

Woman: They're getting closer.

Lieutenant: Why did you do that?

Woman: I want to kill you.

Lieutenant: I wouldn't be able to stop you.

Woman: Of course not. I'm a woman. Something to do with honour. My people don't value it too highly.

Lieutenant: But you do.

Woman: Not honour. Dignity. I can't bear to see us — women and children and the men losing their dignity. It's nothing to do with being without — of being poor. It's a failure of spirit — I resented you to-night. You didn't lose yours.

Lieutenant: I felt as if I had.

Woman: No. We couldn't do that to you. And it wouldn't have mattered if you were a peasant or an officer. You have been gifted with a sense of yourself that nothing can break — Sean had that — He even swung like that — even the husk of the man swung with dignity — such a wild man to do a thing like that.

Lieutenant: Perhaps it's because I didn't resent them.

Woman: Perhaps. You're in danger of losing your dignity now — *(Tugs the rope)* I feel like a woman on the town with a toy dog.

Lieutenant: I'm sorry.

Woman: You don't have to be sorry for anything — Except being. I can take anything in this environment except humanity. It's the one thing that's lacking. And you showed it. You've no excuse *(Suddenly cries)* It's not possible to live very long once you accept that.

Lieutenant: *(Gets up)* It's not a real situation. You know that. We are stranded on some island at the edge of time. There's the sea. And the fog. And occasional sunshine. But nothing grows without the consent of nature. We're captive in a peculiar zoo — It's life and death for the creatures of the island and if we choose to live on it, we can't gentle it in any way — impose an order or a universal design upon it. It's stronger than all of us. Breaks down our individuality. Our race. Our loyalties. Ultimately, we respond to the ferocity of the sea. And the impermanence of life. It's very disturbing. Very beautiful, very primitive, very disturbing.

Woman: It makes us strong and weak at once. Childish and innocent and terribly cruel and stupid at once.

Lieutenant: Why did I want you — watching you by the corpse.

Woman: Why did I want you — watching you who had hung the man.

Lieutenant: I didn't hang him because I wanted you.

Woman: But you would have anyway — if you had.

Lieutenant: Perhaps you're right.

Woman: That's the nature of the place.

Lieutenant: That's the nature.

Woman: I might hang you one day.

Lieutenant: You might.

Woman: But now — I have a rope around you — and you must go where I will you to go.

Lieutenant: Yes.

Woman: Until your sense of duty calls. *(More red flares on cyc)*

D20

They exit.

Gunfire. Sporadic. Following interspersed with cheering of a mob. Cyclorama — outline of the Fort — platform representing Captain's Office. A soldier on guard outside the door. Captain Gross is a fat — dissolute red-faced man in his late forties. He is tired — prematurely aged — as lights rise, he is standing with his back to the audience, looking in the direction of the cyc. The Lieutenant enters.

Lieutenant: Captain Gross. Captain Gross.

Captain: *(Turns)* Ah, Lieutenant — I sent for you.

Lieutenant: I tried to see you yesterday, Sir. Three times.

Captain: Yes. I was busy. Very busy. Dispatches to England and Halifax.

Lieutenant: We have to fight, Sir. And the men are idle. The fortifications.

Captain: What about the fortifications. Do you think the fortifications repaired or broken are going to stop the Frenchmen? They've hundreds of men. We're — we're —

Lieutenant: Eighty-six, Sir. And the Hill.

Captain: Lieutenant. Are you going to be happy to see women and children murdered?

Lieutenant: I'm never happy, Sir, to see anyone murdered.

Captain: What do you think will happen if we resist? Eh. I'll tell you. They'll fire the town and treat every civilian as an enemy. You might be very comfortably off behind these bulwarks, Lieutenant; and confident that you've done and will continue to do your duty until death strips you from your uniform; but those people.

Lieutenant: Most of them will join the French anyway, Sir. They'll be unharmed — We have a duty.

Captain: I have a duty, Lieutenant. I have a duty. And it is not to you. And don't come any

grandiose ideas about having a duty to yourself. Honour is an expensive luxury, reserved for naval battles and campaigns mounted for Imperial gain. This stinking fishing village —

Lieutenant: Is one of the most important trading posts of the empire, Sir. If you refuse to fight, Sir — I feel it my duty to send a separate report.

Captain: Your duty, your duty. How many years have you been here, Lieutenant?

Lieutenant: Seven.

Captain: Seven. I've been here for twenty-three years, Lieutenant. I left a wife and baby in Liverpool twenty-three years ago. Haven't heard from either in ten.

Lieutenant: I understand, Sir — the hardships.

Captain: No, you don't Lieutenant. Do you think I wasn't like you? Spit and polish. Serve King and Country. Promote peaceful trade. Encourage harmony and goodwill and kill a few savages every now and again — Maintain the Law — The Law — the great Imperial pocket book. With justice and fairness and humanity. Thou shalt not steal. Thou shalt not covet his Majesty's goods. Thou shalt not kill his Majesty's servants with impunity. Look at it — *(Strides to edge of rostra and looks out at audience)* Look at it. Fish guts and excrement and stinking hovels and lice and vermin and the pox — and a rabble of Irishmen murdering themselves and anyone who moves in their sleep. *(A woman in disarray dodges past the sentry and throws herself at the Captain — the sentry comes in after her)*

Sentry: Sir — she pushed past.

Gert: You cheap jack. You trumped up turkey cock — what's this? What's — *(Thrusts out her hand)*

Captain: *(Trying to maintain some decorum)* It's your money, woman — I left it for you — Now be off.

Gert: This pittance. It won't even buy a bottle of rum so that I can forget what I had to do for you.

Captain: Get her out of here.

Gert: I'll tell them all. All your fine lads out there — Even drunk, they're better men than you are — crying and whimpering.

Captain: *(Shouting)* For God's sake, get her out.

Sentry: *(Something of a grin on his face)* Come on, Gert. For Chrissakes, come on. Get down to the guardhouse and they'll give you a drop of rum to warm you on your way.

Gert: Filth. Scum — I hope they hang you — I hope they hang —

Captain: I'm sorry *(A pause)* I said I'm sorry *(Lieutenant maintains silence — startingly clear)* I see icebergs in my sleep. All the time.

Lieutenant: Sir. Let me organize the men. I know there's little time, but some earthworks — musket drills — they'll fight if they have to, I know. And they'll —

Captain: They'd kill you first, Lieutenant.

Lieutenant: At your instructions. *(The two men stare at each other. The Captain lowers his eyes — fumbles in his desk for a bottle — drinks — offers it to the Lieutenant who refuses — sound of laughter — the woman's laughter — then the voice of the sentry)* Go on up — the pair of ye — I'm busy right now, as you can see. And make my apologies *(More laughter)*

Murmuring getting louder as the Magistrate and the Merchant enter — the Merchant carries a scroll.

Magistrate: Captain Gross — How nice to see you *(Sniffs delicately)* Quite a nip in the air this morning.

Captain: I hadn't noticed.

Magistrate: Tupper here has something to show you, Sir — The townspeople are getting worried — The French are very close now.

Merchant: They say they've burnt and looted right up the shore — Not a merchant's property left standing — It's outrageous — nothing is sacred it seems — even to men of honour.

Magistrate: The people, Sir, would beg you to consider very carefully your plans for the defence of the town — If you can guarantee their safety — take them all inside the fortifications, perhaps.

Captain: Mr. Nye — You know damn well I can't accommodate anymore than two hundred within these fortifications at least. And then, I couldn't guarantee their safety. A cannonball —

Magistrate: I think, Sir, that within the terms and conditions of your duty as laid down — and as communicated to me — his Majesty's loyal servant who has tried hard these past years, God knows — to keep a semblance of order in conditions of extreme unrest — an unrest generated in part — by the actions of your soldiers.

Captain: I don't need these words, Magistrate.

Magistrate: What do you need, Captain?

Captain: Men. Arms. News of relief from Halifax.

Merchant: I have a petition here, Sir — signed by the chartered citizens of this town — respectable God-fearing men.

Lieutenant: Cowards.

Captain: That will do, Lieutenant. I am in command here.

Magistrate: The Lieutenant perhaps is anxious for the safety of the Irish girl — now that she has turned her back upon her own.

Captain: *(Goes to Lieutenant)* You too. You too — It's your conscience then and not our own impossible position that's exciting you *(Strides back to Merchant — takes petition — reads)*

"As it has been rumoured that Lieutenant Mannon intends to burn the shipping in the harbour before it falls into enemy hands, and that his Majesty's Officers consider defending the town against impossible odds, the principal Inhabitants and Merchants beg and request Captain Gross to request of him that he not burn the

D24

ships but, if he must take action, run them ashore and that if possible, he parley with the enemy and reach an honourable compromise for we are assured that our houses and effects will be burnt if such actions are taken; and, therefore, we humbly petition and beg that you will comply with our request.

Signed — Michael Gill — James Escott — Robert Farnell — James Summers — James Tupper — etc. *(There is a growing disturbance outside — sounds of a crowd — two men enter, dishevelled — armed to the teeth — fishermen.)*

Captain: What's going on — where's the guard?

1st Fisherman: You might well ask at a time like this. But he's passing a wench and a bottle hand to hand in the guardhouse — But that's not our business — Are you in charge, Sir.

Captain: I'm Captain Gross, yes.

1st Fisherman: I've four hundred and fifty men, Sir. We've roused them between here and Portugal Cove to put at your disposal against the French devils, and on behalf of his Majesty the King. *(He speaks with touching dignity)*

Lieutenant: Four hundred and fifty — Why, man, that's miraculous — And you are a miracle. *(He wrings his hand — the fisherman is embarrassed — the Merchant and the Magistrate go off to confer in a corner — the Captain looks at the petition in his hand — nervous — sweating — goes back to his desk under pretence of locking away the petition — pours himself a glass — plays for time)*

Captain: You must have come hard across country, Sir. A drink.

1st Fisherman: No thankee, Sir — I don't expect there'll be time for that — We heard news that the French are past Petty Harbour some time gone. *(The Magistrate and the Merchant go to Captain — much whispering)*

Lieutenant: For God's sake, Gentlemen. This is what we have been asking for. With these men and what we have — why —

Captain: With these men — God knows I appre-

ciate their help and would accept it on behalf of his Majesty — except — except — except that they are not trained soldiers, Sir — they don't know one end of a cannon from the other — and if they were to crack the slaughter would be abominable — I cannot take the responsibility — I'm sorry, Sir — Tell your people to go back to their homes.

1st Fisherman: *(Disbelief)* Did I hear you aright, Sir?

Captain: I thank you — But the offer's come a little too late — I ask you to go back to your homes — and keep the peace.

1st Fisherman: Keep the peace, is it. And what do you think, Sir, will happen to those homes. To our stocks and stores. Our fish flakes. Our boats and gear. When they ask us to take the oath of loyalty to the damn French papist, and we say No — our loyalty is to the King of England — what then, Sir — what protection then shall we have — scattered about the land with our wives and bairns. And yourself, Sir — where will you be?

Magistrate: We shall extract an honourable promise from them — there will be no more looting and burning — we don't want anymore bloodshed — not of you and yours.

1st Fisherman: Nor of yours, I'll be bound. I'll take my leave, Sir — I wouldn't have believed my ears, if I hadn't heard it coming from an officer of the Crown. And believe me — some others will have trouble believing it too. But I'll do my best to drive the point home. *(They leave in anger)*

Captain: Well, gentlemen. It is settled. I would like your presence here when they call to parley — We will settle for as generous and honourable terms as we can get. *(The Lieutenant hurls himself out of the room)*

Merchant: He's young — Sir — hot-headed.

Magistrate: And in love — It distorts a man's sense of balance.

Captain: Indeed it does. *(He stares after the Lieutenant)* A drink, gentlemen. *(A shot — can-*

non — very close — cries of 'The French are here — the French are here' — ragged cheering.)

Captain: I'll make it a stiff one — It's going to be a difficult morning.

(Blackout — principals remain on the rostra — the stage is filled with soldiers — rabble — all in postures and attitudes relevant to their situation and character — light on cyclorama up reveals them in silhouette — none move — sound — a drumbeat — and a voice over the sound system above the drumbeat)

From the Governor of Massachusetts to Sir Jeffrey Amherst, New York — 24th August 1762.

"When the French came before St. John's, the garrison consisted of three officers and twenty-three privates of the train of artillery; and of two officers and fifty or fifty-one privates of the 40th Regiment, Captain Gross commanding. There were thirty-six guns in the fort and battery adjoining, besides six in the south battery, of which twenty were twenty-four pairs eight eighteen pounders, and eight six pounders (including two field pieces, one of which had its carriage broken), ten of which guns pointed towards the ground where the enemy advanced; and there was ammunition sufficient. The people of the country that came into defence of the Fort were three hundred and seventy according to the armourer's account who delivered out so many arms and boxes. This was when the French were above a mile off the Fort. The French that attacked the Fort were about five hundred according to the best account, when they marched from the Bay of Bulls; and some were left by the way. They had no cannon with them, or nearer than Bay of Bulls. At first, preparations were made for defending the Fort. When the French were within half a mile, one cannon (twenty-four pounder) was fired at them with round shot and once with grapes — The French advanced to gain the shelter of a hill about three hundred yards off, and then they were met with a flag of truce which was met and conducted to the Fort. Soon after, a French Major was taken to the room of Captain Gross, where a council was held. The Battery Lieutenant came out of the Captain's room to the platform opposite the French, and wringing his hands cried, "My lads. You are all sold. I have ruined my character forever by coming into this damned place."

Lights up — cheering and jubilation — the French flag being hoisted above the fort — Captain Gross silently reaching for a bottle and then turning his back upon the scene — the Magistrate and the Merchant conversing with two French officers — the crowd singing and dancing.

Spokesman: The bottle, Pat; the bottle. *(The soldiers are now mingling freely with the crowd — carrying stone jars of rum — French soldiers guard stage right and left — in a relaxed fashion.)*

1st Soldier: Here — have a swill of this. The best from Barbados.

Spokesman: Ah, you're not such a bad sort after all, I suppose — we won't hang you today, will we, lads?

A Voice: As long as the rum lasts. *(Laughter)*

Spokesman: After all — he isn't exactly Oliver Cromwell, is he? *(Laughter)*

A Voice: Who was Oliver Cromwell?

Spokesman: What the hell does that matter — it's the cause that matters. *(Drinks heavily)*

A Woman: He was a man who murdered children.

A Voice: But was too much of a Christian to rape.

Spokesman: And therein lies his defects — now our friends here — the redcoats —

Woman: Bastards.

Spokesman: Exactly — Like us, you see. Of doubtful parentage and far from home, being very lonely. *(He pours the rum over the soldier's head)* And smelling as if he'd been drinking all night. *(The soldiers, humiliated are able to do nothing — spokesman slaps him on the back)* Dance. *(Laughter)* Dance for our French saviours now, or by the Lard Jesus I'll feed your liver to Widow Clancy's children — they haven't tasted blood now for at least a year. *(Soldier* *looks helplessly at the French soldier — begins clumsily to do an oafish clog dance. Falls down. Starts again — is pushed and pulled around the crowd who clap and keep time — the Magistrate and Merchant watch — and laugh — but remain close to the French Officers. The whirling gets wilder — rum flows everywhere.)*

Woman Sings:
Old Noll Cromwell was a fool
a man's true God's as big as his tool
and though be burned and pillaged and hung
we know that the man who is well slung
would beat the bastard long before
his soldiers ruled the Southern Shore . . .

Man Joins Her:
For every ball that old Noll tossed
in those times long ago
we'll get our own back two by two
So you're a protestant, how d'ye do
it's no good crying or calling the King
the sound wouldn't reach him till the Spring

Woman:
What we takes we take for good
It's orange child for Catholic blood
and if it was spilled long long ago
That makes no difference to Tom or Joe
We'll do our best to spread the faith
just as the Holy Father says
and it's our duty
and it's your woe
to pay our debts the way we know

Chorus:
Cheers to the French who understand
the dubious ways of the Church and man
While the English write and the English rule
we'll breed bastards to prove them fool
for the poor know that the child of hate
will burn the castles of the state
and ravage and scar like a locust horde
because blood is all that they can afford . . .

Suddenly the Spokesman snatches a grappling hook from one of the crowd — as the first soldier, breathless, falls to his knees — he stands in front of him — the crowd fall silent — the Captain is still standing with his back to the audience — Merchant, Magistrate and French Officers mount the platform. Captain turns — unbuckles his sword belt and gives it to French

Officer. He exits. Magistrate and Merchant and Officer watch as the Spokesman pushes the point of the spike against the soldier's groin. He says one word.

Soldier 1: No. *(The Spokesman presses harder — the soldier's voice rises to a scream)*

Soldier 1: I have a wife and children. *(His hands clutch the spike)*

Spokesman: And this is for mine. *(He impales him — the soldier falls — the French Officer in French — to his soldier.)*

French Officer: Ils avaient besoin de verser le sang d'une personne au moins. Faites-les rentrer maintenant — et qu'on fasse la patrouille dans les rues. Le rassemblement est interdit.

The crowd — as if after a communal orgasm — turn and drift slowly out — the French soldiers ushering, motioning, with pikes -- lights dim save on the upper rostra.

Merchant: Now Monsieur — let us discuss terms.

French Officer: Pardon.

Magistrate: Pardonnez mon compatriote, monsieur. Son ignorance de votre langue vous protège de son manque de politesse — Nous étions sur le point de parler des conditions — le ravitaillement — les articles de la loi et bien entendu la sauvegarde de la propriété — de la propriété chère à votre coeur — et au nôtre, bien sûr.

French Officer: Bien entendu — Messieurs, je crois que le capitaine aura déjà libere mon logement — Continuons notre petite conversation plus a l'aise avec une bonne bouteille de vin.

Merchant: What's he saying, Magistrate? Will he agree? Can we be guaranteed?

Magistrate: For God's sake, Tupper. Hold your tongue before it's cut out.

Merchant: But you are getting good terms, aren't you? I mean, we can't afford —

Magistrate: Tupper — the only reason I do business with you is because your greed blinds the world to everyone else's. My own included. All will be arranged — come —

They exit off rostra — pool of light shows up on body — the second soldier comes furtively on stage — dishevelled — half drunk — goes to body — kneels — stands.

2nd Soldier: I'd say a prayer, Willie, I would. But I've forgotten how. You poor dumb bastard. You'll never get relieved now — The Captain's going to put you down as dying in action, Willie. I've been speaking to him — He said it was the least he could do — The very least — In a funny way, Willie, you've saved us all — I mean — it was like you were a bleeding sacrifice — Funny. *(Moves forward — the Ballad of the Soldier — to audience)* You and me now, we're still warm, breathing. Like bloody cattle in a pen. And it don't seem to matter — when you see somebody dead — whether it's a pig-sty, a mess of fish guts — or linen sheets that you sleep in. You sleep easier 'cos someone else's blood drips on the stones and it isn't yours. I'm glad it was Willie and not me.

One minute, dancing — and the next, skewered.

Begins to parody Willie's fumbling dance — sings disjointed.

All a man is — all a man is — eh,
Willie Boy . . .

When you came from your mother's womb
all you wanted was milk
a clean behind
and a rocking crib
that's all you wanted, Willie Boy

Sings, Dances.

All a man is
is in his eyes
bits of people
bits of sky
bits of grapeshot
bits of blood
bits of grass
and lots of mud . . .

eh, Willie Boy . . .

Kneels

The worms'll be at you soon.
Then the ants and the beetles —
but things'll grow on you Willie —
things'll gow out of you —
And that ain't so bad —

Sings, Dances

All a man is
is in his hands
breast at birth
mud and sand
cloth and paper
breast again
steel and blood
and the wet rain
and lots of mud . . .

eh, Willie Boy . . .

Kneels, Cries

I'm sorry for you Willie
But I'm sorrier for meself —
you see how it is —
I'll remember you Willie
although I hardly knew you, somehow —
as long as it lasts I'll remember you . . .

Sings, Dances

All a man is
is in his head
bits of people
a long time dead
bits of churches
overgrown
bits of loving
long outgrown
bits of light and
bits of dark
and lots of mud . . .

eh, Willie. Eh.

The Girl and the Lieutenant enter.

Girl: They had their sacrifice then.

Lieutenant: Yes. Poor devils.

D28

Girl: A day ago, I would have pushed the spike in.

Lieutenant: Not now?

Girl: Not now. Not ever. There's no sense in repeating anything is there.

Lieutenant: I could lie with you.

Girl: Blood makes you want sex. It makes you frightened — and people want warmth when they're frightened.

Lieutenant: Then there's no sense in repeating love.

Girl: I don't know. I sometimes think there's only ever one time for anything. Hate or love. Killing or suckling or kissing.

Lieutenant: Is it finished then?

Girl: Oh, for you — no. How can it be. There's your wretched honour — and your hurt. You've got to get rid of that. Like my people got rid of theirs — I can't get rid of that for you. I don't want to. That would be to change things. I'm tired of changing things — that don't change.

Lieutenant: People do. See themselves mirrored in other people's actions.

Girl: But nothing changes. My people don't change. Yours don't — change. Everything — just two hours after the French have captured the town and captured your honour. *(Laughs lightly)* and my people have captured one drunken soldier — put him to sleep — Nothing has changed. The Magistrate sleeps the sleep of the Just — and the Merchant puts sawdust in his flour sacks. And the French soldiers lie with us — and keep the peace. And they pay the same price, and we pay the same price. *(Shudders)* Nothing is clean.

Lieutenant: We weren't born clean. It's something we have to work for.

Girl: *(Laughs)* Oh, yes. Wash yourself in the blood of the lamb. It's alright for Jesus — but for Chrissake — you can't fill the world with crucifixes to justify pain. And nobody wants a virgin. And even you — even you, with your dignity ruffled like a sparrow's in the gale — even you — you're not a Roman.

Lieutenant: No. I don't suppose I ever was.

Girl: What will the French do now?

Lieutenant: Under the articles of war, we are prisoners here until an exchange can be made — but the Navy will be here before that time. And then there will be a fight — And we'll win it.

Girl: You see.

Lieutenant: See what?

Girl: Like the sea. Retreat and advance. Occasional storms — shipwrecks — a few lost — a few honours gained — or in your case *(Laughs)* regained — but I feel somehow — that there has to be something else — Everything comes too soon to us — your loyalties, my angers, rule and law and govern and pray — It isn't even any good having children anymore because they grow away from the breast — Once upon a time — that's the way of all stories, isn't it.

Lieutenant: Yes — fairy tales.

Girl: It's not a fairy tale — Once upon a time, I had a man who was a trapper. We lived in the cold woods but there was meat and fire — and the world seemed to be in my stomach every day — and one morning, on the lake — some lake — there are so many — we met an Indian. It was early morning, and he was paddling in a canoe. And the water was still. And the sky, a soft pink — soft — like a child's cheek. And the ripples from the paddle seemed to stretch into the sky. And the drops seemed frozen in the air, and they caught the light. Everything was so still. And he was — well, not happy. I can't speak for sorrow or happiness. But he seemed to be one with the water and the sky and the movement of the water and the sky.

Lieutenant: Did he just stay there?

Girl: No. My man shot him. He didn't stop to think. I didn't stop to think to stop him. He raised his gun and shot him. And the Indian half rose in his canoe and spread out his arms and fell into the lake. And the canoe went floating on-wards — on and on and the ripples streamed out behind it — and the water was tinged with blood — and it seemed as if nothing had happened. I didn't think anything of it at the time — But often since.

2nd Soldier: Excuse me, Sir.

Lieutenant: Yes. What is it?

2nd Soldier: Willie, Sir — Do you think we ought to bury him — flies'll be off the fish in the morning and I don't think he'd like that.

Girl: He's dead, isn't he. Does it matter.

2nd Soldier: Well, yes, it does, you see. He's going to be reported as having been killed in action — and it wouldn't do just to leave him, Sir, would it — for the flies and the dogs.

Lieutenant: No. It wouldn't do to leave any-body like that.

The girl crosses to him — bends down — lifts up the red coat.

Girl: But for that you see — he'd be alive. Just the colour of a piece of cloth.

Lieutenant: I'll speak to the French Major — He'll let us have a detail to give him a decent burial.

Girl begins to laugh.

Lieutenant: What's the matter? *(Laughter con-tinues — she runs about the stage. Doubled up)*

Girl: A decent burial. That's what you said. A decent burial.

Laughter becomes hysterical — lieutenant moves quickly to her and slaps her face — she imme-diately becomes silent — Lieutenant and Soldier pick up body — crouching, like a harpy, she swoops after them.

Girl: Wait for me, Lieutenant. Wait for me — I'm good. I'm clean. And I don't cost very much. *(Laughs)* I don't cost very much — I'm a decent girl, Sir; ask anyone — ask anyone — I'm decent. *(Blackout)*

End of Act One

Act Two
Can be said by Spokesman:

It is six months later — The poor are as poor. The rich are as rich. The rank and file have been transferred to French prisons and hope eventually to get home. Only the Captain remains — a prisoner in name only. He emerges occasionally — free to walk the town — a man carrying ghosts — his uniform tattered — his pride broken — given to strange utterances — denials, self-justifications — and yet is strangely prophetic. The Lieutenant gets leaner, hungrier. Obsessed with that recovery of reputation which has slowly eroded his relationship with the girl. Yet, she too — having denied her people one — is an outcast. They cling to each other wildly — and as wildly — rip each other apart.

The scene opens forestage. The Merchant and the inevitable boy — he is giving him a French lesson.

Merchant: Ou est le rhum? Come on, boy — ou est le rhum?

Boy: Why don't you speak English, Sir? It's over here. *(Scurries madly)*

Merchant: No, you scabrous pauper. In French — answer me in French.

Boy: *(Blankly)* It's over here in French as well, Sir.

Merchant: *(Clutches his head in his hands — says in horrible French)* Le rhum est au-dessus ici — say that after me.

Boy: *(Repeats the phrase)*

Merchant: That's better. How'd you expect us to trade with those Frenchies unless we made some attempt to learn their language. Communication is the essence of trade, boy. Now — ou est le cognac — come on, dolt — ou est le cognac?

Boy: Over here, Sir.

Merchant: *(Screaming)* Answer me in French — In French.

Boy: *(Says his rum line all over again)*

Merchant: That's rum, you mutton head — Brandy — Brandy — Cognac.

Boy: Oh — I know where the cognac is, Sir. That's French for Brandy, isn't it.

Merchant: Yes, you little bugger. And you know the French for "Would you like my sister? "

Boy: Didn't know you had a sister, Sir. *(Merchant enraged picks up a coil of twine — Boy dodges)*

Boy: In any case, Sir — I'm too young yet for that sort of thing — that's what my sister says anyway, Sir, every time I ask her what's she doing.

Merchant continues to pursue.

Merchant: Stubborn — mulish *(Lashing out and missing)* Newfoundland-born dolt.

Boy: Wasn't born in Newfoundland, Sir — was born in Harbour Grace — Sir. *(Merchant gives up, breathless)*

Merchant: What's the use — Fetch my books — Fetch my books. *(He goes and sits on his desk — the boy rummages in a trunk — finds a ledger — then in clear and startling French)*

Boy: Voici vos grands livres, monsieur. *(He and the Merchant exchange a long hard look — the boy goes and busies himself — Merchant mumbles)*

Merchant: Mmmm — we haven't done too badly the past few months — I must say, the French have been very gallant. *(Chuckles)* Very gallant indeed — full price for everything — mmmmmhh —mmmmh *(Suddenly sits bolt upright)* Boy. What ever happened to Mrs. McDonald?

Boy: Oh. She died, Sir. If you remember, Sir — a deputation came and asked you for some vittals for the wake, Sir.

Merchant: Ah, yes, yes. Times were very hard then. Very difficult — But she still owes me money.

Boy: But she's dead, Sir.

Merchant: *(Peevish)* I don't care boy. It was very careless of her — very —

Boy: I expect you'll get it all, Sir, when you get up there — God does keep accounts, Sir — as you're always telling me — Does he have a big ledger like that, Sir?

Merchant: I expect so.

Boy: And we'll all be on it.

Merchant: Of course. That's what the preacher says on Sundays.

Boy: Mrs. McDonald'll be doing alright then, Sir.

Merchant: What do you mean, brat.

Boy: Well, Sir — you remember you sold her husband's boat and gear for thirty-four pounds I think it was, and she only owed you twenty-four.

Merchant: You just don't understand economics, do you — That's why the stupid poor always remain poor and subsequently stupid — credit has to be balanced by my own credit — and I have to pay for that and so.

Boy: I do understand, Sir — In fact — we all understand, Sir.

Merchant: You do.

Boy: Oh, yes, Sir — We all understand — we may be poor and stupid, but we understand economics or whatever you call it.

He has become — suddenly — dangerous — is looking at the Merchant with a pale ferocity — for the first time, the Merchant realises that the boy doesn't fear him. He hates him — he rises.

Boy: Mrs. McDonald died of hunger, Sir — she understood economics — and her — *(Merchant raises his fist — boy snatches a knife from his rags — they look at each other — the Magistrate enters — in fact has entered as the Merchant was expounding economics.)*

Magistrate: But you understand the law, don't you, boy?

The circle of hatred is broken.

Boy: Just a joke, Sir. He was teaching me French, Sir — I never could stand learnin', Sir — makes me all upset.

Magistrate: Get out.

Boy: Yes, Sir — I was waiting for me wages, Sir.

Merchant: Ye murdering brat — There's no wages coming your way.

Boy: But you need someone to deliver your economics, Sir — I mean, I steal less than most — you wouldn't find a better, Sir.

Magistrate: Apologise.

Boy: Beggin your pardon, Sir.

Magistrate: Say you're sorry. *(Boy slowly goes to Merchant)*

Boy: I'm sorry, Sir. (*Merchant cuffs him about the head. Boy doesn't flinch — he cuffs him again — the boy doesn't flinch — Merchant looks at him — fumbles in a drawer — produces a coin*)

Merchant: Here — Go and get drunk. (*Boy doesn't believe the coin*)

Boy: But, Sir — all of.

Merchant: Hurry — Before I change me mind — Oh — The knife.

Boy: Yes, Sir. Of course, sir.

Merchant: Five o'clock tomorrow morning.

Boy: (*Scurries out*) Of course, Sir. I'm truly grateful to your Honour — thank you, thank you. (*He exits*)

Magistrate: (*Comes downstage*) What in God's name did you do that for?

Merchant: I don't know meself come to tell the truth. Just made me feel kind of queasy in the stomach — Young as that — and a knife — and all I've done for him — Oh, I feel quite faint.

Magistrate: (*Looking at him closely*) You're lying, you scoundrel — You've learnt something yourself the past few months.

Merchant: Jesus in Heaven knows that if you hadn't come in at that moment.

Magistrate: You've learnt something at last. No matter how much they hate you — at the moment of violence, weaken — be generous — it destroys the flame of the spirit. (*The Merchant looks up — then laughs delightedly — hugs himself*)

Merchant: We'll break open a bottle of port, my good friend — It has truly been a bumper year. My partners in Bristol are overjoyed.

Magistrate: The French have been magnificent. (*Merchant opens the bottle*)

Merchant: I am owed half the fish in the North Atlantic.

Magistrate: The wives of the malcontents send me their daughters.

Merchant: The population are kept in order.

Magistrate: The Irish have ceased to be a problem.

Merchant: The English have left in their thousands, leaving their valuables behind them.

Magistrate: Which are confiscated in accordance with our fiscal policy. (*They drink*)

Merchant: A magnificent year.

Magistrate: But the leaves are falling from the trees. (*A pause*)

Merchant: What?

Magistrate: I had some news today, my friend — You have kept your English flags.

Merchant: Of course. My first loyalties.

Magistrate: Exactly. (*Chuckles*) You'll soon be able to sell them at a premium, I should think.

Merchant: Then it's happened.

Magistrate: As I forecast it was inevitable.

Merchant: They are on the way then.

Magistrate: The fleet left Halifax five days ago.

Merchant: The French will fight?

Magistrate: With what they leave behind, yes — The fleet will go — Their commanding officer — what they have managed to accumulate — yes — it will go. It all promises to be very exciting.

Merchant: But our position — our collaboration with the enemy.

Magistrate: We are in no danger — I've already sent a trusted messenger to contact the fleet. We have endured only because of threats of the direst kind — We wait anxiously for relief — For the resumption of the benign rule of the great King.

Merchant: But the military will be thorough — They'll take stock — inventories.

Magistrate: Then we just infiltrate our stock into that of the garrison — Inventories will be impossible. More — the French have done what they set out to do — they burnt half the island — there's much rebuilding to be done — great trade concessions and charters to be drafted.

Merchant: But the fighting — the looting — I must get my stock to sea.

Magistrate: You will stay where you are. Decency and fair play will win the day for us. *(Drinks)* War to the English is a game played according to very rigid rules of conduct. Property will not be molested. Treaties will be observed. Loyalty will be rewarded — And fair prices will be paid — Without that you see, the game becomes carnage, brutal, uncivilized — Mark my words, my friend, next year promises to be even better.

Merchant: And the people.

Magistrate: The people. They'd cheer a flag a week. They need emotion to brighten their lives. Need causes. But when one is done, the old order re-establishes itself — They'll follow a saviour one day and hang him the next — Cheer the French for freeing them from British oppression and cheer the British for freeing them from French corruption — As long as they keep cheering, Tupper — you and I are alright. *(Raises his glass — he and the Merchant drink — slow cross fade)*

The Captain and the Lieutenant are walking on the waterfront — approaching from opposite directions — fog rolls — the Captain is as described — the Captain stops — the Lieutenant walks past.

Captain: Lieutenant. *(Lieutenant stops — does not turn his head)* It's a chilly day. *(No response)* Autumnal one might say — Can you hear the swell out there. *(No response)* There's ships out there, Lieutenant. Life. Bodies and sweat and commands and eyes straining. *(No response)* Lieutenant — You don't like me. *(This time the Lieutenant turns)* Would you care to salute me, Lieutenant. Give me the honour of a military greeting. *(No response)* No. I thought perhaps you mightn't — Then I will salute you. *(He draws his tattered frame to attention. And salutes — it is very still — across the narrows — a gun booms — Captain still maintaining his salute)* Would you do me the honour, Sir — of a walk along the promenade. *(Very still — a gun booms — Captain lowers his hand)* Would you care to walk with an old man for a spell, Sir — It's a cold day — and lonely.

The Lieutenant turns and walks to the Captain — in step they begin to pace up and down.

Captain: I have already written my report, you know — I should imagine they'll be coming soon.

Lieutenant: Any day now, thank God.

Captain: Yes, well. You might thank God, Lieutenant — But I will go soon. And leave nothing here. Twenty-five years. You would think a man should leave something in a place, a place he —

Lieutenant: Served, Captain Gross. Were you going to say 'served'.

Captain: No, Lieutenant. Save your anger for the French who have been feeding you. The girl who's been sleeping with you.

Lieutenant: *(The Military role reasserting despite himself)* Sir — I don't have —

Captain: Of course not. But you will. Because you are kind. And you pity me. *(They pace a while)* I was going to say 'lived', Lieutenant. A man should leave something in a place in which he has lived. But this rock now — something in it defeats the spirit.

Lieutenant: Your spirit. *(Both stop)* I'm sorry, Sir.

Captain: Mine was defeated before I got here — a man learns things walking alone in the fog.

Some locals drift by silently — as they pass the Captain, one spits — at him. Lieutenant suddenly enraged — he waits for the Captain to do something — he does nothing — the man has passed — says something indistinguishable to a companion, turns and spits again — Lieutenant leaps after him — seizes him — shakes him like a rat.

Lieutenant: An apology, you rat, or I'll.

Captain: No apology called for, Lieutenant — I can fight my own battles. *(Lieutenant releases the man — he rejoins his companion — words drift back and hang in the air — "Fight his own battles — Jesus, Mary and Joseph —" laughter)*

Captain: I've watched year after year. People build. Then fire. Or drowning. Or famine. Or disease. Or just — failure of the spirit — Somebody else comes and carts the house away — for timber or firewood. The thin scrub marches back across the cleared land — The flake rots into the sea — I have seen places *(Pause)* I have seen places — where people once lived, where even the land no longer bears the scar — It makes me frightened.

Lieutenant: *(More gently)* There isn't enough of a hold yet. That's all. Children and children's children.

Captain: No. Look. I once played on a hill where the scars of the Romans were plain. Sixteen hundred years. If we were all to leave here — you would never know we've been. *(Suddenly clutching the Lieutenant's arm)* I've made my reports — That's tangible isn't it. That's written — I acted out of conscience. *(Lieutenant shakes himself free)* That's history, Lieutenant. Mine. One man's history. One tick of time. It's humiliating. It's defeat. But it's tangible. I will be remembered as the man who surrendered the garrison.

Lieutenant: It would be better that you were not remembered.

Captain: *(Crying out)* No. No. I tell you, Lieutenant — that nothing will be remembered here — That people will be born and live and die and their passage will go unnoticed. That their buildings will fall and rot back to the land. That their history will die in their children. It is not fit — It belongs to the bottom of the sea — to secrecy and silence.

Have you noticed — Have you noticed — How the blood does not sink into the soil. How it stays and clots, and waits for the rain to wash it into the river. Into the sea. But I have made my report, Lieutenant. *(A pause)* It is different for you.

Lieutenant: I have to leave now, Sir.

Captain: It is different for you — Part of you is still alive — Do you know what I always wanted to do, Lieutenant? I wanted to grow roses. But when I tried, the worms always got there first — Did I ever tell you.

Lieutenant: I have to go, Sir.

Captain: Ah, yes. To prepare — To meet our countrymen — to put the past to sleep — I think I'll walk a little longer. The fog I find, always makes life more bearable — Good-bye, Lieutenant. *(Once again he salutes — A pause — Slowly — grudgingly — the Lieutenant salutes back — turns and leaves. The Captain begins his pacing but almost immediately is accosted by the Merchant.)*

Merchant: Ah, Captain — how propitious — yes indeed — how propitious — What a beautiful day.

Captain: Is it?

Merchant: It is indeed. *(He is measuring the Captain with a thoughtful eye)* Doubtless, you've heard the joyful news — our captivity will soon be at an end — ah, what a sad time it's been for us all.

Captain: You look remarkably well-kept, Mr. Tupper.

Merchant: It's business, you know. In business, one has to keep up appearances — Of course — that's really why I wanted a word with you this morning.

Captain: Have you ever been to sea, Tupper?

Merchant: Sea. Goodness — I venture upon it with fear, Captain, as little as possible. When I see what it does to the poor.

Captain: But we are at sea, Tupper. At this moment.

Merchant: What — surely —

Captain: Listen — can you hear it. We're adrift, man. Helpless. The whales and the ice thrash about us.

Merchant: *(Pragmatic to the end)* It's a bit early for ice, Captain. But there's possibly a whale or two past the narrows. Yes, *(Happy with his idea)* a whale or two — having a whale of a time.

Captain: I've made my report. But there it is. Without a rudder, what can a man do. Drifts, Tupper. Only his head showing above the wave. Limbs, loins — ice cold.

Merchant: Come, come, come, Captain. It's not as bad as that. Now what I had in mind was a new uniform. Of course — I realise that you have no money now.

Captain: A uniform *(Stops)* A uniform.

Merchant: That's right, Captain — It just so happens I have one exactly your size — and I might say, your rank — You can't greet the relieving officers like that, now can you.

Captain: A uniform.

Merchant: *(As if humouring an idiot)* A shiny new dress uniform. You'll have six months back pay coming, of course — I can trust you — we men of honour.

Captain: My uniform.

Merchant: It might well have been yours, Captain — I must say, it does bear a striking similarity to your build — But the spoils of war, eh *(Laughs)* Some of your lads brought it in before they left — said the French were throwing it out — I've kept it well — just a little mould on the right sleeve, but after the heat of battle, who'll notice a thing like that.

Captain: *(Realization comes to him)* I take you to mean, Tupper — that you would like to sell me my own uniform.

Merchant: *(Unaware)* Exactly, Captain. Exactly. And for a very reasonable price — I was more than generous.

Captain: Stolen by dogs. Bought by a cur. To be sold back to a coward. *(He begins to laugh)* And I said — I said to the Lieutenant — that a man must leave something — Tupper. You may keep my uniform — I bequeath you my uniform.

Merchant: *(Uncomprehending)* But it's mine, Captain. In good faith.

Captain: In good faith wear it. As for me — if a man is what he wears — then I am properly dressed — Good-day to you, Tupper. *(Exits laughing — two words fall back on the air)* A uniform. *(Tupper makes as if to run after him — stops — shakes his head — puts his finger to his forehead and taps it significantly)*

Merchant: Always was a little funny, that one. *(Perks up)* Never mind — Perhaps one of the relieving Lieutenants will get promoted.

The cyclorama goes dark — then a cold, pale dawn light — occasional flashes of gunfire — coughing and spitting, the denizens of St. John's — the lower world begins to assemble — the two old women — the prostitute — the spokesman — the Merchant's boy — all extras — they seem muted — quieter — exchange greetings — the shape of the hill looms and dominates — the first impression is one of groups meeting, standing — low indistinguishable conversation — occasional laughter — the actors here must improvise around the following.

Spokesman: *(To boy)* No good going to work today, boy — He'll be ironing his ruffles and pressing the Union Jack.

1st Woman: There'll be no work for anyone until the fighting's over.

2nd Woman: Give me back a rest, eh, Gert.

Gert: Last time I slep on me stummick was when I was in me crib.

Some laughter

Man: I see the Frenchies have gone.

Spokesman: *(Spits)* Good riddance. Crept out in the fog — taking many a good man's work with 'em.

Woman: Didn't tell any difference between them and the English.

Man: All fish are alike in the dark.

Spokesman: And for us it always is. *(Two men busy themselves with nets and gear)* You're not thinking of going out today, boys.

Man: Today — yesterday — tomorrow — What's the difference — There's fish and they's got to be caught — whether them silly devils kill each other off or no is no worry of mine.

Boy: At least the French are fighting for what they've got.

Spokesman: Those that are left. What are they fighting for though.

Woman: It's us. *(Cackles)* Heard sometime about a whole army fighting over a woman.

Spokesman: That was in the days when there was a thousand men to every woman — I heard tell of it too.

Gert: Jesus — the thought of it makes me tired. *(She sits — on a bollard)*

Man: Well — one thing's sure — it's not us they're killing each other for. And it's not the place — none of them would live here by choice.

Spokesman: Only us — You'd think we'd have some say in that, wouldn't you — Never mind — when it's done, they'll break open the casks and beat the drum and read a proclamation or two and we'll all cheer and then it'll be back to normal with a bit of fishing, bit of building, bit of growing — bit of breeding.

Boy: I thought you hated the English — when we killed the soldier.

Spokesman: We killed the soldier for a bit of sport — seemed fair at the time — I'd forgotten it. An if I were you, I'd forget it too — It won't be a good thing to remember. *(Arms around each other, the Lieutenant and the girl enter)*

Spokesman: Well, well, well, boys — lookee here. *(A few whistles — catcalls)*

Woman: She's putting on weight.

2nd Woman: Too much plum pudding.

Spokesman: Starting a new breed, Lieutenant. *(No response)*

Gert: That means he's leaving — always leave when a girl's carrying — can't stand the screams.

Woman: The sight of blood.

2nd Woman: Themselves.

Spokesman: Don't worry, Lieutenant — we'll all look after it for you. *(No response)* Used to be able to get a rise out of him — Should have hung him when we had the chance.

Man: If not him, someone else.

Spokesman: For her.

Man: No. To hang — Would ye care to lend a hand today.

Spokesman: With all them English man 'o wars lying outside — You're crazy — you'll end up rowing them in if the breeze stays as it is.

Man: Perhaps. *(The two of them hoist their gear — go off — the group remain still — looking at the cyc — occasional pointing — spotlight on the girl and the Lieutenant)*

Girl: I'm sorry.

Lieutenant: For what?

Girl: For you.

Lieutenant: We'll never agree will we.

Girl: We'll never be together long enough to agree — that takes time.

Lieutenant: I've tried to be honest.

D40

D41

Girl: You're transparent — I'm muddy — We're all muddy — Those of us who stay here — You want to begin and end things — we exist — The French know that you are going.

Lieutenant: Didn't even cross their minds that I'd cross the lines.

Girl: You know them all now?

Lieutenant: Many of them.

Girl: Do you like them?

Lieutenant: We're the same — it's just a question of balance that's all. Who tips the scales — but we're all professionals — it gives us a point of communication.

Girl: But you wish to go and kill some of them.

Lieutenant: No, I don't wish it — But I have to do. Just as they will kill me once they've found I've broken my parole.

Girl: A lie to prove a truth about yourself.

Lieutenant: Look — they understand. I understand. It's all I've got, you see. Certain loyalties. Certain obligations and contracts — That's what you saw in me, you said — that's what you wanted.

Girl: That's true. You were so sure — but since then, I've seen you unsure, hurt — vulnerable — puzzled — just like the rest of us — You've got strong hands — Could build something.

Lieutenant: Is the child mine or Sean's?

Girl: Both of you, you fool. But first of all, it's mine — Don't worry on account of that — he was right, you know — a child gets loved by everybody — it's the only testament we can scribble.

Lieutenant: I'll tell you now — I have thought about it. Thought about abandoning the past. Of moving out around the shore — of building — working — But I'd rot away.

Girl: I know. You don't belong here, that's all.

And you think that you'll win peace in some bloody parody of heroics, but I tell you — I will tell you — that the bravest people I know are the ones who endure. *(She turns and half walks towards the group — turns)* You'll die, you know — that's the only way you can redeem yourself in the cold eyes of the men who will judge you.

Lieutenant: Are my eyes cold?

Girl: I have seen them so.

Lieutenant: Then perhaps I will. I've forgotten the other one, you know. You did that for me.

Girl: I did nothing for you. Put your tears to sleep every now and again — I've got what I want. *(She pats her belly)* But you're not in the business of life, are you.

She walks across to the group — there's a pause — then in a movement that is almost an embrace, they surround her — swallow her up — the Lieutenant hesitates — exits — the Ballad of the Poor — very sudden — upsurge of lights — a barrage of artillery and arms on sound — fades out.

Spokesman: OK, good people — We're nearly at the end — Historically, this has been a pretty inaccurate play; but there's something that could be said was real — I mean — we are — we really are — We're the majority — We keep the Pope in golden chalices, Luther in special ointments for his piles, Kings and Queens in their stupidity; wars ain't no good without us because we're always the casualties and it's our blood that writes the histories — We're the stuff of dreams as some bloody Englishman said, and you all know that dreams are pretty common. And we don't deny that. Being common. We are the nature you try to subvert, divert, convert; and in general, screw up in a lot of ways, refining us into tracts and treatises on morals, politics, all kinds of tics which get incorporated into armies and governments which in turn impose them upon us — which is, or are, or were according to whether you are living, dead, or only partially deceased — the raw stud which you've stolen — We're copyright — We're not really interested in God — but since you insist that he was created for the poor, we pay occasional attention — just in case we might miss something. We're not really interested in government or causes — but we react to people who get all excited about us, by adding a bit of fuel to the fire, burning somewhere here, running somebody through there — cheering on appropriate occasions — We don't know much about business because that means robbing your neighbour and in the way we live, that makes life difficult. As a result, we don't rob our neighbour and we're happy, and the merchant robs all of us — our neighbours too — and he's happy, and we're happy because suffering has got to be shared to be enjoyed — We don't particularly like work, but it's a way of getting away from the women and the children; and there's a measure of satisfaction in putting the muscles of your arms against the muscles of the sea. It's hardly wrestling with God or devils in the wilderness of the south, but it's something — We don't really like sex all that much either — It's a joke really — we know that — hump-backed and sweating, we grind away to perpetuate our own mythologies, most of which I'm sure you'll agree are better left unborn — But we like to laugh about it — That's the best part of it really — We like to get drunk and roar. We tolerate the blind and the lame and the idiot and the old — because we see a bit of each one of them in ourselves — We accept the prostitute because she's honest — she just sells a commodity that's all. The rest of us sell ourselves — And most of the things you do to us in the name of King or Country or Decency or Church or God or Right and Wrong, we accept with a minimum of protest — But one day, we'll kill you all. Because there'll be nothing else left to do.

Turns his back on the audience — the Battalion, the cyclorama grows — the crowd begin to get excited — sound — as realistic as possible — crowd shouting above it.

There's one Frenchie down.

Woman: And one poor soul with grapeshot right in the heart of him.

Gert: *(Clutching herself, sinks down)* Oh, I can feel for the poor feller.

Boy: Look — Look. It's the Lieutenant.

Man: Going straight at them.

Another: Bayonet — look at the way it shines in the sun.

Boy: There's something on it.

Man: Blood, boy — what d'you think a man's made of — sawdust.

Woman: Only if he eats the merchant's bread.

(A cannonball speeds overhead — they all throw themselves down)

Spokesman: You see how it is — we'll lose more than the enemy.

Man: Which is the enemy.

Spokesman: Both. *(Faint cries of pain — off)*

Boy: The French are giving ground.

Woman: Lookit here — lookit — a whole head — just bouncing — bouncing.

2nd Woman: Tis a pity. The brains are no longer working in that one.

Another: Hand-to-hand now — look at them go at it.

Woman: Such a beautiful morning too. You'd think they'd have something better to do.

A bugle sounds.

Spokesman: That's it. *(A bugle sounds again — the gunfire gets sporadic and dies away)* OK lads. Who's for the undertaking business. *(Chorus of assent)* Half a crown a coffin — at a rough guess, we'll be five pounds to the good — But first let's greet the conquering heroes. *(Suddenly — very clear — a last cannon shot — all look)*

Woman: It's the Lieutenant. *(A sudden sharp cry from the girl — piercing — like a bird's)* One of his own too — from behind. *(Again that cry)*

2nd Woman: There's two of him now — tsk, tsk — that's a terrible mistake for them to make now.

D44

Spokesman: It's half a crown.

Man: Perhaps we can claim two bodies — that's five shillings.

Again a bugle — all firing ceased — light on cyclorama glows to reveal a bright, a perfect autumn day — they all look at the woman.

Spokesman: It's all in a day's work. *(He moves across stage to greet the English)*

Woman: You know where to find us.

2nd Woman: When the time comes. *(Follow Spokesman)*

Boy: I'll get you some flour — if you don't mind the sawdust. *(Follows)*

Man: It's best, girl — you belong here. *(Follows — and so the ritual goes on — until all have gone across stage — there's the sound of a drumbeat — splendidly clad, the Merchant and the Magistrate arrive and join the crowd — the noise grows — the light grows — a stirring drumbeat)*

Merchant: Well, lads, it's a great day — a great day. Tyranny has been overthrown.

Voice: What's tyranny?

Spokesman: Being alive.

Drumbeat very close — English Officer and two Soldiers arrive. Drum stops — crowd cheer hoarsely. Caps — shawls in the air — cries of God Save the King — etc. — Merchant and Magistrate step through the crowd and bow.

Officer: Who are the leading citizens? We had a communication from a magistrate.

Magistrate: My honour, Sir. My relief. Thank God the ordeal is over — These honest men. *(Indicating the rabble)* have suffered.

Officer: I understand. But so have my men, Magistrate. We have many casualties — and so have the enemy. They must be cared for — provisioned.

Merchant: It so happens, your Honour — that

we have managed to put things aside for this emergency.

Officer: If you two gentlemen will care to join me in my quarters — The French will have vacated by now — over some spirit perhaps.

Magistrate: We'll be honoured, Sir. *(Officer turns to Soldier)*

Officer: See to it that these honest citizens are rewarded for their loyalty — Tonight, gentlemen, ladies — you will drink the King's health. *(Cries — you're right, Sir. God Save the Queen — we will — we will —)*

Officer: Come. *(All exit save the girl — she sits — bent like a broken bird — the Captain enters — goes to her)*

Captain: The tide is running. *(Girl makes no response — he lowers his tattered frame beside her)* I made my report — A man has to write down what he does. *(No response)* Isn't that right. Isn't a — doesn't a sentence — weigh — the word — the word remains doesn't it. What we speak dies. But what we write — now there's something no iceberg can do. *(Girl suddenly begins to sob — the gross, tattered old Captain cradles her in his arms)* There — there — It's alright — There's life in you yet. There's life in you. I have to go and make my report. *(He strokes her hair)* But there's life in you yet. *(Gets up)* I will tell them that you live here — That I did what I did because you live here. *(Girl looks up at him)* No, no. I will just say — I will just say —

Girl: Tell them to go to Hell. *(Very clear)*

Captain: That would be nice. Yes — that would be nice — I don't think I'll be able to do that — Good-bye, my dear.

Girl: You were nothing to anyone, but me; and your sense of honour, your King and Country. Now you're dead. And the honour and the King and the Country lie dead with you. And there's only me left — me and him — me and her — what's it matter.

Sings:
Swing by the neck,
hang by the toes
from birth to death
the swinging goes
But it's a fool
who doesn't trust
to give himself
because he must . . .

The lights die save for the spot on the Girl —
clutching her belly and crooning — crooning —
The lights fade.

The End

Exit Muttering

Donald Jack

Donald Jack started out as a documentary film writer, researching and preparing scripts on a wide variety of subjects, including banking, labour unions, Naval communications, Western wheat, electronics, road safety, high-speed welding, civil and military aviation and deep sea fishing. (For this last film he spent two weeks on a trawler in mountainous seas off Newfoundland, gaining new insights into the life of the Maritime sailor, and losing eleven pounds).

Since 1957 he has been writing for television. His second play, Breakthrough, was the first Canadian TV play to be simultaneously telecast tothe U.S. Others have been produced all over the world, including Poland and Russia. His most recent work for the medium includes six plays for the McQueen series and three for the current CBC series of half hour adaptions of Canadian short stories.

Mr. Jack's first two stage plays were Minuet for Brass Band and Flamacue Serenade. His third play The Canvas Barricade (first prizewinner in the Stratford Shakespearian Playwriting Competition 1960) was produced in Stratford in 1961. It was not only the first Canadian play produced there but also the first play not written by Shakespeare produced there since Oedipus Rex in 1955. A year after the production of this play, which broke the ice for Canadian playwrights, Exit Muttering was produced in Toronto.

"Since 1955, four years after he emigrated to Canada (his mother was originally from Charlottetown), he has been supporting his family . . . entirely out of his earnings as a thoroughly-disciplined, nose-to-the-grindstone freelance writer. Apart from the novel, he has hammered out 40 television plays, about 35 scripts for documentary films, several radio plays and four stage plays . . . (Douglas Marshall, Books in Canada)."

The novel referred to is Volume I of a series of comedies on the life and times of a Canadian warrior, covering the period 1916-1929. The first volume is the internationally-praised Three Cheers for Me. It was republished simultaneously with Volume II, That's Me in the Middle, by Doubleday Canada Limited, in October 1972, a publishing event of some note.

Volume III is in progress, and the research for Volume IV, which is set in Russia, has been completed. At least three more books are planned.

"Exit Muttering is the play of mine that people seem to remember the best."

"Exit Muttering" was first produced at the Grenville Street Playhouse under the direction of **Hugh Webster** with the set designed by **Vincent Vaitiekunas.**

Cast of characters

Ludovic Tappin
Barington
Gloria
Eleanor
Sybil
Bishop
Jane

©Donald Jack 1974

Picture by J. Jensen Books in Canada

Act One

The stage is completely bare except for a two dimensional flat with three doors in it, and downstage, an office chair with a clapper board lying on it, and a handbell underneath.

Ludovic Tappin comes on slowly and thoughtfully, carrying a clipboard. He tries out a tap dance or soft shoe shuffle. He is rueful when it doesn't come out right.

Barington enters, carrying a blackboard. On it is a simple graph with the line falling off sharply. He also hugs a portable tape recorder.

Barington: Tappin, I want your ideas, ideawise, on this graph of our business operation.

Tappin: Wait a minute. Where are we?

Barington: In your office, of course.

Tappin: But — who am I? What am I?

Barington: Cut!

Barington goes off impatiently, returns with a script. He shoves it at Tappin.

Barington: Read your script!

Tappin takes the script. Barington jabs at it.

Barington: Look, you're Ludovic Tappin. You're comptroller of this outfit — Romance Films. I'm Barington the president. Now have you got it?

Tappin: Oh, yes, of course.

Barington: Right. *(Tappin takes up the clapper board and holds it up)* Turn it over!

Tappin: Speed.

Barington: Slate!

Tappin: Scene one, take two. *(He claps the board then takes it off)*

Barington: Action! Wait! Where's my tape recorder? I must have my tape recor — Ah, there it is. *(Barington has laid the recorder aside; he picks it up and hugs it to him. Gloria comes in with an easel. She wears a black dress.)*

Gloria: You wanted this brought on, you said, Mr. Barington.

Barington: Yes, put it there, Gloria.

As Barington rests the blackboard on the easel, Gloria smiles at Tappin and goes off, hipswinging.

Barington: Tappin, I wanted your ideas, ideawise, on this graph of our business operation of the past several years. It shows that we're losing business badly. *(He indicates a point on the graph)* At this point here, we expanded as you know, to accommodate that television film series, with the result that our overheads shot up, forcing us to raise our prices. But raising our prices lost us the television film series.

Tappin: It's like a Greek tragedy, sir.

Barington: Yeah. In fact it's so bad that according to this graph we went bankrupt three years ago. Well, you're the comptroller. It's up to you to get us out of this jam. We're all relying on you, Tappin — so think, man, think! *(Tappin thinks. He snaps his fingers)*

Tappin: I have it, sir. *(He turns the graph around so that the line ascends instead of descending)*

Barington: Say, that's much better. Now we're making a profit. That's brilliant, Tappin.

Tappin: It's nothing really.

Barington: Not at all, not at all. How much are you earning now, Ludo?

Tappin: Back to fifteen hundred a month, sir.

Barington: You're fired.

Tappin: Fired?

Barington: Fired. Better clear out your desk.

Tappin: I don't have a desk.

Barington: Well, clear out your clipboard, then. *(Going)* There'll be a new man taking over your job on Monday.

Tappin : Who is this new man, sir?

Barington: It's you, of course. See me on Monday, and I'll take you on again — at eight hundred a month.

Tappin: Thanks. *(Tappin wanders about gloomily, then takes up a large handbell and rings it loudly. Gloria enters with her notebook)*

Gloria: Did you ring, Mr. Tappin?

Tappin: Yes. Take a letter, Mrs. Cammbridge. To Mr. Barington.

Gloria: Our Mr. Barington?

Tappin: Yes, President, Romance Films etcetera. Dear Mr. Barington. With regard to your dismissal of me as per the above date, I understand you will be taking me on again at a reduced salary on Monday. I know of course, that this is in accordance with company policy, but you're pushing me sideways, Mrs. Cammbridge. *(Gloria has been leaning against him, pushing his chair sideways)*

Gloria: Oh, sorry.

Tappin: But I'm getting tired of having my salary reach 800 a month then having it reduced time and time again to 500. It's not the principle of the thing, it's the money I'm concerned about.

Gloria: I wish there was somewhere for me to sit.

Tappin: Ah, I'm sorry, love, sit here.

Gloria: Oh, thank you. *(Before he can move, she sits in his lap. Tappin looks surprised, and gently urges her up)*

Tappin: Er . . . *(He gets up. She sits)* Now a letter to National Illusions, Limited. Dear Sirs: *(Then he sees)* I see you're not wearing a bra, Mrs. Cammbridge.

Gloria: Is anybody?

Tappin: To continue: Dear Sirs: With regard to the film that we have just completed on your behalf — the final cost of which is forty thousand over the estimated budget . . . I have examined . . . And you're not wearing any pants, either.

Gloria: No. I like the feeling.

Tappin: So do I. That reminds me — I have a letter to write to Quimbies, Limited. Where was I?

Gloria: You were examining.

Tappin: Yes. The final cost of which is forty thousand over the estimated . . . *(His eyes can't help straying to her slightly exposed buttock)* . . . buttock . . .

Gloria: The estimated buttock?

Tappin: Budget. Yes. The final estimate of which is two . . . I'm sorry, Mrs. Cammbridge somehow I don't seem able to concentrate to-day. I suppose Mr. Barington has upset me slightly.

Gloria: All right. I'll type the one I have.

Tappin: Mrs. Cammbridge?

Gloria: Yes, Mr. Tappin?

Tappin: I couldn't help noticing you've been wearing mourning for some time. More or less. There's nothing wrong, is there?

Gloria: No. It's just that my husband died . . .

Tappin: I am sorry.

Gloria: It's all right. Anyway, black suits me.

Tappin: *(Sitting down, looking at his clipboard, making a note)* Yes . . .

Gloria: I go to the cemetery every Saturday, you know, to lay a fresh phonograph record on his grave.

Tappin: A fresh —?

Gloria: Phonograph record. Last week it was ex-cerpts from Il Trovatore. The week before something by Verdi. Tomorrow it will be Boris Goudunov.

Tappin: *(Losing interest)* Mm.

Gloria: He was very fond of opera, you see.

Tappin: Mm.

Gloria: Are you fond of opera?

Tappin: Can't stand it, I'm sorry.

Gloria: I'm glad. It was my husband's one weak point. After sitting through ringing Wagnerian operas, and trying to follow the plottings of Fasolt and Faffner, Donner and Fricka, Freicka and Erda, Woglinde, Wellgunde, Flosshilde and well, he used to come to bed so damned con-fused that we had to wait for morning before he'd — Well, you know.

Tappin: Know what?

Gloria: To *(spelling it out)* f-u-c-k. I'm sorry, I can't bring myself to pronounce the word. I'm an old-fashioned girl. That's the worst of the arts. They take your mind off the things that matter. You don't think I suit mourning? I'd be glad to change into something brighter, if you wanted. After all, I can't go on mourning my husband forever. Can I?

Tappin: No, it's not healthy.

Gloria: After all, it's almost three weeks; and abstinence doesn't make the heart grow fonder. As a matter of fact, I've — I've been looking around for a **grand passion** . . . *(No response)* I said I've been looking around for a grand passion.

Tappin: *(Looking up vaguely)* Hm? *(Returning to his work)* Perhaps one of the department stores might have one . . .

Gloria: Oh, for heaven's sake!

Tappin: *(Looking up startled)* What?

Gloria: Why won't you — ! Why do you never look at me!

Tappin: *(Rising)* Mrs. Cammbridge. Is there something wrong?

Gloria: Of course there's something wrong! With you! Have you no red blood in your veins?

Tappin: Only red ink — I live on the debit side of life. *(She burst into tears and rushes out. Tappin stares after her, astounded and bewildered. Finally he goes hesitantly to the door)*

Tappin: Mrs. Cammbridge? *(No answer)* Mrs. Cammbridge?

Gloria: *(Off)* What?

Tappin: Would you come in a moment, please.

Gloria: No!

Tappin: Please?

Gloria: Go away.

Tappin: Please come in. *(After a moment he sees she's coming. He waits for her agitatedly. Gloria comes in, dabbing her eyes)*

Tappin: Please sit down, Mrs. Cammbridge.

Gloria: *(Sitting)* I have to get on with my typing.

Tappin: I just wanted to explain.

Gloria: There's nothing to explain. You're just not interested in me, that's all.

Tappin: No, it's not that. I . . . well, you see, sex and all that, I don't feel the need for it.

Gloria: Oh, I am sorry, Mr. Tappin. I didn't realize . . .

Tappin: No, no, don't misunderstand. It's just that . . . Well, I haven't gone in for that kind of thing for over five years.

Gloria: Five years!

Tappin: Yes.

Gloria: How can you stand it!

Tappin: The usual way . . . I mean, I try not to stand it. I have spiritual and intellectual companionship, and I find that's sufficient. I have a feeling you've been trying to become friends for some time?

Gloria: I was trying even before my husband died.

Tappin: *(Working at his clipboard)* Were you?

Gloria: Did you never get any of my hints?

Tappin: Hints?

Gloria: Like the time I invited you to my bedroom, and suggested we turn the four-poster into a five-poster?

Tappin: No . . .

Gloria: Or the time I hinted that my shoulder blade was itching, and asked you to put your hand up my skirt and scratch it — hints like that?

Tappin: I thought it was a slip of the tongue.

Gloria: How very preoccupied you are.

Tappin: With becoming a whole man. My dear Mrs. Cammbridge, I see I owe you an explanation. Simply that my life is complete as it is. The spirit and the intellect are enough.

Gloria: Your life can't be complete, because sex is quite necessary.

Tappin: I assure you, I can struggle along without it.

Gloria: Can you? Can you really, Mr. Tappin? *(She is pressing against him)*

Tappin: Are you suggesting we have an affair?

Gloria: Certainly not. That would be unladylike. I wouldn't dream of suggesting such a thing. It's up to you to suggest it. Well, go on, suggest it.

Tappin: *(Hypnotised)* Shall we have an affair?

Gloria: Certainly not. I'm surprised at you, Mr. Tappin.

Tappin: I'm surprised at myself.

Gloria: Making a proposition that sounds like a flat tire.

Tappin: Sorry. I'm out of practise.

Gloria: Well? Oh, for heaven's sake. It was just the same with my husband. I had to play tape cartridges of Rachmaninov before I could screw him —

Tappin: What?

Gloria: — up to the point where he'd become elated enough, keyed up enough to come to bed, in F minor. And then the fool insisted on getting married. Said he wanted to be made a respectable man of. I've always had to take the lead. What's wrong with you men? I thought at least you were different, Mr. Tappin.

Tappin: I used to thrash around with girls in motels and things. Until it no longer meant anything. I was looking for more than that. But you . . . How desirable you are . . . I wish I could tell you your eyes are deep pools in the gentle landscape of your face, or something poetic like that, but . . . All the same, my fingers tingle for some tactile espionage . . .

Fascinated, he is about to kiss her. At the last moment he turns away.

Tappin: No! Mrs. Cammbridge —

Gloria: Gloria.

Tappin: Mrs. Cammbridge, I have constructed my life very carefully — Don't look at me like that — There is no room for sex — *(She looks astonished)* It gets in the way of fulfilment. *(She looks forlorn)* I won't allow myself to . . . *(She looks unhappy, then appealing)* I tell you it's hopeless! It's . . . It's selfish . . . it's destructive . . . *(He suddenly seizes her and kisses her passionately)*

Tappin: Oh, damn.

Gloria: Oh, Tappin . . . I will call you Ludo when I know you better.

Exit. Tappin looks after her a moment.

Blackout.

When the lights come up again, Eleanor enters

with a book. A chesterfield is brought on. She sits, reads with concentration, making notes.

Tappin enters with a briefcase. He kisses her on the cheek.

Eleanor: Hello, dear. Here's your favourite seat. I'll get dinner.

She goes out. Tappin sighs, sits, relaxes, stretches, looks round with a satisfied expression.

Tappin: It's good to be home.

Eleanor: *(Entering)* Did you have a hard day at the office, dear?

Tappin: Very hard.

He realizes he is sitting on a book. He takes it up. She sits beside him.

Eleanor: Tell me your news.

Tappin: Jane Ramington our negative cutter, has bought an abstract painting to go with her new seat covers.

Eleanor: *(Looking under his shirt)* You forgot to put on your woollen vest this morning, dear.

Tappin: I hate to give in to winter. Did you say you'd dinner ready?

Eleanor: I thought we could stay home for once. I thought of cooking a TV dinner.

Tappin: There's a very good lecture at the main library tonight. It's on Kierkegaard's Fear and Trembling and Sickness Unto Death.

Eleanor: I just thought it'd be nice to sit before the imitation fireplace, just you, and me.

Tappin: I must admit it's very pleasant, all this. You really are wonderful, Eleanor. The only woman I've ever met who can not only discuss everything from the tragedy of the ingrown psyche to the Toynbean theory of challenge and response, and understand my esoteric references, and I yours. Yes, it's very pleasant, being with you.

E8

Eleanor: Then you'll eat at home?

Tappin: No, let's eat out.

Eleanor: All right, dear. I'll get my coat. *(Exit)*

Tappin: By the way, I was re-reading Dr. Wiener's chapter on Time Series. You know, I don't quite follow his communication, Eleanor. You have a degree in mathematics; I thought we might discuss it over dinner.

Eleanor: *(Calling)* What part is that?

Tappin: It's his prediction problem following theorem 3.905, the Fourier Transforms.

Eleanor: *(Entering)* The Fourier Transforms? Oh yes. *(She cleans the blackboard and writes on it:*

$$q_{,2}(\tau)\int M \kappa (\sigma+t) = N q_{,2}(\tau)_u \kappa(\sigma+t)(t)s$$

Now let me see — how does that resolve...? *(She strokes out everything on the right hand side, until all that is left is: $-N u (t) S$)* Nuts? Hm. No, that can't be right.

Tappin: Dr. Wiener must have made a mistake somewhere.

Eleanor: Yes . . . *(Laughs)* I know it's very frivolous of me, Ludo, but the most interesting part of Wiener, I think, is his speculation on the reversibility of time.

Tappin: Oh, yes.

Eleanor: You know the part, where he considers the time implications of an intelligent being in the cosmos whose time runs the other way.

Tappin: Yes, I remember.

Eleanor: So any message being sent us we'd already know. It's a fascinating thought.

Tappin: Except he wouldn't be a being, but a been.

They laugh in comradely fashion.

Eleanor: Well, if you're sure you don't want to stay home — and celebrate?

Tappin: Not — it's not — not our — ?

Eleanor: Yes. Five years today.

Tappin: Our anniversary! Of course! *(He shakes hands)* And how well I remember our first meeting. It was at that exhibition of Picasso's paint rags.

Eleanor: It's been good, hasn't it, Ludo? I'm very happy. We couldn't possibly be closer, could we?

Tappin: No, we couldn't.

Eleanor: How wonderful life is. To be so close to somebody. When we talk so excitedly, Ludovic, I feel all tremulous inside, and want to throw my arms around you and hug and kiss you.

Tappin: Sisterly.

Eleanor: Out of gratitude, because I'm elated. And nothing gets in the way, does it? None of the distractions that clutter lives and drive people apart.

Tappin: Pure thought! Pure ideas!

Eleanor: It's so good to rise above one's animal programming!

Tappin: Of course, the biologists have shown that basically we still are animals.

Eleanor: But animals that have struggled out of their territorial and aggressive bonds!

Tappin: Yes! We at least are free!

Eleanor: Oh, I love you, Ludo! *(Kisses his hand)*

Tappin: Easy, Eleanor. You're coming perilously close to the raw material of comparative ethology.

Eleanor: Sorry, I was carried away. Shall we go?

Tappin: I mustn't stay out too late again, though.

Eleanor: Do you have a hard day at the office tomorrow?

Tappin: No, it's Saturday. But I really ought to be home by midnight, or my wife will be wondering where I am.

They go out. Blackout.

Lights up, revealing Sybil in night attire entering, sewing a sackcloth garment. Tappin enters bringing on a hatrack on which he hangs his hat and coat. They kneel side by side. (They don't put their hands together)

Both:
In the beginning the fire
In the ending the fire
Neither end nor beginning
Both free and confining.

Tappin: But what is godhead?

Sybil: It is neither this nor that, nor that, nor the other, nor this, until all of the universe has been accounted for, and only godhead remains, through the fire we burn with.

After a moment they get up and silently, lightly embrace.

Sybil: Late again, dear.

Tappin: Yes.

Sybil: How are things?

Tappin: I was fired today. Back to five hundred a month. I'll have to curtail my expenses again.

Sybil wanders about a moment, sewing thoughtfully. At last —

Sybil: Is it all right if I descend to the level of the senses for a moment, and complain?

Tappin: Of course, dear. Even a saint has a right to descend now and then.

Sybil: We never buy anything. I'm still slaving over the same hot stove we had when we were married. We eat only the simplest food. We haven't even a telephone. What, in other words, do you spend your money on?

Tappin: Dear Sybil, you've descended too far.

Sybil: I know, but —

Tappin: You know it's good to have few possessions.

Sybil: Yes.

Tappin: *(Putting his arm around her)* And the proof is in your inner serenity.

Sybil: But — Oh, Ludovic! Do you think, just this once, we could go out? To paint the town, if not red, at least a reddish-brown? Could we, Ludo? Tomorrow?

Tappin: Isn't tomorrow your day for contemplation of the infinite?

Sybil: That was today. *(Holds up the sackcloth nightshirt)* I stood in my sackcloth shirt and thought about the Divine. But . . . it's difficult to consider heaven, when there's a hell of a draft blowing up your back. No, tomorrow's my day for reading the good book; and also the Bible. Also I have to waterproof the dripping stone walls of my bedroom. But my afternoon is free.

Tappin: Sybil! You've put a lining in the sackcloth!

Sybil: Only a cotton lining, not a silk one, Ludovic.

Tappin: Sybil, what's come over you?

Sybil: Goosebumps.

Tappin: It's not like you at all.

Sybil: I know. Oh, Ludovic, I feel myself slipping. Sometimes I seem no nearer to Atman-God, than Mrs. Chamberlain next door, who has broadloom wall to wall, and an automatic toaster so up to date it even butters the toast. And sometimes even eats it.

Tappin: I wouldn't exactly call Mrs. Chamberlain close to God. She watches soap operas.

Eleanor: And reads the Reader's Digest — under plain covers. But still.

E10

Tappin: *(Embracing her fondly)* But still, you'll take that lining out of the sackcloth, won't you, dear?

Sybil: *(After a moment, smiles)* All right.

Tappin: *(Yawning, stretching)* Well, it's time for bed and board.

Sybil: Which happens to be one and the same thing. Sleep well, my dear. And I'll swap you prayers.

Tappin: *(Kissing her tenderly)* Good night, dear soul.

He goes out. (Through upstage left door) Sybil looks after him fondly for a moment, suppresses a sigh, then exits through the upstage right door. The lights fade out. In the darkness.

Barington: Lights, lights, lights! Give me some light! *(The lights come on — a flickering light, as from a movie projector)* That's better. *(Shields his eyes and looks into the auditorium)* Is the sponsor here? The sponsor? Come on, speak up, don't be ashamed. *(No response)* Hm. *(Gloria comes on, notebook in hand)* Is everyone else still here?

Gloria: *(Checking over the audience)* Director, assistant, continuity, sales, camera, sound, art —

Barington: I want everyone's reaction afterwards to the insurance commercials we've just seen — Oh, make a note, Mrs. Cammbridge: in the third commercial there's something about bosoms.

Gloria: "There's nothing like being home in the bosom of your family" —

Barington: Yeah, that's it. It'll have to come out.

Gloria: *(Making a note)* 'Bosom — to come out.'

Barington: *(Shielding his eyes)* Where's Tappin?

Gloria: Just gone to his office, Mr. Barington.

Barington: Didn't he watch all the commercials?

Gloria: Oh, yes, Mr. Barington.

Barington: Call me Simon.

Gloria: *(Making a note)* 'Simon.'

Barington: Remind me to give you a raise, sometime.

Gloria: *(Making a note)* 'Raise.' *(Barington starts to feel her buttocks)* Would you mind, Mr. Barington?

Barington: I wouldn't mind in the least.

Gloria breaks away with difficulty. Barington follows in silent-movie fashion in the flickering light. There is the sound of a silent-movie style piano.

Gloria: Mr. Barington, what's come over you?

Barington: The commercials have got me all excited.

Gloria: You'd better lie down until the feeling goes away.

Barington: If you'll join me.

He gives a villainous laugh, and his hands reach out for her. Gloria seizes first one wrist, then the other, and a stylized wrestling match ensues.

Gloria: Have pity on a poor working girl.

Barington: I can make you **rich** poor working girl! You want a raise, don't you?

Gloria: If that's the kind of raise you had in mind.

The flickering light effect ends.

Barrington: You don't mind Tappin supporting you, though, do you?

Gloria: Will that be all, Mr. Barington?

Barington: Yeah, looks like it. *(Gloria goes with dignity. Barington stumps about)* Don't know what secretaries are coming to, these days. No goddam morals at all.

E12

He stumps out, clutching his tape recorder. Tappin enters, studying his clipboard.

Tappin: Would you come in a moment, Mrs. Cammbridge?

He waits, still apparently preoccupied with his correspondence. Gloria enters, her notebook at the ready.

Gloria: Yes, sir?

They look at each other. They embrace.

Tappin: Oh, Gloria, you were right. I do feel complete, now. That was a lovely Saturday.

Gloria: All our Saturdays have been lovely. There's nothing like love in the afternoon, I always say. You can see what you're doing.

Tappin: When I look at you I feel like dancing.

She holds out her arms. They dance. Barington comes in. He glares at them jealously. Seeing him, Gloria sweeps gracefully out. Not realizing either that she has gone or that Barington is there, Tappin finds himself executing the dance steps by himself. He stops embarrassedly as he sees Barington.

Tappin: Oh; *(Laughs)*

Barington: And how is your wife?

Tappin: Fine, thanks.

Barington: Yes. I'm very fond of that woman, Tappin, and I don't like to see you carry on this way. One mistress is okay, I guess, but two — well, all I can say, Tappin is, it smacks of inflation. Tell me, Tappin — sexwise, don't you find it hard, living beyond your means?

Tappin: Well . . .

Barington: My wife Louise . . . I don't know . . . For one thing she smokes too much. Our bedroom's always so full of smoke I hardly ever see her. She may have left three months ago, for all I know. Her epitaph will be 'ashes to ashes' all right. What salary are you earning now?

Tappin: Back to eight hundred, sir.

Barington: Remind me to fire you this afternoon.

Tappin: You'll take me back in the morning, of course.

Barington: Of course. Say, Ludo, I don't like to harp on it, especially as I don't play the harp, but what do you get out of this domestic quadrangle of yours?

Tappin: Merely the best of all possible worlds. Sybil is spiritual, Eleanor is intellectual, and Gloria's purely physical, and so between the three of them —

Barington: You lick the platter clean, eh? *(He laughs and digs Tappin in the ribs)* And everybody's happy, eh?

Tappin: I might go so far as to say that.

Barington: Lucky dog.

Tappin: Not luck but planning, Mr. Barington.

Barington: Yeah. Anyway, what I came in about was those commercials we just saw.

Tappin: Oh, yes.

Barington: I heard you making appreciative noises during the screening.

Tappin: M'm.

Barington: Or were they appreciative noises? What did you really think of them, Ludo?

Tappin: Oh, they were splendid, Mr. Barington.

Barington: Naw, come on, Ludo, you can trust me.

Tappin: You're sure I can speak frankly, Mr. Barington?

Barington: Sure you can. Call me Simon. We're friends, eh, Ludo?

E13

Tappin: You see — I realize, of course, that we have to keep the home fires of our high standard of living burning, with the dross of advertizing, Simon. It's a reasonable price to pay, so I've no quarrel with advertizing, per se.

Barington: It's good to hear you say that, Ludo — especially as we're practically in the advertizing business.

Tappin: You're — you're quite sure you want real loyalty — in other words my honest opinion?

Barington: Ludo, we prize loyalty above all else at Romance Films.

Tappin: Simon — most advertizing takes liberties with the truth, but to an acceptable extent. But those commercials aren't acceptable, they're completely unreasonable, Simon. To sell insurance they tell us that merely being together is the answer to the isolation we all live in. And that's worse than a lie, it's a distortion, a drug, a —!

Barington: No need to get excited, Tappin — Ludo.

Tappin: But you see, deeply to know another and to be known, is — That's what my life is about. Trying to foil this isolation by knowing one person profoundly. But I found that it was impossible to achieve this ideal closeness with one woman.

Barington: So you got hold of three of them. Yeah.

Tappin: Dividing the theme, you see, between three instruments, to produce a harmony — Oh, such a harmony — !

Barington: Yeah. Anyway, you think our work here is lousy, eh?

Tappin: I didn't say that, Simon. I —

Barington: You answer me one question, Ludo, then we'll forget all about it, eh? Tell me, which is better: a picture of Hamlet brooding like a hen, or a nestful of soliloquies?

Tappin: Well, a picture of Hamlet can convey a great deal, but there are certain perceptions that our language, imperfect though it is —

Barington: That's all I wanted to know. (He starts to go)

Tappin: I just wanted to make it plain, Simon, that I wasn't being disloyal —

Barington: Course not, Ludo, course not! By the way, you've caught up on all your work, have you? Got the financial statement prepared?

Tappin: Yes.

Barington: Good, good. Well, Ludo . . .

Barington hesitates, then nods briskly at Tappin and goes out.

Tappin gazes thoughtfully out for a moment. Then first making sure there is nobody about, hitches up his trousers and tries out his tap dancing again.

He is in the middle of this when Barington comes back in.

Barington: What's this?

Tappin: Oh. (Laughs embarrassedly)

Barington: Dancing?

Tappin: Just — trying out a little step, Mr. —

Barington: Dancing when you should be working?

Tappin: I — Well, there's nothing to do for the next day or two, now the financial statement is out.

Barington: That's nothing to do with it. I've had my eye on you from some time, Tappin, and I can't say I'm completely satisfied.

Tappin: What's the harm in — —

Barington: It's flippant, that's what it is, Tappin, flippant. I know your type. Starts out dancing and end up in all kinds of excesses, like murder, drugs, perversion, or taking seventy minutes for lunch! I'm tired of it, Tappin, I won't stand for it any more.

Tappin: Mr. Barington, I only —

Barington: You'd better — yes, I'm sorry, but you'd better go.

Tappin: But you'll take me on again to —

Barington: If there's one thing I won't tolerate, it's tap-dancing to company tempo!

Tappin: But you'll take me on tomorrow?

Barington: Take you on again? What kind of an organization do you think this is? When a man is fired he stays fired, as far as I'm concerned.

Tappin: You mean I'm — really fired?

Barington: I'm sorry, Tappin. But if there's one thing I won't stand its dancing in office hours. It's flippant, that's what it is. I never have been able to stand flippancy. No, sir. *(Waving)* You'd better clear out. *(He goes out then returns immediately)* And you can take your secretary with you. I'm not having that kind of flippancy in my company!

Exit. Gloria comes in and sits on Tappin's knee, notebook at the ready.

Gloria: Ludo, what's going on?

Tappin: He's — actually fired me . . .

Gloria: Oh, dear. And on a Monday, too.

Tappin: What am I going to do? *(He paces)*

Gloria: You shouldn't have too much trouble. You're an accountant.

Tappin: I'm — not fully qualified.

Gloria: Oh, dear. What are you going to do?

Tappin: Of course, money isn't a long-range worry. My Aunt Jane is leaving me a great deal of money in her will. I've great plans for that money . . . for all four of us.

Gloria: All four of who?

Tappin: But that doesn't solve the problem of the moment. I haven't much money saved up. I spent most of it on your little flat, and Eleanor's apartment.

Gloria: Eleanor?

Tappin: My other mistress.

Gloria: Your — ?

Tappin: Other mistress.

Gloria: Oh.

Tappin: Didn't I tell you?

Gloria: No.

Tappin: I thought you'd have heard.

Gloria: No.

Tappin: I thought everyone knew, except my wife.

Gloria: Your wife?

Tappin: Sybil.

Gloria: You didn't tell me you had a wife. It slipped your mind, did it?

Tappin: I thought you knew. I'm very sorry Gloria. I do love you very much.

Gloria: Do you?

Tappin: Yes, I love all three of you. You and Sybil and Eleanor.

Gloria: Oh.

Tappin: What shall I do? I can't afford to maintain a house as well as two apartments — Oh, by the way, Mr. Barington's fired you, too. *(Gloria shrugs as if this is a mere bagatelle)* I'm very sorry.

Gloria: Don't keep saying you're sorry. This is impossible — I like chaos as well as the next woman, but this —

Tappin: I'm sorry. I mean I'm not sorry.

Gloria: Not sorry, after what you've done? Men! So it's goodbye.

Tappin: (Almost inaudibly) No.

Gloria: What? 'Course it is.

Tappin: I can't let you go. I won't.

Gloria: Perhaps I've something to say about that!

Tappin: I love you.

Gloria: Love! You must have worn the word to shreds, using it on all three of us.

Tappin: Gloria —

Gloria: Don't touch me! Never touch me again! (She rushes off. She comes back almost as swiftly) Don't worry. I can soon get someone else to love me. I've never had the slightest difficulty. I can get someone else at the drop of a — at the drop of a . . . (Tappin takes her in his arms) But it's not so easy finding someone I can love back.

Tappin: I need you, Gloria.

Gloria: (Holding him tighter) Dirty dog.

Tappin: I won't let you go. I'll think of something . . . I'll think of something . . .

The lights fade. They go off. Sybil enters.

Sybil: Is that you, Ludovic? You still haven't found a job?

Tappin: No.

Sybil: Oh well, Atman will provide. (Tappin gives her a kiss on the cheek)

Tappin: I have a present for you.

Sybil: A present? Oh, how wonderful! (Frowns) Oh dear, I'm overjoyed, that's terrible. (Jumping for joy) What is it? Tell me! (Her face falling) Ashes to go with my sackcloth?

Tappin: No.

Sybil: The lives of the saints — uncensored?

Tappin: I'll get it. (He goes, returns with a portable TV set)

Sybil: A television! Oh, Ludovic, how simply — dreadful!

Tappin: It's just a used TV set.

Sybil: I don't know what to say, I'm so utterly shocked. Ludo, do you think we might actually have it on for a minute?

Tappin: (Plugging it in) We could try it out.

Sybil settles herself eagerly in front of it.

Sybil: How thrilling — it's the news!

Tappin: I'll turn up the sound.

Sybil: No, I'd rather not hear — the news is bound to be bad.

They stare at the TV set.

Tappin: He's got egg on his tie.

Sybil: No, dear, that's decoration. See, it's some kind of embroidery.

Tappin: Sybil?

Sybil: Yes, dear?

Tappin: We have a big house, here. Two spare bedrooms. It seems a pity to waste them.

Sybil: You're not — you're not suggesting we have in . . .? Not — infants, Ludo?

Tappin: Er — not exactly, no.

Sybil: Do you know, I really believe he does have egg on his tie.

E16

Tappin: (Switching off TV) Do you think we could have the TV off for a minute.

Sybil: (Disappointed) Oh. Perhaps there'll be a church service later.

Tappin: I shouldn't think so. They've very poor ratings, I understand. Sybil, I've a confession to make.

Sybil: Oh?

Tappin: It's . . . well, I have, as a matter of fact, two mistresses. (Pause. She looks up at him, her knitting needles slowing to a halt) I was wondering if you'd mind if they came to live with us.

Sybil: You were wondering if I'd mind if they came to live with us . . . Your mistresses . . . Ludo, would you mind starting again? I seem to have dropped, not just a stitch but a whole set of combinations.

Tappin: I have two mistresses, Gloria and Eleanor.

Sybil: I've got that, I think.

Tappin: I've paid for their love nests to the end of this month, but I can't afford to keep them after that.

Sybil: And you were suggesting they stay with us? Yes, I've almost caught up with you now.

Tappin: I thought that Gloria could sleep with me, and we could put Eleanor in the back bedroom.

Sybil: (Dropping her knitting and getting up) No, I haven't caught up. I haven't even passed the starting line. Let's take it from their staying with us.

Tappin: (Putting his arm around her and patting her shoulder) I knew you'd agree! I knew you wouldn't be selfish, Sybil.

Sybil: (Faintly) Don't mention it . . .

Starts to wander out dazedly.

Tappin: Wait, Sybil. There are one or two practical details to discuss.

Sybil: Are there? Their mere existence is practical enough for me . . . (Pause) On the . . . On the surface of it, Ludo, I'd say you'd been very — I hate to put it quite so bluntly, but the only way to describe it is evasive. Wouldn't you agree?

Tappin: Yes.

Sybil: I feel inclined to throw a rolling pin at you.

Tappin: Please do it if it would help.

Sybil: I'd have to go out and buy one first, of course . . . What would the bishop think, for one thing.

Tappin: Bishop?

Sybil: Uncle Linus.

Tappin: Oh, Uncle Linus. Well, he's in the Arctic with the Eskimos, so that's safe enough.

Sybil: Well, what about Aunt Jane? You know how moral she is.

Tappin: Yes.

Sybil: She won't leave you her money when she dies, if she finds out you're a dirty rotten bottle, filled to the neck with moral turpitude.

Tappin: That's all right — I won't tell her. Anyway she's in Prince Edward Island.

Sybil: And what about Mrs. Chamberlain next door.

Tappin: But the point is, what do you think?

Sybil: Well, I can hardly cultivate the non-attachment to the flesh, and make a fleshly scene. I begin to understand why it's so hard to be saintly. To do without the luxuries of jealousy is very hard!

Tappin: What is your answer, Sybil?

Sybil: I may have an answer as soon as I've worked out what the question is. It's such a questionable question requiring such an answerable answer. Whatever I decide I'm sure I'll be able to work out a decent Christian reason for it. Especially if it's no. *(She starts to go, sees the TV set)* Oh!

Tappin: What?

Sybil: So that's why you bought this TV set. For them to look at.

Tappin: No.

Sybil: Don't lie to me. You did.

Tappin: I didn't buy it. It belongs to Eleanor.

Sybil: Oh! That settles it! That . . . that certainly settles it.

She flounces out. The lights go out.

When the lights come up again we see all three women sitting side by side on the sofa. Sybil is knitting, Eleanor is reading in the middle, and Gloria on the right is lounging in her dressing gown. Underneath she wears only bra and pants. Most of one leg is showing.

The ladies knit, read and lounge in absolute silence for sixty seconds. Then Sybil, her elbows moving with her knitting, begins to jab Eleanor in the ribs, apparently accidentally. After the third 'accidental' jab Eleanor begins to drag herself from the depths of her book. She glances annoyed at Sybil. Sybil knits obliviously. Eleanor goes back to her book. Sybil jabs her again. Eleanor looks up again. Then goes back to her book. Sybil jabs her again. Eleanor stares pointedly at Sybil. She moves further away from Sybil. In so doing she jogs Gloria, who is painting her fingernails. Gloria gets paint on her fingers. She gives Eleanor a look. Eleanor returns it, then goes back to her book.

Gloria turns away from Eleanor, resumes painting her nails.

After a moment Sybil half turns away, too, knitting.

Gradually Eleanor becomes more and more irritated at the sight of their backs.

Finally she puts the book in her lap.

Eleanor: Perhaps you're proud of your backs, but I find them quite characterless.

They ignore her. She goes back to her book. But their backs irk her. Finally she gets up and goes out.

Gloria immediately puts her feet up.

After a few seconds her feet, only inches away, begin to annoy Sybil. She keeps glancing, glancing at them angrily.

Sybil: Do you mind?

Gloria: Mind what?

Sybil: Your feet.

Gloria: I don't mind them at all. In fact I'm quite attached to them.

Eleanor returns with a drink in her hand. She paces.

Eleanor: This is absolutely intolerable. I can't understand how he persuaded me.

Gloria: Me, too.

Sybil: And me.

Eleanor: I must have been mad to agree to this.

Gloria: Me too.

Sybil: And me. Except I don't remember agreeing.

Gloria: Neither do I.

Eleanor: Nor me.

Gloria: It's his eyes.

Eleanor: What?

Gloria: When he looks at me, I go all wibbly.

Sybil: Speaking for myself, I accept this situation in the right spirit. I've been trained to selflessness; and when I look around and see how tortured by pride people can be, I know

I'm right. So I feel quite impersonal about all this, perfectly serene. It's just that I can't stand you two being in my house!

Gloria: I guess I agreed because I'm a slave to his passion. Well, why not — sex is everything.

Sybil: Death is the only thing worth living for.

Gloria: Eh?

Sybil: The death of the passions.

Eleanor: Rubbish. Reaching the mind of another — that's the real contact, the real ecstasy.

Gloria: How can there be anything more thrilling than sex?

Eleanor: Maybe not, if sensuality is all you want.

Gloria: You bet.

Eleanor: But that's not love. Love is getting so close that — Oh, how often I've envied men's ability to get so close without sex as to make an embracing couple seem on separate mountain tops. My father the professor had that kind of friendship. He loved my mother, but it was from the Dean of Philosophy that he drew his strength. But whenever I tried to achieve a deep friendship with a man, **that** would get in the way. Until Ludo came along.

Gloria: So when he went to your apartment, all you did was . . .?

Gloria and Sybil wait tensely.

Eleanor: Our minds met. We became one.

Gloria and Sybil relax, catch each other's eye, and look away.

Tappin enters. He beams at the three women proudly.

Spontaneously he breaks into his dance.

In the middle of it, Sybil jumps up, throws aside her knitting and stamps to one side and folds her arms, seething.

Tappin: What's up? You haven't been quarrelling, have you?

Gloria: Oh, good heavens, no. Why on earth would we quarrel? (*Tappin takes up three parcels*)

Tappin: I have a present for you Gloria. With my love. (*She unwraps it. It is a bunch of strange, artificial flowers*)

Gloria: Oh, thank you, Ludo, darling. They — they're artificial flowers!

Tappin: And this is for you, Eleanor dearest. (*Eleanor unwraps her present. It is a vase*)

Eleanor: A vase! Oh, Ludo, it's beautiful! Thank you! Isn't it exquisite?

Tappin: And for my most dear Sybil.

Sybil: (*As she unwraps her present*) Hope it's a horsewhip. (*It is a plantpot stand*) Oh — thank you very much, Ludovic. But you really shouldn't always be giving me presents, though.

Gloria: What is it?

Sybil: It's a stand!

Eleanor puts her vase on it.

Eleanor: Just what I needed — for my vase.

Gloria puts her flowers in the vase.

Gloria: And my flowers.

So all three women are mad again.

Tappin: There, now, everybody's happy. (*He looks at their angry backs*) Of course I know things will take a bit of getting used to. (*Sybil stamps her foot*) Before, we were separate but close —

Eleanor: Now we're close but separate.

Tappin: No, not really.

Gloria: I don't think it's going to work, Ludo.

Tappin: It must, it will. Oh, it will take time — just as it takes time for a string quartet to achieve a perfection of harmony. Yes! The Tappin Quartet! Oh, my dearest ones, we will learn to play such variations on our single soul that all humanity will be enraptured, and enriched!

As he speaks, the women gaze at him spellbound, not so much by his words as by his conviction.

Eleanor: Ludo, is it possible?

Tappin: Yes, Eleanor. We have each so much to give the other. As for us, we can't fail to be better off than we were.

Eleanor: How?

Tappin: Our opportunities for discussion will be all the greater, won't they?

Eleanor: Yes, but —

Tappin: It should make not the slightest difference otherwise.

Eleanor: I suppose not, theoretically; but —

Tappin: So nothing has changed, has it?

Eleanor: I suppose not, but . . .

Gloria: It has for me.

Tappin: How?

Gloria: How can we get together with all this horde of women around?

Sybil: Are you calling me a horde?

Tappin: Living together permanently will give us even greater opportunities for physical oneness.

Gloria: Theoretically, maybe, but —

Tappin: Before I could afford only occasionally evenings at your little apartment. Now we'll be able to concentrate.

Gloria: M'm.

Sybil: And what about me? How much of your time is left for me?

Tappin: It stands to reason, more than ever.

Sybil: Huh!

Tappin: The time I spent travelling to visit Gloria and Eleanor will now be shared at home with you. Isn't that right, dear?

Sybil: Well, well, yes, but —

Tappin: Dear Sybil, you know it can't make the slightest difference to us. What we have isn't divisible by time or other people. Why, even if I had a dozen women in the house, it couldn't —

Eleanor: What's that? You're not thinking of bringing any more women in, are you?

Tappin: No, no, what an absurd idea. I was just . . . I was just . . . *(He thinks about it for a moment)*

Gloria: Now, Ludo!

Tappin: Where was I?

Eleanor: You were busy juggling. You'd got to Sybil.

Tappin: I don't juggle with human beings, Eleanor. I've always tried to give all of myself honestly, so's to get honesty back from you. I love you all devotedly, you are my need, my reason, my life.

There is an emotional silence.

Gloria: Oh, Lude! Come upstairs!

The spell broken, Sybil draws in her breath and stamps out.

Tappin: In spite of herself, she perhaps still clings to the old idea of marriage as a business arrangement. As if we'd put ten per cent down and were making monthly payments for the exclusive use of each other. But she'll come round. She's not selfish. *(He sits beside Gloria, caresses her)*

E20

Gloria: How did you two get onto this mortification of the flesh routine?

Tappin: My eyes first fell on her in Yoga class. She was in the lotus positon.

Gloria: What nice hands you have.

Tappin: She was the only one, I think, who had taken up Yoga for the proper reason — dedicated to the detachment of the mind from the body for union with the godhead. So I married her.

Gloria: And spent your honeymoon contemplating each other's navels.

Sybil enters, trying not to sound glad.

Sybil: Ludovic. The bishop.

Tappin: Bishop? What bishop?

Sybil: Our bishop.

Tappin: Our bish—? What? Not Uncle Linus?!

Sybil: He's musing his way up the street.

Tappin: Oh, good grief!

Doorbell chimes.

Tappin: Oh, no — Quick, everyone, hide! He mustn't find out what's going on here!

Sybil: He's not likely to, since none of us knows.

Tappin: Hide, everyone, please, don't just hang around!

Eleanor: *(With dignity)* I'm not hanging around; I never hang around.

Tappin: Hide, quick, he'll come in by himself in a —

Sybil: I'll go upstairs. *(Exit Sybil)*

Tappin: Yes, that's right, go up — No, no, not you, you're the one he's supposed to see — Sybil! Oh, hell — You two get out of sight — please!

Eleanor: Well, all right, as long as he doesn't stay too long. *(Exit)*

Tappin: Quick, he's coming in! *(Gloria starts to hurry off)* No, no, not that way — for heaven's sake, Gloria —

She is about to hurry off in the other direction when the Bishop enters, wearing a dog collar and purple vest and clerical suit, and carrying a suitcase. Glasses suspended from one ear.

Bishop: Ah, Sybil! It is Sybil, isn't it? I can't see a thing without my glasses. I'm sure I had them a moment ago. Now where . . . *(Searching the floor for glasses. Tappin gently removes them and gives them to Gloria)*

Tappin: *(Urgent whisper)* Hide them. *(Gloria hides them)*

Tappin: Uncle. How are you?

Bishop: Ah Ludovic! How pleasant to see you. *(Shakes hands with Tappin, squinting at Gloria)* At least it would be pleasant if I could see you. But my eyes are not what they were, you know. Short sightedness in a clergyman is rather a hard burden to carry, letting me in for all kinds of digs, japes and joshing from pagans, agnostics and our Catholic confreres. You've grown, Sybil. Isn't that unusual at your age?

Tappin: Uncle, what brings you here? *(Anxiously)* I don't suppose you can stay. Oh, hard luck.

Bishop: Certainly, my boy. What brings me here? On the surface I'd say my legs bring me here, bring me here on the surface indeed. *(Gloria is starting to sneak out)* By Job, Sybil my dear, you certainly have changed. *(Looks at one of her long, bare legs)* Er — for the better, I see — or at least I think I see. Where are my glasses? I don't often wear them as usually I've only my colleagues to look at. But this seems like an occasion for celebrating, optically speaking. Where are my glasses?

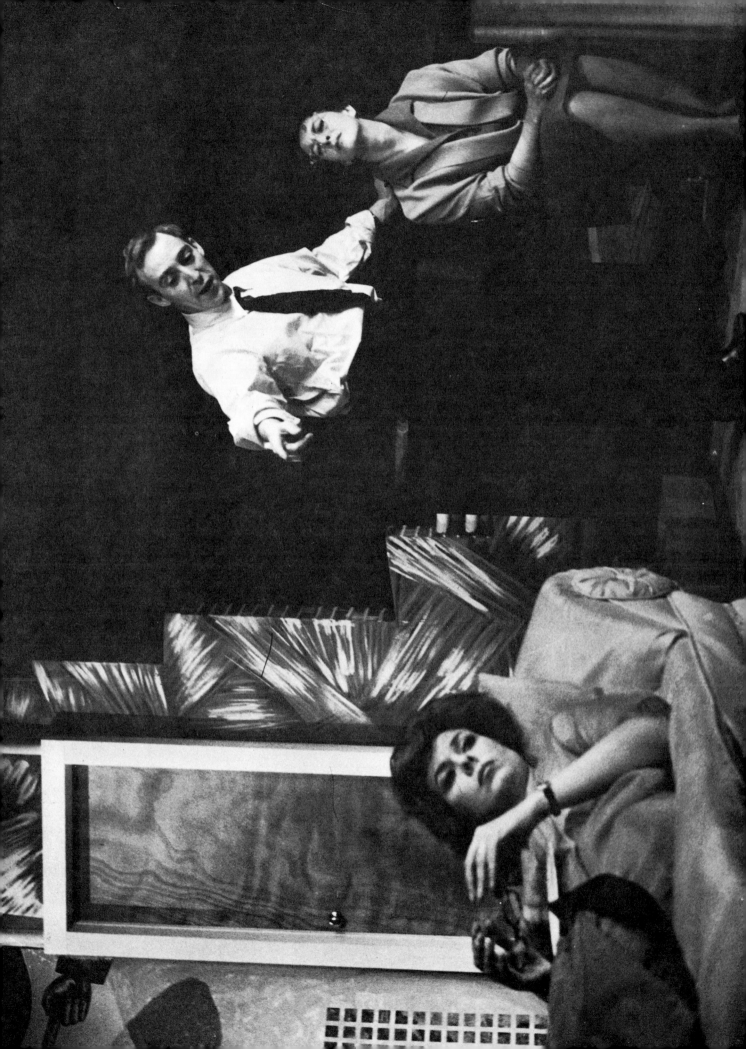

Tappin: You had a good trip down from the Arctic, Uncle!

Bishop: *(Turning)* Oh, did I?

Tappin: Yes. Your diocese in the Arctic, you live at Tuktoyuktuk.

Bishop: That's remarkably accurate. *(To Gloria)* You must come up to my room and see my Eskimo carvings.

Gloria: *(Coyly)* Oh, Uncle!

Bishop: *(Patting her hand)* No need to be formal. Just call me Right Reverend.

Tappin: Uncle Linus is Aunt Jane's brother.

Gloria: Is that the Aunt Jane that . . .?

Tappin: Yes, who's leaving me all her money —

Gloria: That's great.

Tappin: Provided I get a clean bill of health from the bishop, morally speaking.

Gloria: Oh dear.

Tappin: Aunt Jane and the bishop are very close.

Bishop: Dear sister Jane . . .

Tappin: And equally moral.

Gloria: Oh — oh.

Tappin: So the bishop has me covered. One false move — and he has me uncovered.

Bishop: Precisely. So, if I may venture a little jest, you will have to "watch your step". Ha. Yes. Well, Ludovic, which room can I have?

Tappin: Oh, you can have the one that's — what? Which room? You're — you're not staying here, are you, Uncle?

Bishop: You asked before what brings me here. I can answer in just one word: one word, namely, I come here to refresh myself, Ludovic, to stif-fen the sinews of my spiritual arm, through the sublime abnegation of your mystical household, with its renunciation of the things of the flesh —

Gloria: Renunciation of what?

Bishop: Flesh.

Gloria: Oh.

Bishop: *(Striding up and down, inspired)* To refresh myself with the example of a couple unattached to the perverse universe, this continent of incontinence — in a word, to refresh myself with the example of a couple who have renounced —

Gloria: What couple are you talking about?

Bishop: Hm? Why, you and Ludovic, of course . . .

Gloria: Oh, yes.

Sybil comes on. Tappin desperately waves her out. She stares blankly. He goes on gesturing. She gets it and goes out just before the Bishop turns.

Bishop: Why else would I want to sojourn in your ascetic house. It's abominably cold — *(Sits on the sofa)* there's no comfortable place to sit, the beds are like Stryker frames for people with ruined spines. *(Reclines luxuriously)* But it's good for me. I need to get away from the fleshpots of the Arctic. I need to have my inner coils renewed. *(To Tappin)* That's why I've decided to stay a few days. To mortify my flesh. Hello, a TV set. Is there anything on? I'm particularly partial to Cecil and Beany.

Tappin: But Uncle —

Gloria: *(Snuggling beside the Bishop)* I just love the way you use a thousand words where one will do.

Bishop: Yes, it's my ecclesiastical training. I —

Tappin: But you can't stay here, Uncle. I mean?

Bishop: I've already explained, my boy, why I've chosen to spend a few days here, but if you like, I'll go over it again. In a word —

Tappin: Don't bother, Uncle. I think I've got it. (Exit.)

The Bishop pats Gloria's hand.

Bishop: Well, my dear, you're looking very ... (He peers, sees she's wearing very little) — cool.

Gloria: Tell me what you do in the Arctic, Uncle?

Bishop: God's work, Sybil. It's very hard.

Gloria: It must be.

Bishop: The Eskimos are confoundedly virtuous it almost makes one want to give up.

Gloria: You look after the Eskimos, do you?

Bishop: And Looshoo Indians, yes.

Gloria: Is it true the Eskimos offer their wives for the night as a mark of hospitality?

Bishop: Oh, we cured them of that. We've taught them to cling to their possessions. (He gets up) I think it's time to take my bag up to my room.

Gloria: (Jumping up) Oh. Wait, Right Reverence — I'll get it ready for you.

Bishop: But I also need to go upstairs to —

Gloria: (Pushing him down) You make yourself comfortable. Have a drink or something. I'll be right back.

Bishop: But I need to go to the Jonathan.

But she grabs his suitcase and hurries off, passing Eleanor re-entering.

Gloria: I'm getting the bishop's room ready.

Eleanor: Your job is to herd your flock into the ritual corral where they might understand the meaning of things by faith and visceral acceptance rather than through, to, and beyond conscious comprehension to superconscious union.

Bishop: (Uncomprehending) Er ... yes. (Getting up) I think I'll lie down for a moment ...

Tappin enters. He sees Eleanor now, with the Bishop.

Tappin: Oh — oh.

Bishop: I do wish you wouldn't keep dribbling in and out, Ludovic. It seems to have an unsettling effect, not merely on me but on Sybil here.

Tappin: Sybil? Oh, yes. Show Uncle to his room, Sybil.

Eleanor: (To Bishop) All right. Which room are you in?

Bishop: Dash it all, you should know — you've just been up to get it ready.

Tappin dodges out.

Eleanor: Are you staying then, Uncle?

Bishop: (Sitting, holding his head) I begin to wonder ... Ludovic — Tchk! He's done it again! (He gets up and stumbles over his bag) Oh, so that's where my bag is.

Tappin comes in.

Tappin: I've found out. Yours is the back bedroom, Uncle.

Indicates centre door. Eleanor starts to protest. Tappin silences her.

Bishop: Good. Well, I'll go up and unpack.

Tappin: I'll show you the way.

Bishop: It's quite all right. I know the back bedroom. It's the one with the window jammed open, allowing all that lovely fresh air to howl in.

He shudders involuntarily and fumbles his way out with his bag.

Eleanor: That's my bedroom. Where am I going to sleep?

Tappin: I don't know. He's staying for a few days. It'll mean some adjustments.

Eleanor: Adjustments. That probably means I'll have to sleep in the cellar.

Sybil comes in, dressed to go, carrying two bags, one the Bishop's.

Tappin: What? Oh, yes . . .

Bishop: Well, how are you getting on, Ludovic?

Tappin: Not so good at the moment.

Bishop: *(Looking for his suitcase)* I do wish I could find my glasses so I could see whether you've developed a mystic aura yet. I had a close look at Sybil and I must confess I perceived little sign of anything mystic about her as yet. *(Can't find his suitcase)* Oh, dear — *(Tappin goes out again)* Now I can't even find my bag. Ludovic, can you see my — Indeed, now I can't even see you, Ludovic.

Eleanor sticks her head in cautiously and looks around. The Bishop sees her.

Bishop: Ah, there you are, Ludovic, have you seen — Oh no, it's Sybil isn't it?

Eleanor: Sybil? Yes, I suppose so. *(She comes in with the Bishop's suitcase)*

Bishop: Can I go up to my room now?

Eleanor: I don't see why not. *(Puts the bag down. The Bishop doesn't see it)* I found this in my room.

Bishop: What? Your voice seems to be very changeable, Sybil. *(Peers closely)* Oh, I see you have your clothes on.

Eleanor: I beg your pardon?

Bishop: That was quick. *(Confidentially)* Tell me — Ludovic seems to be somewhat vague today — are you and he any closer to mystic communion yet? I'm most interested. You see, my dear, I'm so busy ministering to the physical welfare of my people I've so little time left for mystic speculation.

Eleanor: *(Interested)* Really?

Bishop: Yes, I —

Eleanor: Surely it's not your business anyway.

Bishop: What do you mean?

Eleanor: *(Sitting, interested)* Well, your line is religion. Surely it's merely your job to give your flock a fix.

Bishop: A fix?

Eleanor: To inject them with the forms but not the content of the sublime. To hypo the body politic into the mindless acceptance of the spiritual, rather than the spiritual acceptance of the mind.

Bishop: What a changeable person you are —

Tappin: Sybil? What are you doing — dressed —

Sybil: I'm going. There's no room for me here.

Tappin: There is! You're essential! You mustn't!

Sybil: I'm going away until all this blows over.

Tappin: Oh, I thought you meant — for good.

Sybil: Why shouldn't I? I'm not going for good, but if I was going for good, why shouldn't I — go for good? I must say I think most women would find the presence of an adulterer, a bishop and two mistresses — I think they might find that sufficient justification for leaving.

Tappin: Don't go. I can't do without you, Sybil.

Sybil: I'm sorry, but you'll just have to. *(Relenting)* I'll be in the Gaiety Hotel.

Tappin: All right. I suppose . . . Damn, all I needed was a little time. Why did he have to turn up? Oh well — in the circumstances. You won't stay too long, will you? I see you've two bags. I didn't know you had that many possessions.

Sybil: I found this one upstairs, outside the bathroom.

Eleanor: You've brought the bishop's bag down again.

Tappin: Look out, here he comes!

Eleanor hurries out just as the Bishop enters.

Bishop: This is too much! My bag's wandered off again! *(Sees Sybil dressed to go out)*

Sybil: Uncle! *(Embracing him)* How lovely to see you again!

Bishop: Sybil? But it's only a minute since you saw m— *(Wearily)* Oh, never mind.

Sybil: How are you, Uncle?

Bishop: I haven't the faintest idea. *(Looks at her closely)* Now you're dressed to go out. Are you taking lessons from a quick change artist?

Sybil: *(Kissing the Bishop)* Well, goodbye, Uncle.

She takes up one of the bags. It is the wrong bag.

Bishop: Why, where are you going?

Sybil: *(Looking at Tappin soberly)* I'm not at all sure. *(Exit)*

Bishop: Peculiarer and peculiarer . . .

He turns dazedly to go, stumbles over his bag.

Bishop: So this is where you got to . . . *(The Bishop addresses the hatrack which has a hat and coat on it)* You know Ludovic, considering there's just two persons here, not counting myself of course — this house seems unnaturally crowded.

Exit. Tappin sits and mops his brow. Gloria looks in.

Gloria: Has he gone?

Tappin: What? Yes.

Gloria: Was that Sybil I just saw, going in a taxi?

Tappin: Which Sybil? Oh, you mean Sybil. Yes. *(Startled)* Leaving in a taxi?

Gloria: Yes.

Tappin: She'd only a few miles to walk. What extravagance . . .
The Bishop re-enters.
Bishop: *(Muttering)* This is really the limit! I'm quite sure I packed in my bag my clerical pyjamas, but the first thing I unpack is this object! *(Holds up a sackcloth nightshirt)*

Tappin: What are you doing with Sybil's nightdress?

Bishop: I'm not doing anything with it. I — I just don't understand. My bag after wandering upstairs and downstairs, in here and out, has now changed its sex; it's full of women's clothes! Ludovic!

He looks at Gloria in her bra and pants, goes out, returns, his eyes bulging.

Sybil! Great Job! She's undressed again!

End of Act One

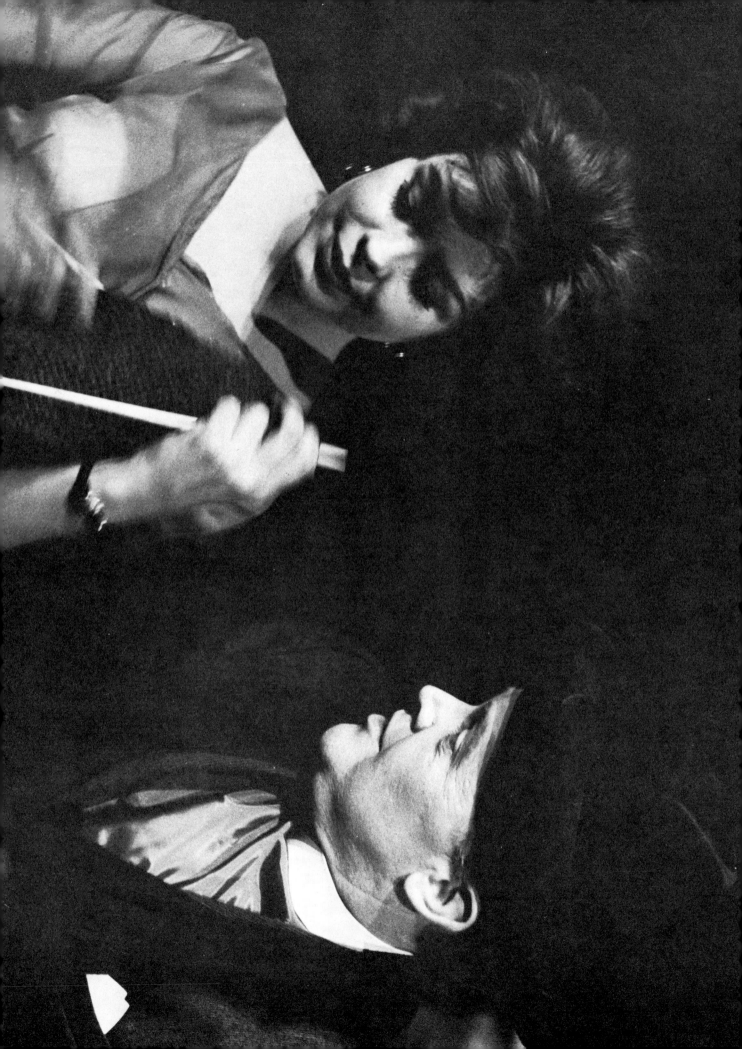

Act Two

By now the stage holds an office chair, handbell, blackboard and easel, sofa, hatrack, plantpot and stand and flowers, TV set, luggage.

In addition it now contains a portable computer, a bar and two stools on one of which Sybil is sitting, holding a bunch of balloons, and with a few coloured streamers hanging from her hair.

Music is playing. Sybil is dressed in a fashionably altered version of the Bishop's clothes.

Sybil: Here at the Gaiety Hotel, all is gaiety, I suppose.

Barington comes in clutching his tape recorder, carrying a drink.

Sybil: Hello, Simon.

Barington: Sybil. What are you doing here?

Sybil: Ludovic has a bishop and two mistresses at home.

Barington: Oh. *(He pours two drinks)* What are you drinking? Ginger ale? Come on, have something stronger.

Sybil: Even this is an indulgence for me.

Barington: I'm darned glad to see you.

Sybil and Barington look at each other in silence for a moment. Barington reaches out and touches her hand.

Sybil: Simon?

Barington: Yes, Sybil?

Sybil: Why do you always carry that tape recorder around?

Barington is confused.

Barington: What? Cut! I think we'd better take that again.

Sybil: All right.

Barington: Turn it over.

Sybil: Speed.

Barington: Action.

Sybil: Simon?

Barington: Yes, Sybil?

Sybil: Simon, why do you always carry that tape-recorder around with you?

Barington: Are you sure those are your lines?

Sybil: Yes.

Barington: I've never told another soul about this. Not even my wife. Are you sure you want to know?

Sybil: Is it dreadful?

Barington: Yes.

Sybil: All right.

Barington: (Bracing himself) Well — here goes.

He starts the tape recorder. The recorder speaks in Barington's voice, very hearty.

Recorder: You are Mr. Simon Barington! Cheerful, successful, well-liked. Not exactly handsome, but smart!

Barington: Yes, that's right.

Recorder: You have everything a man would want, from monogrammed long johns to a personal psychoanalyst. What more could anyone want?

Barington: Absolutely nothing! No, sir, absolutely nothing!

Recorder: You have two cars, a boat, six insurance policies and you don't owe the income tax a damn thing!

Barington: But do people really like me, Simon? I mean, do they really? I mean, Louise doesn't seem to, much.

Recorder: You are popular as hell! People laugh at your jokes, dogs adore you, and women breathe faster whenever you come near them! You are brave, generous, kind, convivial, resilient, volatile, effervescent! You are Barington! The salt of the earth!

Barington: (Convinced) You're sure, eh? I mean, really sure?

Recorder: Yes! (Laughs heartily)

Barington: (Laughing, too) Yeah. (But though the recorder is still chuckling away, a gloomy look comes on Barington's face) Well, I wouldn't have got where I am today if I hadn't been a bit unscrupulous now and then.

Recorder: You are successful, that's all that matters! ! ! You've got to do what's best for yourself, Simon!

Barington: Damn right!

Recorder: Everything is worthwhile. You've got the most out of life! You're happy! Happy, do you hear?

Barington: Yeah, I hear. (He switches off the tape recorder. Sybil looks at him compassionately) Well, now you know. You won't tell anyone will you?

Sybil: No.

Barington: You want to hear more? It gets worse.

Sybil: If you want me to hear. (He hesitates, then switches on again)

Recorder: You are Mr. Simon Barington.

Barington: I know.

Recorder: Born in Regina in nineteen-twenty, you had a distinguished academic career at the Brannigan High School where you did damn well in such diverse subjects as arithmetic, woodwork, football and French.

Barington: Wee wee, Monsewer.

Recorder: And today if you don't have everything you want, you certainly have everything you need.

Barington: Yeah. There's just one thing wrong.

Recorder: What's that?

Barington: Oh, nothing.

Recorder: (Angrily) Come on now, out with it? What is this one thing that's wrong?

Barington: No, honest, it's nothing.

Recorder: Listen, you started this now come on! Come on now!

Barington: Well, it's just that I — I don't feel anything. *(He laughs: his laugh fades as he looks at Sybil)* I don't feel anything. No anger or — or even disappointment much. And — you know, I've got a lot to be disappointed about.

Recorder: You're a liar!

Barington: I'm not.

Recorder: You're a liar, I say!

Barington: *(To Sybil)* I don't even think I'd feel much if I saw an H bomb dropped — so long as I was safe. Why don't I feel, like I ought to, Sybil. Why don't I care about anything, or even just feel — humility or something? You know what I am? I'm half-dead, Sybil.

Sybil: Oh, Simon . . .

Barington: You know how I can tell? *(Gestures at the recorder)* Because I can't even feel anything about that. If I was really alive, I'd kick it in the capacitors. You know why I don't? Because all I can think of is — it cost three hundred bucks . . .

The recorder chuckles malevolently. The lights go down. When the lights come up again, mainly on the three doors, Tappin comes on slowly.

Tappin: Well, time for bed, I guess. I hate confusing Uncle Linus, but I need that money to pay my union musicians. I wonder why it is that the higher the ideal, the more money you need to achieve it; while the more money you have the further the ideal recedes?

He goes into the right hand (R) door, leaving it open: then re-emerges with toilet bag and towel.

(All the directions are stage directions)

Tappin goes off towards the bathroom.

The set is empty for a moment, a few seconds. Then the Bishop comes on, goes through the centre (C) door and closes it.

Gloria comes cautiously up the stairs, hesitates. She doesn't know which room she is in. She tries the (L) door.

Gloria: Ludo?

No response. She taps at the centre door. The Bishop opens it, in his trousers and purple vest and collar.

Gloria: Oh, sorry.

Gloria backs away. She hesitates, then goes into the (R) door. The bishop stares after her. Gloria re-emerges cautiously. She sees the Bishop. She has to go back in. She closes the door.

The Bishop looks after her curiously, then goes back into his room.

Tappin enters and makes for the (L) door. Gloria looks out of (R) door.

Gloria: Psst! Which is our room?

Tappin is about to answer when the Bishop's door starts to open. Gloria returns to the room. The Bishop comes out with his towel and toilet articles.

Bishop: Goodnight.

Tappin: Goodnight.

The Bishop beams at Tappin. Tappin enters (L) door and closes it. The Bishop starts off, then comes back and stares at both (L) and (R) doors, puzzled. Then shrugs and goes off.

Eleanor enters and goes into the (R) door. After a moment she and Gloria emerge. Eleanor indicates the (L) door.

Eleanor: That's it.

Gloria: Thanks. *(Gloria goes into the (L) room, closes the door. Then before Eleanor can enter (R) door, Gloria comes out and hurries across again to (R) door.)* Forgot my towel and things.

Eleanor is still outside. Gloria comes out again with her towel and things, and is about to cross back when she sees the Bishop coming and goes back into the (R) room.

The Bishop waits. Immediately, Tappin comes out of (L) and starts to lead Eleanor towards (R): then sees the Bishop and in a continuous movement, leads Eleanor back into (L). The Bishop, considerably puzzled, goes into (C) and closes the door.

After a moment, all the doors open and every-one sticks his head out. The Bishop stares at Tappin and Eleanor at (L). He starts to turn his head to look at (R) door. Gloria gets it closed just in time. The Bishop stares straight out for a moment, then closes his door again.

Gloria comes out and makes a dash for the (L) door and gets in just before the Bishop hurries out of his room and sneaks to the (R) door and peers inside. Seeing nobody, he goes in.

Eleanor emerges from (L) and sneaks across to (R). She is about to go in, sees the Bishop backing out, and in a panic rushes into the Bishop's room.

The Bishop goes back to his own door, tries it. It is locked. He goes to (L) and knocks.

Bishop: Ludovic?

Tappin looks out cautiously.

Tappin: Yes, Uncle?

Bishop: My door is locked.

Tappin goes over and tries (C) door.

The Bishop, hearing Gloria singing to herself feels his way cautiously into the room.

Tappin, meanwhile has made a quick check of (R) and not finding Eleanor, goes to (C) and taps hurriedly.

Tappin: Eleanor?

Eleanor: Yes?

Tappin: Quick!

Eleanor hurries out of (C) and into (R): just as there is a scream, and the Bishop backs hurriedly out of (L).

Bishop: I beg your pardon, Sybil, I'm terribly sorry, I—

He hurries into C and closes the door as Tappin hurries into (L). The Bishop opens (C) again, and stares towards (L).

Bishop: That wasn't — Sybil?

Eleanor looks out of (R).

Eleanor: Yes?
She sees the Bishop, dodges back into (R). The Bishop whirls, stares at (R) then rushes to (L) knocks. As he does so Eleanor hurries into (C) Tappin looks out of (L).
Bishop: Ludo, there's something fishy going on here! Come and see for yourself!

As the Bishop and Tappin go into (R) door, Gloria rushes from L door to (C) door. The Bishop and Tappin emerge from (R) door, go in (L) door.

Bishop: Well then, she's in here!

They go into (L) door. Eleanor and Gloria dash from (C) door back to (R) door. The Bishop emerges from (R) and makes for (C) door.

Bishop: Then she must be in my room!

He hurries into (C) door. Tappin rushes to (R) door, joins Gloria and Eleanor. The three of them run across to (L) door. The second they are in, the Bishop looks out of (C) door. Eleanor comes out of (L) door, walks past him to (R) door, goes in, closes it.

Bishop: I really must find my glasses. I really must.

Blackout. Lights up. Eleanor comes on. Seeing nobody around she tries to do a Cha-Cha and to swing her hips seductively.

Eleanor: Cha-Cha.

There is a crash off. She hurries to the computer. The Bishop enters, limping and rubbing his knee.

Eleanor: Good morning. I hope you slept well.

Bishop: Oh, good morning, Sybil. The wooden bed was perhaps a trifle uncomfortable. I awoke this morning with my epidermis full of splinters. *(Hearing the computer buzz, warble, and click, he feels his way over)* What is this?

Eleanor: Computer.

Bishop: A computer? Is it really? May I try? Will it do sums?

Eleanor: It's not for simple arithmetic, you know.

Bishop: What shall I ask it to do? I know: how about two and two? *(He taps out this sum. The machine rattles)* Four! Isn't that marvellous! Ten times ten, is . . .?

Eleanor: *(Worried)* It's used to more complex things.

Bishop: I'm sure it won't mind ten times ten. Ten times ten is — a hundred! Wonderful! But I don't understand what this has to do with you, Sybil.

Eleanor: I'm not Sybil.

Bishop: You're speaking metaphysically, of course.

Eleanor: I'm not Sybil, I don't want to be Sybil, I refuse to be Sybil.

Bishop: Is nobody making breakfast?

Eleanor: I went through all this religious stuff. I was brought up in unquestioning faith, I nodded over the church's undebateable sermons. Then I went to university.

Bishop: That's where we lose a lot of people.

Eleanor: And there people did question, did debate. And I'd no answers. Especially to the one vital question.

Bishop: But I thought you had the answer, you and Ludo?

Eleanor: Uncle — I mean, Linus. Linus, couldn't you talk to me just for a moment as, well, as a stranger called Eleanor.

Bishop: Really, Sybil —

Eleanor: Eleanor!

Bishop: Very well, Eleanor, if you insist, but I think it most unfair of you to be metaphysical, especially before breakfast. When are we going to eat, anyway?

Eleanor: I've put some beef in the oven. But listen —

Bishop: Roast beef for breakfast. It wouldn't surprise me in the least.

Eleanor: Will you listen! Tell me the difference between those who believe, and those who don't.

Bishop: He works in a mysterious way, his wonders to perform. *(Eleanor makes an exasperated noise)* Belief, my dear, is a matter of —

Eleanor: Never mind.

Bishop: The spirit, you see, is not something —

Eleanor: Excuse me. *(She goes back to her computer)*

Bishop: You're quite right. I haven't much left save honesty, so I should stick to that, like a drowning man clutching even at the flotsam from a sundering ship. Or is it jetsam? The fact is, I don't know.

Eleanor: You don't know?

Bishop: It's like asking me the difference between life and death. I don't know the difference. The theological implications of the confession have wide ramifications . . . No, no, I must speak more directly, for once in my life. But — could you allow me just one biblical quotation?

Eleanor: Go ahead.

Bishop: For if the trumpet give an uncertain sound, who shall prepare himself for the battle? One Corinthians, fourteen, eight.

Eleanor: You have doubts?

Bishop: Not so much doubts as — I'm so busy with religion I've no time left for God. When I preached in this city, I couldn't get through to the people. And I blamed them. But when I went to the Arctic, among the Eskimos and Looshoos, with their truer understanding . . .

He gestures hopelessly.

Eleanor: But I think you try.

Bishop: I used to.

Eleanor: I think I understand. Your doubt is not in the message, but in yourself as the messenger.

Bishop: You do understand, Eleanor. How strange: now I think of you as Eleanor, I find you much more real than Sybil.

Eleanor: I am glad.

Bishop: I'd no idea one could get across one's meaning so simply — what a wonderful discovery. Of course, now I think of it, the Bible is in simple language . . . H'm . . . I really must get some new glasses. Is there an optician in the house? No? I'll have to go out and get some . . .

He wanders out, muttering. Gloria looks in cautiously.

Gloria: Has he gone?

Eleanor shrugs. Gloria comes in with a heavy book and a plate of sausage rolls. Eleanor works

at her computer. It buzzes, warbles, clicks and pops. Gloria feels the Bishop's glasses in her pocket, tries them on as she looks at the books and eats a sausage roll.

Gloria: How can he see through these?

Eleanor: Damn.

Gloria: What's the matter?

Eleanor: The equation won't come out.

Leaning over Eleanor, Gloria goes over the equation, looking learned.

Gloria: Let me see, now . . . (*After a moment Eleanor looks at her. Realizing her presumption Gloria desists and holds out the plate*) Have a sausage roll. (*Eleanor takes one, goes back to work*) Must be wonderful, knowing how to add up and divide and subtract. All I know is how to multiply. Is mathematics really fun?

Eleanor: If you only knew what ecstasy it can be, to follow an equation of thought to its conclusion.

Gloria: I wish I was clever, like you. I guess it must be wonderful, being able to talk to Ludo and get all excited over ideas and things.

Eleanor: Yes . . . Of course you have compensations.

Gloria: But afterwards, we've nothing to say. He seems quite happy that way, but . . . I don't know, I feel cheated, somehow. I suppose it's my own fault for being ignorant. I do envy you, Eleanor.

Eleanor: You **envy** me?

Tappin enters, and beams at them.

Tappin: Good morning, Sybils!

He dances happily but again the step won't come out right.

Eleanor: Ludo, I'm not satisfied with my role.

Tappin comes over and takes up her sausage roll and examines it.

Tappin: What's wrong with it?

Eleanor: It hasn't enough meat.

Tappin sees Gloria toying with the Bishop's glasses, as she looks at the large volume she has brought in.

Tappin: Look after those glasses, Gloria. Where is the bishop, anyway?

Eleanor: Gone to look for an optician.

Tappin: Oh. Oh, well, it'll take some time to get another pair.

Gloria holds out the glasses.

Gloria: They're getting bent in my pocket, Ludo. I'd feel better if you looked after them.

Tappin is about to take the glasses —

Tappin: What's that smell?

Eleanor: Oh, the roast beef!

Tappin: Roast beef?

Eleanor: Well, it's time I learned to cook — and other things. *(She dashes out)*

Tappin: What's come over her? That's not her line.

He is even more bewildered when he sees Gloria puzzling over the book.

Gloria: Ludo, this book.

Tappin: *(Looking at the title)* Quantum mechanics?

Gloria: I think I understand the Quantum Theory all right, except for this word here.

Tappin: That's the name of the author. What's going on here?

Eleanor comes back with the roast beef on a plate. It is smoking and blackened.

Eleanor: Just look at it! Like something out of a horror movie!

Tappin: Well don't bring it in the living room! Oh, Eleanor!

He takes the plate and goes back to the kitchen, Eleanor following.

Eleanor: Well, nobody ever taught me how to operate an oven.

They go out just as the Bishop enters.

Still absorbed in her book and not realizing Tappin has gone, Gloria again holds out the glasses.

Gloria: Here, I'd feel much safer if you looked after these.

Bishop: Oh, certainly. *(He takes them)* I'm afraid somebody will have to guide me to the opticians; I nearly fell down a coal chute. *(Gloria reacts as she realizes what she has done. The Bishop starts to put the glasses on)* I had a terrible job finding my way back, let alone forward. I thought I'd never — *(He stares at Gloria)* Oh, Oh! I'm terribly sorry! *(He hastens back to the door)* I really must apologize, my dear, I seem to have entered the wrong house, I — Please forgive me — How utterly stupid — But I was sure I had the —

He hurries out. A few seconds later he returns slowly, taking off and peering at his glasses, then putting them on again.

Bishop: But these are my glasses . . .

Tappin and Eleanor enter.

Tappin: Oh, oh!

Bishop: Ludo! So it is the right house!

Tappin tries to sweep Eleanor out again.

Tappin: Excuse me.

Bishop: Just a minute, Ludo!

Tappin: I'll be back in a minute, Uncle, I just have to show Sybil how to clean an oven —

Bishop: Show Sybil; yes, but where is she? *(Gestures at Eleanor)* Who is this lady?

Tappin: Oh, that is no lady, that is my — my . . .

Bishop: I'm waiting for an explanation, Ludo.

Tappin: Well, as a matter of fact — Well, this is Eleanor. She's my — Are you sure you want to hear this, Uncle?

Bishop: I'll decide that after I've heard it. Now, sir!

Tappin: Well, this lady is my . . .

Eleanor: Mistress. Sort of.

Bishop: Mistress. Oh.

Tappin: She's called Eleanor.

Bishop: So you said. And this? *(He gestures at Gloria, who is trying to hide behind the furniture)*

Tappin: Gloria.

Bishop: Gloria, I see.

Tappin: She's my mistress, too.

Bishop: I see. And where is the real Sybil?

Tappin: Staying at a hotel.

Bishop: Staying at a hotel. Yes. No wonder I've been experiencing little spiritual recharging. It seems instead I have wandered into a den of iniquity. *(He starts up, staring at Eleanor delighted)* Oh! Then — you're not my niece — you're Eleanor. You are — *(His face falls)* But of course you are still Ludo's . . . Yes. I think I'd better get up and lie down so I can rise to the occasion and stand up to all the — I'm babbling, excuse me.

He looks at Tappin sadly.

Bishop: Oh, Ludo, Ludo. I know you want to get genuinely close to people; but this is really going too far.

Blackout. In dim light, Sybil comes on cautiously from the left, Barington from the right.

Sybil: Simon?

Barington: Sybil?

Sybil: Where are you?

Barington: Here. Where are you?

Sybil: Here. *(They meet. Up lights a little. Sybil is superbly dressed. They embrace)* Oh, Simon.

Barington: Sybil. Where is everyone?

Sybil: They all seem to be sulking in their rooms.

Barington: What are we going to tell Ludo?

Sybil: The truth.

Barington: *(Embracing her)* I feel like hollering whoopee.

Sybil: Do you really?

Barington: Yes.

Sybil: Then —

She takes a pistol out of her bag.

Barington: What's that for?

Sybil: You know, Simon. It's the only way out.

Barington: You're asking me to — kill myself?

Sybil: Yes.

Barington: No — anything but that, Sybil.

Sybil: Simon, I can be a crutch for a time — but not a wheelchair.

Barington: Sybil, don't ask me that. I've only got one life, I know it's not much but — *(She holds out the gun)* I can't! Sybil — I'm too old to die.

Sybil: All right, Simon.

Barington: You do understand?

Sybil: Yes. *(He tries to embrace her)* But it's all finished between us.

Barington: No!

Sybil: You'd better go, Simon.

Barington: All right. All right, I'll do it. Leave me alone.

She gives him the gun and goes out. He seems about to shoot himself.

But then he rushes to his tape recorder and switches it on.

Recorder: You are Mr. Simon Barington!

Barington: Yeah.

Recorder: You are forceful, dynamic, dauntless and fearless!

Barington: You said it.

Recorder: You are the salt of the earth!

Barington: Damn right I am!

Recorder: You are chivalrous, heroic, adventurous, bold, gallant, intrepid, splendid and **resolute!**

Barington: Yes!

Recorder: Then what the hell are you waiting for? Go ahead and shoot!

Barington: *(Raises the gun, then lowers it, turns away)* I can't.

Recorder: There's no such word as can't! Point the gun. *(Barington slowly points the gun at the tape recorder)* No, not this way. No, no! Stop! Don't shoot!

Barington fires. The recorder gives a cry and dies away. Barington stares at the dead tape recorder, trembling.

Barington: Oh, my God — I've done it! Sybil! I've done it!

Sybil rushes in and embraces him.

Sybil: Oh, Simon!

Tappin rushes in, followed by the Bishop.

Tappin: What's happened? What were those shots? Sybil! Barington — what are you doing here?

Barington: I'm embracing your wife. Being in the motion picture business, I thought I'd better show you rather than just tell you about it.

Bishop: Yes, yes, I see.

Barington: After all, that's the essence of films — showing rather than talking about it.

Bishop: Yes. I saw an excellent movie at Tuktoyaktuk last summer. It was called The Great Train Robbery.

Barington: I want her, Ludo. I need her. I was with her all last night.

Bishop: I hardly think that was very ethical. But I may just be wrong about that . . . it could be highly ethical for all I know.

Tappin: You? *(Laughs)* You couldn't interest a woman like Sybil in a thousand years.

Sybil: Ludovic —

Tappin sees the superb way she is dressed and made-up.

Tappin: Sybil! Look at you!

Sybil: Like it?

Doorbell sounds.

Bishop: Hell's bells, now what is it?

He goes out.

Tappin: What's happened to your rejection of the flesh?

Sybil: I have something to tell you, Ludovic —

Tappin: I can't quite put my finger on it, but you've changed, somehow.

Barington: I was going to tell you that I might just be persuaded to take you back, Ludo.

The Bishop enters with a telegram.

Bishop: Ludo —

Tappin: Take me back? You really mean it?

Barington: It would depend on your being reasonable, of course.

Tappin: Believe me, I'd do anything if it meant getting my job back.

Bishop: Ludo —

Tappin: You really mean it, Mr. Barington?

Barington: Well, of course we have to clear up this other business first.

Tappin: What other business?

Bishop: Ludo. *(He hands Tappin the telegram)* It's from your Aunt Jane. She's coming.

Tappin: When?

Bishop: On the ninth of this month.

Tappin: But it's already the nineteenth.

Bishop: She does tend to be a bit late sometimes.

Sybil: *(Whispering)* Simon, you're not making any deals.

Barington: But it's the only way, Sybil!

Sybil: It doesn't matter. *(She leads Barington out)*

Tappin: Just a minute — what's this about —

Bishop: Ludo — about this *ménage* of yours — I'll have to tell Aunt Jane. It would not be right for a man in my position to remain silent about your peccadillo. Peccadillo — doesn't seem quite the right word in the circumstances . . .

Tappin: Uncle, you can't! I need the money! How can I keep Sybil, Gloria and Eleanor without it?

Bishop: How can you keep . . .! Great Job, what sophistry is upon us! He wants me to keep quiet about his sin in order to get the money to go on living in it!

Tappin: You don't understand —

Bishop: For the first time since entering this sinful household I understand. Now that, that's all, Ludovic. Not another word! You forget what I stand for. *(Tappin is silenced. The Bishop strides about in increasing agitation, removing his glasses)* But — I know what you're thinking. Oh, yes, I know what you're thinking.

Tappin: My mind is numb.

Bishop: It's nothing of the kind. I know, Ludo, oh, I know only too well — I have eyes, Ludo. I can't blame you for thinking about that — but I assure you most sincerely that I am being strictly objective.

Tappin: I don't know what you're talking about.

Bishop: It's very honorable of you not to have mentioned it, Ludo, I will say that for you.

Tappin: Mentioned what?

Bishop: Or perhaps you're being subtle and cunning. But it won't work, Ludo.

Tappin: What won't?

Bishop: Now stop that. You know very well that I am a not disinterested party. That by telling Jane the truth I stand to gain.

Tappin: *(Getting it)* Yes . . . Of course . . . I forgot all about that. If I don't inherit her money — **you** do.

Bishop: My church does, Ludo.

Tappin: Yes . . . You are an interested — a biased party in this affair.

Bishop: (Unhappily) It's true, it's true.

Tappin: Are you quite sure, therefore, that it isn't a matter of self-interest.

Bishop: Oh, oh, you've hit my one weak spot. No, no, it's not true! But it is true I did very much want to build a cathedral at Tuktoyuktuk . . . No, I'm utterly objective! No, I'm not! Yes, I am, I'm sure of it — Except that — No, no, I have no doubts — Oh, you devil — twisting the knife this way!

Tappin: Dear Uncle Linus — it's not the way it seems. If the sin you mean is the one in the sexual sense, then — Uncle, I'm only sleeping with one of them.

Bishop: (Startled) With only one? Great Job, why? I mean — But my boy, that makes all the difference. Oh, I'm — You give me your word of honor that's true?

Tappin: Yes.

Bishop: Oh, my dear Ludo, I'm so happy — especially for Sybil. Things may be a bit queer round here, but at least, thank God, nobody can accuse you of adultery.

Tappin: Well, they can actually, because it's Gloria I'm sleeping with.

Bishop: Great Job! (Jumping up) Wait! Does that mean — Ludo, does that mean that Eleanor — that Eleanor and — you and Eleanor — you don't — Well, tell me!

Tappin: No.

Bishop: (Overjoyed) Oh — Ludovic.

Doorbell rings.

Tapping: Then you won't tell Aunt Jane?

Bishop: Of course I'm telling her. What a strange person you are, Ludo . . .

Bishop exits. Barrington enters.

Barington: Look here, Tappin, we've got to get this settled right now.

The Bishop re-enters.

Bishop: Ludo — she's here! Your Aunt Jane!

Tappin: Oh, gosh — oh lord! (Tappin pushes Barington out) Quick — It's complicated enough without you! Get into the bathroom! (He pushes Barington out) Uncle — It's not as if I wanted the money for the sweet life! I need them all, I can't do without them!

Jane enters — a tiny little white-haired woman.

Jane: (Striding in) What the devil d'you mean, keeping me waiting? Linus, are you staying here?

Bishop: Yes —

Jane: What are you doing out of the Arctic? (Shaking hands vigorously) How do you do?

Tappin: Hello, Aunt Jane. (Embraces her)

Jane: I am hungry, Ludo. Exhausted with beating at your door, tired and hungry! Linus, go and bring in my things.

Bishop: Yes, of course. (Exit, Bishop)

Jane: Well, let me look at you. Ludo, you haven't changed a bit — and that's as deadly an insult as you're likely to encounter. Shivers, you don't look all that glad to see your dear, rich old Aunt Jane, though.

Tappin: You're not old, Aunt Jane. Whatever you say your age is, I'm sure you're exaggerating.

Jane: (Slapping him on the back) Well said.

Tappin: Well, this is very nice. Which hotel are you staying at this trip, Aunt?

Jane: You know perfectly well I always stay at the Majestic.

Tappin: (Hurrying out) Fine, we'll all go right now and have dinner at the Majestic —

Jane: I'm not staying at the Majestic.

Tappin: What?

The Bishop comes in, struggling with three or four suitcases and a trunk and various other items of baggage, including a stuffed animal, a stuffed bird, a male mannequin in top hat and tails, a palm tree, and a machine gun.

Tappin: Oh, no!

Jane: Yes, this time I'm staying here. If Linus can stand the hardship, so can I.

The stage is now so crowded, everybody has to climb over things to get about.

The Bishop sits, breathing hard and fanning himself.

Tappin: But you can't! You — Oh, Lord!

Jane: Why not, pray?

Tappin: Because . . . because all the bedrooms are taken.

Jane: Then I'll sleep down here.

Tappin: But . . . but . . .

Jane: Of course if you prefer I can always spend a nice busy evening in the Majestic — altering my will.

Tappin: Ordinarily you'd be very welcome —

Jane: You're very agitated, Ludo. Linus! Has he been behaving himself? *(The Bishop opens his mouth to reply)* Of course he has. I know how much my money means to him. And it won't be long now Ludo. As you know — *(Thumps her chest vigorously)* with my heart I'm liable to drop dead any moment. In fact a lot of people have advised me to. Where's Sybil?

Jane hits the male mannequin with her fist.

Tappin: She's out shopping at the moment.

Jane: Well, Linus, let me have a look at you. *(She does so, and frowns)* Yes . . . Still, it's good to see you. *(Jane sits on the sofa. She pats it)* Come and sit beside me. I've lots to tell you. Do you remember Mrs. Ding of Charlottetown? She's just bought her boyfriend a pair of leopardskin pyjamas.

Bishop: My goodness.

Jane: Where on earth is my dear niece, where's Sybil?

Tappin: She's out shopping at the moment.

Jane: You've said that before. You're repeating yourself, Ludo. That will never do. Go and get Sybil.

Tappin: Yes, sure, Aunt Jane!

Exit Tappin. But, distracted, he returns almost immediately.

Bishop: You're as rude as ever, Jane.

Jane: What me, rude? Yes, I suppose so. Perhaps that's why I never married. Whereas you never married because you were never rude enough. Well, it's too late now.

Bishop: I — don't feel it's too late. After all, I'm — not much more than the age at which life is said to begin. As a matter of fact —

Jane: What?

Bishop: Oh, nothing. A foolish notion . . . Who, after all, would have me?

Jane: Nobody.

She kicks the male mannequin on the shins.

Tappin enters.

Tappin: I've put the kettle on, Aunt Jane.

Jane: Your trouble, Linus is you live as if you owed the world a debt for living in it. In spite of which I can't get over this bad habit of mine of trusting your judgement and looking on you as my mentor. Strangely enough it has always worked. You have never let me down, ever since the never-to-be-forgotten crisis in my affairs when you stopped me investing in Syrian Silkworms Ltd. Or was it Bulgarian Borax?

Bishop: *(Distressed)* No, no.

Jane: Now don't argue. You know you've always done the right thing. I have always been able to trust your integrity.

Bishop: It's true, it's true. I must, Ludo. I can't help it.

Jane: Eh? What's going on here?

Bishop: Jane.

Jane: Yes? Out with it, man.

Bishop: I'm not telling you this because of your will going in my favor . . .

Jane: What are you talking about? It isn't going in your favor.

Bishop: I know, but . . . I mean if Ludo here . . . Your money not going to him if he isn't . . .

Jane: If he isn't ethical? We all know that. It's not so much that I'm moral myself, but I do demand morality in others; for where would we be if we condoned other people's excesses? It would be the end of the world as we know it.

Barington: *(Entering)* Look here, Tappin, I haven't got all day, I want this matter cleared — Oh.

Jane: Who the devil is this?

Tappin: *(With a effort)* This is my boss, Mr. Barington. Miss Jane Begshot, my aunt.

Barington: *(Nods)* Yeah. Look, Tappin, how much longer do I have to stay in the bathroom?

Jane: Shivers, if **you** don't know, nobody does! *(Whispering very loudly to Bishop)* I've taken an instant dislike to his face.

Tappin: I'll be with you in a minute. Mr. Barington.

Barington: I want this matter cleared up.

Tappin: I said I'll be with you in a minute!

Barington: *(Backing down)* All right. There's no need to shout. I can take a hint. *(But he stays where he is)*

Jane: *(Whispering hoarsely)* He's an exhibitionist, going around with a face like that. He ought to cover it up — it's making me blush. *(In her normal voice)* Now, what was it you were going to tell me, Linus? About Ludo?

Tappin hesitates, then takes Barington's arm.

Tappin: Come on, Mr. Barington.

Exit Tappin and Barington.

Jane: You know, I'm almost sorry my money is going to Ludo instead of you . . .

Bishop: Yes. Jane — what?

Jane: I had such grand plans for your cathedral at Tuktoyuktuk.

Bishop: Plans?

Jane: In my imagination. But I suppose Ludo's lifelong dream of making himself complete — or whatever the devil it's all about, comes first. Especially as his ambition is so deliciously mad. But, oh, the cathedral I'd have built . . .

Bishop: *(Dreamily)* Yes . . . the cathedral . . .

Jane: All in prickly Gothic, towering out of the muskeg!

Bishop: Yes! Not exactly Gothic, Jane, but of rounded concrete, blending with the Arctic. Do you know, I've even dreamed of designing it myself! I studied architecture before I realized it was the architecture of the spirit —

Jane: And stained glass and lots of tombs and things, and Eskimo choirboys!

Bishop: Eskimo choirboys?

Jane: Dressed as angels. Oh, that dangerous-looking spire soaring haughtily out of the snow! Can't you just see it?

Bishop: Not actually soaring, but blending, Jane, the whole church blending with the —

Jane: Rubbish, Linus, soaring.

Bishop: No, it's very important it doesn't soar, Jane.

Jane: Of course it soars! Shiver, how can you overawe everybody without carved Gothic?

Bishop: No, no, it's very important it doesn't overawe! Jane, it has to blend!

Jane: To soar! I insist it soars!

Bishop: It must be modern.

Jane: Gothic!

Bishop: Modern!

Jane: I insist on Gothic! That's how I see it and that's how it is, take it or leave it!

Bishop: Do you mean it's a condition that if I get your money the cathedral must be Gothic?

Jane: And that it soars.

Bishop: Then I won't have it, I won't have the money!

Jane: You will. How dare you refuse my money!

Bishop: It's too important to compromise over, I'm sorry —

Jane: You'll take my money when I die if it's the last thing I do!

Bishop: I won't!

Jane: You will!

Bishop: I won't!

Tappin looks in to see what the argument's about.

Jane: You — What the devil are we arguing about? The money's going to Ludo, not you.

Bishop: It certainly is!

Tappin: Then you — you aren't going to —?

Jane: What? He isn't going to what?

Bishop: Nothing, everything's all right, Jane.

Jane: Then where is Sybil? You've divorced her — that's what it is, isn't it? You know I can't leave my money to —

Bishop: No, no, everything's just fine, Jane, not a thing wrong, everything's just perfect, just perfect.

Eleanor and Gloria wander in. The Bishop groans and holds his head.

Gloria: Ludo, darling —

Bishop: Great Job.

Jane: What's this? Who are these broads?

Bishop: What? What broads? Oh, you mean those broads. They're — they're —

Tappin: Maids!

Bishop: Yes, maids!

Jane: Maids?

Tappin: *(Delirously)* Yes. You may serve lunch now, er, maids — Get back to the kitchen, there's good — maids.

Jane: Just a minute, there's something going on here —

Tappin dashes out. Meanwhile the Bishop is fishing a pinafore and a frilly bedcap out of one of Jane's bags.

Jane: Ludo, since when did you go in for domestic servants? Ludo!

Tappin dashes back, hiding a mop and floor brush behind his back.

Tappin: Here I am, Aunt. Look!

He tap dances. As she distracts Jane, the Bishop dresses Gloria and Eleanor in the pinafore and bedcap.

Jane: Very impressive — but what's it got to do with anything? (Sees the Bishop busy with the girls) Linus, what are you doing with those women?

Tappin: *(To the girls)* Well, don't just stand there, do something!

Dazed, Eleanor and Gloria start some house-work.

Jane: They're the most damnably inefficient maids I've ever seen —

Barington dashes in, followed by Sybil.

Barington: No, Sybil, I'm having this out right now.

Sybil: I'm sorry, Ludo, I couldn't hold him back any longer. *(Embraces Jane)* Hello, Aunt Jane, how nice to see you.

Jane: Sybil! Sybil, what's going on here — are you holding a convention?

Barington: I'm going to speak and nobody's going to stop me, Tappin, I'm not having Sybil exposed to this immoral place any longer, having to live here with your mistresses. So she's coming to live with me.

Jane: Living with his what?

Bishop: Mistresses, my dear. Come, I'll explain.

He takes her arm and starts to lead her out.

Jane: Living with Ludo's — What on earth is he talking about, who is that man, what does he mean about —

Bishop: I'll tell you all about it . . .

He leads Jane out, her protesting voice fading into the distance.

Barington: As I was saying, Ludo, I might be persuaded to take you back.

Tappin: Give back my job? Yes?

Barington: It would depend on you being reasonable about this, of course.

Tappin: I told you I'd be most reasonable, if it meant getting my job back. But —

Sybil: Simon —

Barington: Let me handle this, Sybil. *(To Tappin)* Sybil is the other business we have to clear up.

Tappin: Oh, I see. The job in exchange for my wife?

Barington: There's no need to be crude, Tappin.

Tappin: Get out!

Barington: Now look here —

Tappin: I'd starve first, I'd — Get out.

He moves towards Barington. Barington dodges behind the furniture.

Sybil rounds on Barington.

Sybil: How dare you try and blackmail Ludo!
Barington: Sybil, I've got to! You know what he's like!

Sybil: I am not for sale. You said you badly needed him back. Well, if you're offering him his job back, you do it without strings.

Barington: But he'll twist you round his little finger — He can make you do anything!

Sybil: We can't do it that way, Simon.

Barington: All right. *(To Tappin)* All right. You can come back on Monday, Ludo.

Sybil: Whatever happens?

Barington: Yeah.

He looks tragically at Sybil, and goes out hopelessly.

Tappin: This is all a joke, isn't it, Sybil? You know you can't leave.

Sybil: You've told me often enough that marriage isn't a matter of monthly payments for the use of each other. Well, I'm taking you at your word. I'm going, Ludo.

Tappin: You can't! Sybil, I — I love you!

Sybil: Ludovic — whatever else you say, don't say that. Please don't say that.

Tappin: But — Barington?

Sybil: Why not? He needs me. To you I'm nothing but part of a quartet.

Tappin: Dearest Sybil — is a fiddle the less for being part of a quartet? It becomes all the more meaningful, through the harmony it helps to create.

Sybil: Oh, yes, oh yes! You can — fiddle the words to prove anything! Just as you can switch on your magnetism and arrange women around you like iron filings! But I'm a woman, not a fiddle — a woman, a woman, a woman!

Tappin: If you love me, you won't go.

Sybil: I do love you. How else could I have put up with the sackcloth racket all these years!

Tappin: Sybil!

Sybil: Oh, Ludovic — even now I'd come back, if I though you really wanted me.

Tappin: I do — I'm done — for, without you!

Sybil: If only it were true!

Tappin: It is true! I swear it, I can't do without you.
Sybil: But Simon needs me more, and I can do so much for him, and — Oh, I don't know what to say, to explain how I feel — Yes, I do! I can simply tell the truth! The fact is — I need him at least as much, at the very least as much as he needs me!

Tappin: How can that be? I don't understand you.

Sybil: And that's why I can't explain.

She looks at him a moment; then embraces him quickly: and goes.

Gloria enters, looking back at Sybil.

Gloria: What was Sybil crying about?

Tappin: She's gone.

Gloria: Oh, darling.

She sits beside Tappin and comforts him.

Tappin: What am I going to do?

Gloria: It must hurt terribly, I know. There, there.

Tappin: I can't do without her, Gloria.

Gloria: I know, darling, but you'll get over it, time will heal everything.

Tappin: I'll just have to replace her, that's all.

Gloria: Yes, of course you will, darling, you'll just have to — what? You'll have to what?

Tappin: After all — there are other Sybils.

Gloria: There are?

Tappin: Of course! There's no need to get upset.

Gloria: There isn't?

Tappin: I'll find someone else.

Gloria: Someone else . . .

Tappin: It's essential, don't you see — for the quartet. Let me see now, who else is there . . .? Yes, I remember, there was another girl in the Yoga class, what was her name, now?

Gloria: You're joking. Tell me you're joking?

Tappin: She's so ugly it's highly unlikely anybody will have married her. What **was** her name?

Gloria: Sybil's only just left. She — she can't mean that little to you!

Tappin: I remember her so well — she was in such a sincere Lotus position . . .

Gloria: Oh, my God. You — inhuman . . .

She retreats, staring at him.

Tappin: Inhuman? What do you mean?

Eleanor comes in, dressed to go out.

Gloria: She doesn't mean a damn thing to you. None of us do!

Tappin: But I must have someone for spiritual contact.

Gloria: Then why don't you just get a — a computer! Just feed in all the right responses — it'll do just as well! And while you're at it, you can sleep with it as well!

She dashes out, weeping, passing Jane and the Bishop.

Tappin: What's the matter with her?

Eleanor: She's discovering you have a heart shaped like a brain.

Jane starts to collect her baggage.

Jane: I'm getting out of this shambles while there's still time.

Bishop: I think perhaps I also ought to be moseying along; back to the Arctic where I won't be in the way.

Eleanor: Why do you have to say things like that! As if you were nothing! You're a wonderful person, you — Oh, hell! *(She draws on her gloves agitatedly)* I'm going too, Ludo.

Tappin: No! Not you as well!

Eleanor: We used to soar on wings of words, didn't we?

Tappin: We still can, Eleanor!

Eleanor: How hot our arguments sometimes raged. Our eyes sparkled. We became breathless.

Tappin: Yes! Well, then?

Eleanor: We were thrilled to heaven when we reached fresh revelations, and I might seize your hand in the excitement, and clasp it to my breast.

Tappin: Yes, that's right!

Eleanor: And embrace you, laughing with joy!

Tappin: Yes!

Eleanor: And then you'd pat me on the back.

She turns to go.

Eleanor: That's why. Goodbye, Ludo.
Tappin: But I'll be alone. I'll be alone.

Bishop: You've been alone all along, Ludo.

Tappin: What?

Bishop: Both alone and, in a sense, not alone.

Jane: Eh?

Bishop: You see, if I may be permitted to disagree with John Donne's sentiment — he was not entirely correct when he said that no man is an island. Every man, in fact, **is** an island, "entire to it self." Of course I understand what Donne meant within the terms of reference of his "Devotions", and therefore in a sense every man is **not** an island. Incidentally, Eleanor, there's an interesting parallel between the non-insular 'responsibility' of the Donne mystics, and the 'agonizing choice' of the existentialists . . . However, I digress. Therefore, one is both an island of aloneness, while at the same time being joined to the continent of humanity. This indeed, is my text for today. "He that findeth his life shall lose it, and he that loseth his life shall find it" St. Matthew ten 39. "He that findeth his life shall lose —"

Jane: Get on with it, man; you're not in your pew now.

Bishop: Oh . . . No . . . *(Irritably)* Incidentally, Jane, it's pulpit, not pew. Yes — I was explaining how Ludo is both alone and not alone. I am reminded of the words of Horace . . .

Jane: Horace who?

Bishop: *(Laughing indulgently)* Oh, Jane . . . How does the quotation go now? Ah, yes: Caelum non animum mutent, Qui trans mare current. And this is not entirely inapposite: "They change their sky, not their soul, who run across the sea". *(Enthusiastically)* In fact, how splendidly apposite it is! One's soul is not changed by crossing the sea from one's island of aloneness, to the continent of humanity. Navibus atque, Quadrigis petimus bene vivere. *(He chuckles and slavers a little)* Though one might in this context, substitute 'tape recorder' for the word quadrigis, without undue confusion, wouldn't you agree? *(He chuckles and looks around. By now everyone is slumped over)*

Jane: *(Wearily)* Pull yourself together, Linus.

Bishop: Completeness exists only where no search for it is made. We pass, you see, in the dark, sending snatches of light. But, it is only in the sending of light that we can receive it. *(He goes to the computer)* There. I think that answers your question. Four divided by four is . . . *(The machine clatters)* is . . . nothing? *(The Bishop puts his hand gentle on Tappin's shoulder)* But be of good heart. Wasn't it Krishna who said no one who seeks spiritual union ever comes to a bad end?

Jane: Not come to a bad end? After indulging in lies, deception, adultery and unemployment?

Bishop: Come, Jane, we mustn't split hairs.

Jane: Though in the circumstances, Ludo, I might just reconsider the money business.

Tappin: There's no point in it now, Aunt Jane. I've become meaningless.

Bishop: Nonsense, Ludo, you'll see. Incidentally, Jane, I am not having that gothic church, you know.

Jane: Oh, well. You know best, I suppose; in spite of your warped affection for people. As for me — *(She wallops the mannequin over the head with her umbrella)* That's what I think. *(Exit)*

Eleanor: Goodbye, Ludo.

She starts to go. The Bishop hurries after her.

Bishop: Eleanor — you're really leaving?
Eleanor: Yes.

Bishop: Eleanor — come with me to the Arctic! *(Faltering)* That is, if you've nothing better to do?

She looks at him a moment, then embraces him gently.

Eleanor: No, I haven't anything better to do, Linus.

Bishop: You see, I have this terribly weak feeling whenever I hear you and see you, and I can only assume it is love, at last. *(They start to go out, smiling at each other)* Just a moment, I really must — *(He hurries back to the computer)* Four divided by four — is —

The warbling, bleating, clicking and chattering of the computer reaches alarming proportions: then it blows up, producing a small mushroom cloud.

Bishop: Oh, dear . . .

Exit hurriedly.

Tappin sits in a slumped attitude. Gloria comes in.

Gloria: I don't care. Ludo, I'll stay if you want.

Tappin looks at her, then reaches under the sofa and takes out the script and leafs through it.

Tappin: I'll stay if you want? Where does it say that?

Gloria: It doesn't. I made it up. *(He looks at her sadly)* No?
She goes. The lights go down until Tappin is held in a spotlight.

A door closes quietly off. There is dead silence.

Tappin gets up hopelessly. He walks a few steps. As if on their own accord, his feet execute the step he has been trying to work before. He realizes what he has done. He tries it again. It works.

He is overjoyed. Up music. He dances. He is complete.

The End